POLISH YOUR STAR

POLISH YOUR STAR

*Three-Minute Daily Lessons to
Become an Extraordinary Leader*

VOLUME ONE

VALERIE L. BÉRUBÉ

NEW YORK

LONDON • NASHVILLE • MELBOURNE • VANCOUVER

POLISH YOUR STAR

Three-Minute Daily Lessons to Become an Extraordinary Leader

VOLUME ONE

Published in New York, New York, by Morgan James Publishing. Morgan James is a trademark of Morgan James, LLC. www.MorganJamesPublishing.com

The Morgan James Speakers Group can bring authors to your live event. For more information or to book an event visit The Morgan James Speakers Group at www.TheMorganJamesSpeakersGroup.com.

ISBN 9781683508854 paperback
ISBN 9781683508861 eBook
Library of Congress Control Number: 2017918567

Cover & Interior Design by:
Christopher Kirk
www.GFSstudio.com

In an effort to support local communities, raise awareness and funds, Morgan James Publishing donates a percentage of all book sales for the life of each book to Habitat for Humanity Peninsula and Greater Williamsburg.

Get involved today! Visit
www.MorganJamesBuilds.com

DEDICATION

This book, and all of my work, is dedicated to everyone seeking a second chance in life; who seek to empower themselves and others as authentic leaders, no matter their background or current shortcomings; and, who understand that their true legacy isn't their fame or fortune (or lack thereof), but the lives they impacted in a positive way.

OVERVIEW

Volumes one and two contain seven series collectively: four in volume one and three in volume two. Each series consists of about thirty or so, three-minute lessons (two pages of reading). Some lessons contain exercises that may take a little longer than three minutes, but not much. If you complete one lesson a day, you'll finish volume one in just over three months. Since the material is easy to read, you might choose to read several lessons at once, which will certainly speed your progress. You may proceed as fast or slow as you'd like; it's not a race. Just remember, *personal transformation takes time and effort.*

Given the two-page, three-minute design of this book series, references are not noted in the body of the lessons. References and resources are listed in their own section at the end of both volumes one and two. Several resources are world-renowned scientists, thought leaders, and field experts. Many have shared their wisdom for decades while others are newer to the scene. You're invited to explore these sources further when your time permits to expand your understanding of the concepts addressed in the lessons of this book series.

VOLUME ONE

BRAIN RESET: You'll begin a journey to clear your mind of thought patterns holding you back and sabotaging you. Fresh, beneficial content is introduced and healthier thought patterns encouraged. The BRAIN RESET series attempts to get you some quick results early on, but these results are unsustainable without the remaining body of knowledge to reinforce them. Hence, the remaining six series.

AWARENESS: You'll enter the fascinating world of personality traits, emotional intelligence, and hot buttons that lead to drama. Awareness of your personality, emoting habits, and hot buttons is critical to personal growth. Awareness of how your personality, preferences, and habits impact others will help answer why you get along with some people and not with others.

COMMUNICATION: What you say *matters*. Your communication habits play a crucial role in your relationships and your response to challenges. How you communicate is largely a function of automatic programming. If your programming is faulty, then you could be sabotaging yourself without even knowing it. Here we explain the dynamics of communication and give you practical tools for communicating in healthier, more effective ways.

NEURO-SCIENCE: Here we'll explore the physical parts of your brain, your paleo past, and connect it all to help explain why you behave the way you do. If you've ever wondered why you get upset at certain things, or behave irrationally sometimes, then this series will answer many of those questions. When you understand the driving forces in your brain, you gain the upper hand instead of letting these forces control you without your knowledge or permission.

VOLUME TWO

WISDOM: Eye opening, inspiring, and insightful lessons building upon the material from volume one. We'll challenge common, self-sabotaging thinking traps and help you escape them with the tools of *rational thinking*. Rational thinking leads to much healthier thinking, emoting, and behaving than irrational thinking, and more importantly, to better outcomes. This series adds high octane fuel to resetting your brain.

LEADERSHIP: This series synthesizes learning from the last five series into a powerful leadership framework. This series explains how to leverage the best "you" as an authentic leader, no matter your place in life. It doesn't matter if you're a food service worker, grocery cashier, stay at home mom, front line supervisor, middle manager, or president of a company. The better your leadership abilities, the better the outcomes in every area of your life—both professional and personal. You'll learn valuable leadership truths and tools in this series.

SELF-CARE: Health and well-being are critical to looking and being your best. The health of your body impacts the health of your brain, which impacts every aspect of your life. Health doesn't happen by chance. It takes actionable knowledge and a committed decision to balance your life. In this series, you'll learn some of the latest and most interesting discoveries about nutrition, exercise, sleep, and more. While health is addressed last in this series, it is not an afterthought. Great health enhances your ability to be your best self and inspiring leader.

TABLE OF CONTENTS

PART 2

PART 3

PART 4

The NEURO-SCIENCE Series 189

FOREWORD

Leadership and influence is one of the most important skill sets of modern day professionals. In fact not only for professionals, but on a personal level too. However, few people ever discover the science behind leadership and influence, and even fewer people discover the deep transformation that can take place when one commits themselves to a lifetime of discovery on these topics.

Over the past 20 years, our dive into leadership and influence has taken many forms, from professional to political, across twenty-five countries and hundreds of thousands of people, but it has always come back to the lowest common denominator of the human spirit and values.

The journey for someone to become a great leader starts with questions; questions about oneself. The quality of the leadership reflected into a team or surrounding community is always a mirror of the original leader. As one develops oneself, the reflective quality of leadership into the community becomes distinctively different. And so the evolution of leadership begins.

It turns out though that in observing and developing thousands of leaders globally, there are three follies that can slow the evolution of leadership quickly and, in some cases, devolve leadership capabilities and impact.

The first one is placing function over form. When leaders chose to prioritize the methods, systems and outcomes over humans and feelings, they forget the spirit of leadership. Historically, until now, in highly competitive environments the outcomes were placed at the highest level of values. This has led to a global burnout of professionals, tired of trading their humanness, satisfaction, and fulfillment for achievement. Although it used to be that leaders would simply "stuff their feelings" in exchange for a more certain life, today that is no longer the paradigm. Today, professionals are demanding more of a balanced life, and leadership that represents holistic and integrated ideals, instead of segmented and isolated slivers of life.

The second folly of modern leadership is lack of urgency. Leaders who place comfort over discomfort let down their own leadership, teams, themselves and most importantly their destiny. Today the need to take action quickly and massively is more important that ever. Competition for ideas and execution spans the globe and makes driving urgency a necessity today for leaders who want to challenge the status quo. Leaders have historically been incentivized for urgency with the carrot and the stick. Today's paradigm is to inspire urgency through connection to one's highest purpose. Energy, action and focus are indicators of everyone's connection to their calling. Today, being connected to that calling is essential for the top leadership.

The third folly of modern leadership is that leadership is an individualized activity. Many leaders have their own evolution and growth at the forefront of their leadership and the most powerful leaders of today actually have a different distinction around leadership—it is a team sport.

Today more than ever, leaders are reflecting their skills into their networks and teams to ensure their peers are becoming the leaders they always wanted to be and defining leadership in their ability to influence and design other leaders.

This book is a brilliant guide through the exploration of the mind of great leadership, twisting and turning with dimensions of tactical and strategic suggestions. Enjoy each concept and try them on to evolve quickly past the three largest follies and into a life of authentic and powerful leadership.

Enjoy your journey!

Kane & Alicia Minkus

INTRODUCTION: HUMANS COPY EACH OTHER

The human population of the world is *exploding*.

It took over one hundred thousand years to reach the first one billion people on earth.

Since the early 1800s, the human population grew by another *six* billion.

As of 2017, seven and a half billion human souls inhabit the earth.

One and a half billion in growth took place in only the last fifteen years.

In other words, we've grown faster in fifteen years than in the first one hundred thousand years.

Growing at equal speed is the ability of information to travel around the world.

We all know the quality and truthfulness of this information varies widely.

Children, young adults, and good people like you are exposed to this content on all fronts and struggle to make sense of it. What should we believe? What does "right" look like?

Two facts make this situation concerning:

1. Information, whether right or wrong, tends to get copied and distributed.
2. Humans tend to repeat what they hear and copy what they see.

Today's situation creates a tinder box of uncertainty.

For example, the hate message of terrorist groups like Al Qaeda, Taliban, and ISIS spread globally like wildfire to recruit millions to their genocidal cause.

Children are increasingly subject to sexual abuse and slavery facilitated by global information networks.

The world is becoming more polarized into "us" and "them" based on information (much of it false or twisted) about the "other" side.

You might feel like you're helpless to make a difference in this situation, but that's not true.

The truth is *you*, one of seven and a half billion people in the world, *contribute* to the outcome. You contribute to outcomes in your family, work, and community that in turn impact others.

By being the best version of yourself, a role model for others to emulate, and a *leader* of yourself and others, you make an impact in enormous ways.

Your thinking, emoting, and behaving *matters*.

The things you do (or don't do) *matter*.

The words you speak and write *matter*.

You might think you're not worthy of being a role model and leader. Sadly, too many people think themselves unworthy, which is why they feel helpless to improve their lives or make a difference in the world. It's why we have a critical shortage of role models and leaders to follow.

This must change.

You don't have to adopt a new religion, give up your most treasured values, or abandon your lifestyle, and you don't have to be perfect.

All you need is to strive to be more mindful, positive, and resilient. Striving helps you lead yourself and others to truly make a difference in the world.

If impacting the world is too big a stretch for you, then just consider the following benefits you personally gain by being your best self:

☆ More wealth building opportunities (promotions, business, investments, publicity)

☆ Better health and fitness across the board

☆ Increased attractiveness and stronger, healthier relationships

☆ Faster, more qualitative, more lasting results in pursuing your personal goals

This book series is designed to transform you into a confident, highly productive, and genuinely admired version of yourself.

By being your best self, you automatically become a better role model and leader without having to think about it.

Life is happier and more joyful for you.

Others watch how you do it, and they copy you because they want what you have. When they copy you, others copy them, and the process spreads.

If you're a parent, coach, teacher, co-worker, supervisor, team member, engage in social media, or go out in public, then other people are watching you—particularly children.

You *are* making an impact, either positive or negative—whether you want to or not.

The world *needs* you to be the best version of yourself.

What's more, to get the most out of your own life, you *need* to be the best version of yourself.

Fortunately, you've found precisely the right tool to help you: *this book series.*

The wisdom of millennia and scores of thought leaders is organized into seven learning series, and condensed into *three minute* lessons (two pages of reading).

It's structured to help you achieve meaningful results in consideration of your busy life.

It's designed to transform you into the best version of yourself *at your own pace.*

It's not a get rich quick, lose weight fast, or attract a mate tomorrow program, but with time and effort, this book series will help you achieve your life dreams while changing the direction of our collective future to more happy tomorrows.

Now, with no time to waste, let's get right into the lessons.

PART 1
THE BRAIN RESET SERIES

IT'S NOT YOUR FAULT, AND AT THE SAME TIME, IT IS

You work extremely hard. You put in the extra hours. You bend over backward for others. You're generous and kind. You advance your education. You sacrifice.

It seems as though after putting in so much effort and energy you'd get something out of it, right?

But you don't.

You work diligently for little in return. You're not getting hired or promoted. You're rarely recognized or appreciated. You have little time to yourself. Your relationships are strained. You don't have a lot of things you hoped for by now in life. You've experienced multiple disappointments.

On the other hand, you see people out there who seem to have it easy. They don't work nearly as hard as you do. Getting hired or promoted is no problem for them. They have lots of free time on their hands. They have everything anyone could want in life. Their relationships are happy. It just doesn't seem fair.

Let me tell you something right now. It's *not* your fault! And, at the same time, it *is* your fault!

What's not your fault is you don't know what you don't know.

In other words, if you don't even know you're subconsciously sabotaging your best efforts, time and time again, then it's *not* your fault.

What *is* your fault is you are, indeed, sabotaging your best efforts! You just don't know you're doing it.

It's not that people who seem to have it easy are any smarter or better than you, because they're not. What's going on is they're benefitting from more optimal programming in the automatic part of their mind. Many of these individuals aren't even aware this is going on.

Nature and nurture have a lot to do with programming of the automatic part of your mind. When nature and nurture don't give you the best programming, education and a conscious, committed decision to optimize your programming *does* work.

This book series is designed to provide the education you need to optimize your automatic programming so you can become the best version of yourself, a role model for others, and an effective leader of both yourself and others. The conscious, or *manual*, decision to optimize your programming is up to you.

Again, people who seem to have it all together might not understand why they are the way they are, or why they're successful. They might figure their hard work or a bit of luck got them through. In the next lesson, I'll explain why this reasoning is not true. What got them to where they are today is the programming in their automatic mind, but they have no idea how or why it works. They're unable to share their techniques with others because they don't know themselves.

Soon *you* will have it all together, and you will know why you are incredibly resilient and successful. You'll understand what's happening in the automatic part of your mind, and how to manually refine, or even completely change, your own programming.

To maximize your positive impact on the world, you'll want to *share what you know*. Tell people the story of how you got to where you are, once you've completed your transformation. You have no idea how powerful your message is in changing people's lives until you do it.

I'm modeling what I want you to do by sharing what I know in this book series. Nothing contained here is secret. My ultimate hope is if everyone understands how to become the best version of themselves, while serving as role models and leaders, together we can alter the course of our global future to better health, peace, and prosperity. I need your help to accomplish this vision.

You can mentor friends, teach students, or simply share your wisdom on the Internet. It's all good and it all makes a difference.

To start, I will let you in on a shocking secret. That juicy bit is next.

2 POSITIVE THINKING, EDUCATION, AND HARD WORK DO *NOT* GUARANTEE SUCCESS

Sure, they help, but what really determines your success in life is *brain programming*.

There are two parts of the brain, the conscious mind and the subconscious mind. These two parts of the brain, and everything inside, forms your total brain programming.

In this book, we call the conscious mind the "manual" mind, and the subconscious mind the "automatic" mind. Here's why.

The conscious or *manual* mind is exactly like the *user* of a computer. The user processes information much more slowly than the computer, but has the power to control the computer's outputs. If the user makes no effort to control the computer, then the computer will merely run its programming indefinitely. The results could be good, bad, or random. The user may not be aware the computer is not running optimally and may think everything is fine. The reality is the computer can operate much better if the user is aware of the possibilities and knows how to program the computer to achieve them.

The subconscious or "automatic" mind is the *computer*. This computer executes all the programs running your life. Unless your manual mind is aware and engaged, or unless through extraordinary luck your automatic mind is pre-programmed optimally, then your automatic mind could be executing programs that are actually sabotaging your life, unbeknownst to you. Here's how it happens.

Throughout your life, beliefs get deposited into the programming of your automatic mind. For example, if you were ever bullied as a child, then your automatic mind might have deposited one or more of the following beliefs into its programming:

Wealthy kids are mean and nasty –

Good looking kids are mean and nasty –

Smart, assertive kids are mean and nasty –

Kids who seem to have everything are mean and nasty –

Therefore—I don't want to be wealthy, good looking, smart, assertive, or have nice things because I don't want to be mean and nasty.

Even though you would like to be wealthy, good looking, smart, assertive, and have nice things, your automatic mind says, "Oh, no you don't!" and sabotages you.

Traumatic or unhappy experiences of just about any sort have the potential to deposit *false* beliefs into the programming of your automatic mind.

What's worse is once these false beliefs are deposited into your programming, you unknowingly go about life looking for revalidation of them. You unknowingly focus on the negative while your programming filters out the greater number of examples of people who are wonderful, loving, giving, charitable, smart, wealthy, good looking, caring, and nice. It's not fair your automatic mind does this to you, but it does.

This kind of filtering, along with constant revalidation of the *wrong* beliefs, can lead you to reinforce negative stereotypes about *yourself*, others, or whatever the subject might be.

It can lead to a lack of empathy for others.

It can draw negativity into your life.

It can draw the wrong people into your life.

It can deny you opportunities because you were unable to see them, or afraid to accept them.

It can cause you to procrastinate.

It can seduce you into generating all sorts of excuses as to why you can't do something.

You can think positive thoughts. You can get an education. You can work hard. But if your automatic mind is not programmed right, you're not going far.

What you must do is *reset your brain*. That is the objective of this first series.

We'll challenge those false beliefs and *deposit* new, healthy beliefs into your programming. We'll boost your manual mind's awareness so you have greater control over the bad programming of your automatic mind.

We'll find what you're truly passionate about so you're *excited* to get out of bed in the morning. We'll leverage set-backs to your advantage rather than allowing them to dump yet another false belief into your programming. We'll teach you to harness the immense power of your thoughts to create your ideal reality.

Your relationships, your career, your health, your goals—everything about your life will improve if you successfully reset your brain to consistently run the right program of thoughts.

3 ARE YOU IN YOUR RIGHT MIND?

Your *right* mind is loving, caring, understanding, calm, receptive, confident, and joyful. Positive, happy thoughts or emotions indicate you're in your *right* mind. It's where you want to be.

Your *wrong* mind is angry, selfish, closed-minded, judgmental, anxious, fearful, and depressed. Negative thoughts and emotions indicate you're in your *wrong* mind. It's not where you want to be, but you're there nonetheless. You might be trapped there for long periods. Beating yourself up about it will only make it worse.

You'll know if you're in your right or wrong mind through awareness of your feelings at that time. It's common to have a mix of feelings. You might even quickly move from your right to wrong mind with little provocation. This is very common.

Listen carefully. If you happen to find yourself in your "wrong" mind, you are *not* wrong, bad, evil, nasty, mean, selfish, dirty, or any other silly, unhelpful adjective you might conjure up to describe yourself. Don't go there!

You're an amazing human being with an unoptimized automatic mind, just like most people. Remember, we're going to reset your brain. To start, we must learn and continually practice self-awareness of your emotions.

Self-awareness is vital to our important work of resetting the brain. It's also vital to reinforce the new programming in the brain. We have a whole series on awareness because it's that important. For now, we just need to start building self-awareness of our emotions sufficiently enough to reset the brain.

Self-awareness starts with continually asking yourself how you feel about a certain person, place, or situation. We are *not* judging ourselves, we're simply making a conscious effort to observe our mind *objectively* at that moment in time.

For example, when you saw all the dirty dishes in the sink you felt…Anxious? Weary? Delighted? Ok, maybe not delighted.

When a hummingbird drank from a feeder on your patio you felt…

When a close friend or family member started acting strangely you felt…

When a stranger helped you with your flat tire in the rain you felt…

When you didn't get the job, you knew you should have had you felt…

When you watched twenty hot air balloons ascend simultaneously from the earth you felt…

When the tailgater behind you flashed you a rude gesture you felt…

The list can go on endlessly, but you get the point. Everyday situations and new situations alike will trigger some sort of emotion—good, bad, or indifferent.

Stopping yourself and thinking, "Gee, how do I feel about this right now?" can prove difficult in the moment. If at times it's too hard, then give yourself a moment later when you can calmly reflect upon it. There's no right or wrong answer, only the *honest* answer.

You might want to keep a little diary or make frequent mental notes. "When this happened, I felt this." You don't have to say much, just a few words on what you were feeling. Identifying your feelings can be challenging at first because you might not know what you're feeling. Don't worry. You'll get better with practice and time.

Self-awareness of your emotions is a critical skill that will serve you well for the rest of your life. It's totally understandable if you're afraid to do this. Fear of getting in touch with one's emotions is a common problem. It's ok, we're going to get through this together.

For now, we'll take baby steps into the strange and spooky land of emotions. For transformation to truly take place, it's better to go slow anyway.

For those of you more advanced and ready to take big leaps in emotional self-awareness, please have patience. Some people do struggle with emotional awareness, yet here we are putting it right up front. It's sort of like learning to swim. Some people can dive right in while others need a little more time. The goal is for *everyone* to learn, and to leave no one behind.

VISITING YOUR EMOTIONS IN THE SUPER MAX

Many of us have no earthly idea what we're feeling. We go about our daily lives completely unaware of our range of emotions: irritation, anxiety, amusement, curiosity, contentment, melancholy, impatience, and so on.

Have you ever looked at an infant's face and noticed how it expresses a wide range of emotions in rapid succession? Delight, bewilderment, irritation, curiosity, panic, surprise, back to delight—all in a span of one minute. These emotions are freely expressed up to the toddler age, then things start to change.

Many toddlers are taught certain emotions are not ok to express. This isn't because they have uncaring parents. Many toddlers have excellent, loving parents. The problem is many parents don't know how to have a good relationship with the most complex part of being human, their emotions, so their toddlers grow up placing their negative emotions into maximum security prison, just like their parents did when they were toddlers.

The problem with locking up emotions in the Super Max is they wreak even *more* havoc there. While this sounds counterintuitive, we'll explain why later in this book. For now, just trust that emotions in the Super Max *will* cause problems with relationships, communication, self-motivation, and achieving your big goals in life. Of course, this is not ideal, so we're going to muster up the courage to visit our emotions in prison. Don't worry, they're behind bulletproof glass. But more importantly, we'll learn how to make peace with them. We'll start with an analogy about toddlers.

Toddlers *need* their emotions acknowledged, no matter how icky, and then told they are *loved*. If this doesn't happen, then they'll have problems later in life. It doesn't mean they get their way. It just means their emotions are recognized and not shamed or punished. "I know you feel upset, I love you, and you're not having the donut." Notice the toddler is not being shamed for feeling upset, is still loved, while simultaneously not getting its way.

You want to treat your own icky emotions the *same* way. All you must do is acknowledge your emotions, *without judgment*, regardless of what they are, and then decide to love yourself anyway. It doesn't mean you act out the emotion. It just means you *acknowledge* the emotion rather than continue to ignore it.

To get you started on this important life skill, try using the list of emotions below to help you identify your feelings in response to any given person, place, or situation. You're not at all limited by the words below. For example, how did you feel when you arrived at work this morning? How about on your drive home? You might have many feelings, and that's ok.

Afraid	Curious	Frustrated	Jealous	Resentful
Amused	Delighted	Grateful	Leery	Sad
Angry	Depressed	Happy	Lonely	Secure
Anxious	Disappointed	Helpless	Loved	Sorry
Ashamed	Discouraged	Hopeful	Melancholy	Suspicious
Awkward	Elated	Hopeless	Nervous	Tired
Bored	Embarrassed	Humiliated	Optimistic	Uncertain
Cheerful	Empowered	"In Flow"	Overwhelmed	Uneasy
Concerned	Encouraged	Insecure	Peaceful	Unmotivated
Content	Enthusiastic	Inspired	Proud	Vengeful
Confident	Excited	Intimidated	Relieved	Vulnerable
Contempt	Fearful	Irritibale	Remorseful	Worried

Remember, it's fine to acknowledge that in any given situation you're feeling anxious, aroused, jealous, scared, contempt, or even rage. Do not criticize yourself for the emotions you feel. And don't try to justify them either. In fact, if you do judge or justify your feelings, you could do more harm than good. This is important to remember. You are merely *acknowledging* the feeling without *any* judgment or justification whatsoever.

Practice noticing your emotions as often as you can, starting right now. I promise you it'll all make sense soon.

5 WHAT FREQUENCY ARE YOU TRANSMITTING?

Your brain is a physics wonder. Your thoughts are electric. In fact, there's enough electrical energy moving through your brain to power a light bulb.

Your thoughts generate vibrational frequencies called *emotions*. Remember those things? We just spent the last two lessons on them. Now hang on. We're about to get a little scientific.

In physics, waves traveling at the same frequency attract one other. When they combine, they amplify each other in a situation called *resonance*. Waves in resonance become bigger and stronger. The same principle applies to emotions.

People with similar emotions attract each other. When they're together, their emotional frequencies are amplified. When this happens, they're emotionally *resonating* with each other. Emotions in resonance become bigger and stronger.

In physics, waves traveling at opposing frequencies will repel each other. If they're forced to combine, they'll dampen each other in a situation called *interference*. Waves in interference become smaller and weaker. The same goes for emotions.

People with dissimilar emotions repel each another. If they're forced together then their emotional frequencies will interfere with the other and dampen its strength. If they remain together, then they might start to take on the emotional state of the other person.

Have you ever heard the phrase "misery loves company"? This term means people in a sorry state of mind tend to hang out with each other. They amplify each other's negative emotions. The negativity isn't good for them but the resonance *feels* good. Their brains, thoughts, and emotions are stuck in the badlands while trapped in the "feel good" world of resonance.

Maybe you have a great friend or relative with whom whenever you're together you can't stop laughing. You're constantly cracking jokes and telling funny stories. You two amplify each other's positive mood. Positive emotional resonance also *feels* good.

Resonance of either negative or positive emotions feels good. This is important to remember. Negative emotional resonance is destructive. Even though it feels good, it's bad for you. Positive emotional resonance, on the other hand, is good for you.

Now on to interference.

Have you ever been in a crabby mood, only to be greeted by a nice person with a big smile and some kind words? You felt a little better afterward, didn't you? That person countered your negative mood with interference. This is an example of the good kind of interference.

The opposite happens when your sunny mood is dampened by Mr. or Mrs. "wet blanket." Their complaining and grouchiness can sour your good mood. You don't want to be in a bad mood, but now you are because of this experience. This is an example of the bad kind of interference.

Interference feels good when you *want* to change to a different emotional frequency. You'll invite the new emotion into your mind and adjust your own emotions to match it.

Interference feels wrong and intrusive when you *don't want* to change your emotional frequency; rather, you prefer to remain in your current mood. You'll resist the intrusive emotional frequency, even resent it.

Your emotions and feelings *are* your vibrational frequency. Despite your efforts to hide them or lock them up in the Super Max, your frequencies still emit out into the world, whether you want them to or not. You're always transmitting. *Always!*

During transmission, those *same* frequencies also shape the programming in your automatic mind.

Your emotions are extremely powerful. Out of control, they are *dangerous.* When tuned into the right frequencies, *great things happen.*

Fascinating, isn't it?

You can manage your emotional frequency by directing what trails your thoughts travel in your brain.

In the next lesson, you'll find out how.

THE FIRST LAW OF THE AUTOMATIC MIND

Over the course of life, as you learn new things and make deposits into your automatic mind, thought trails become burned into your brain. Your thoughts love to bounce along these well-worn trails because it's just so easy to do. Remember, thoughts are electricity so as they move through your mind they burn trails wider and smoother.

Remember how we can deposit false beliefs into our programming?

Silly beliefs like: I don't want to be wealthy, beautiful, fit, smart, famous, attractive, successful, happy, or popular, because I don't want to be mean, nasty, foolish, a loser, a failure, unkind, selfish, or pushy?

If you don't think any of those beliefs are buried in your automatic mind, sabotaging your greatest potential and heartfelt dreams, then you wouldn't be reading this book. So, we know they're there.

Once these beliefs are deposited they start to burn little trails. We don't realize it's happening, but electricity (your thoughts) takes the easiest path and simply stays on these trails. Your automatic mind constantly revalidates these beliefs by filtering out information showing otherwise. The trails grow deeper, forming super highways trapping you into habits of unhelpful thinking and feeling.

The best way to get off these old trails (which are superhighways by now) is to create *new* ones in new territory.

To find out *where* those new trails should lead will require some work up front. We don't want those trails just going any old place. We want them aimed toward our goals.

The up-front work consists of creating your *Life Vision* statement, your *Who I Am* statement, and discovering your passions and values. We'll leverage this information to generate powerful statements called *deposits*. We'll match these deposits with accompanying visual images to create a powerful tool to help build new trails in the right direction, and reset your brain. We'll call this tool your *Reality Show*. Once you build this tool tailored just for you, you will use this tool every day for three minutes.

To understand how this tool works, and why it's so powerful, we must first explain the First Law of the automatic mind, which states:

The automatic mind does not recognize the difference between imagination and reality.

In other words, whatever you envision in your manual mind, your automatic mind thinks it's true. Additionally, when the imagery is accompanied by emotion, the impact on the automatic mind is even more powerful.

As you complete the next few lessons, you're creating the content for your Reality Show. Your Reality Show is the show of the person you want to be and the life you want to have. Watching your Reality Show often will greatly facilitate building new trails in your brain. As you traverse this new terrain, new emotions will vibrate into the world, and new behaviors will come alive. The world will respond to these new emotional vibrations and behaviors and your life will start to change. You are effectively thinking, emoting, and behaving *differently*.

As these changes become permanent, reinforced by good habits and practices, you'll become, in time, everything you see in your Reality Show.

Let's make it a great show!

THE POWER OF YOUR HAPPY PLACES

Your *Happy Place* marks the beginning of your Reality Show, but it's much more than that. It's also a safe place to go when you're stressed, scared, bummed, trying to sleep, or making a big decision.

When you're in your Happy Place, you're in your right mind, your emotional frequency is positive, and you're removing yourself from ugly old trails. It's like a giant stop sign in your mind keeping you from negative thought paths. This stop sign gives you a moment to *manually* choose what thought trails you want to traverse rather than letting the automatic mind choose for you, according to its faulty programming.

You see why it's so important?

You can have as many versions of your Happy Place as you like. To get there, take a deep breath and close your eyes. In your mind, imagine your favorite place, your favorite people, or your favorite situation. This can be a getaway, a beautiful scene, a delightful experience, anything that brings you joy, peace, and light. It can be real or imagined. It doesn't matter.

If you're having trouble getting there you can try focusing on your breathing and letting your mind go blank for a bit. Of course, your mind might not go blank and all sorts of thoughts might enter your head. If that happens, just observe them with no judgment and focus on each individual breath. As you settle, your mind will enter a more favorable state for accepting happy images.

A helpful technique is to write down a few words describing each Happy Place and create a menu for yourself. Your menu can help when you're not in your right mind and have trouble thinking and settling down your mind. You can spend anywhere from a moment to several minutes there, whatever time you need to re-direct or settle your mind toward its better self.

15

Over time, you'll improve at reaching your Happy Place quickly. This is a critical skill because you're not always going to have a quiet place to go, or much time to get there. You might be in a noisy place with other people around, and only a few seconds to change the course of your thoughts and emotions. This ability is of paramount importance.

You'll know you need to enter your Happy Place when you realize you're in your wrong mind. You'll realize this through awareness of your feelings. Remember that little exercise about awareness of your feelings? Well here it is again, and it's never going away. It's a *life* skill.

This commercial interruption on your way to creating the content for your Reality Show was brought to you by the letter *V* and the number *8*.

Ok, I'm revealing my age and watched *Sesame Street* as a kid.

The point is little disruptions like this work to get off a subject. Your Happy Place can be used as a powerful disrupter, when you need to get your mind out of a rut and into a better place fast.

You may find this difficult to do at first, but it gets easier with practice.

Like awareness of your emotions, the ability to quickly enter your Happy Place, even when the world is falling apart around you, is an important *life* skill. It's also a life skill that will help maintain optimal programming in your automatic mind.

MY MENU OF HAPPY PLACES

This space is offered for you to draft your menu of Happy Places. You can have as many as you want. You can use just a word or two to describe the place, or you can be descriptive. You're not limited by the space below, nor are you required to fill it.

Happy Place #1: _____

Happy Place #2: _____

Happy Place #3: _____

Happy Place #4: _____

Happy Place #5: _____

8 YOUR *LIFE VISION* STATEMENT

Inside your soul, you probably know what you want. At the same time, you might feel guilty for wanting it, fearful about it, or think it's impossible to achieve. These feelings are the tentacles of your automatic mind holding you under water.

Let's say you want to be amazingly fit and beautiful. Who wouldn't want that? But your programming says it's selfish, self-absorbed, or narcissistic to want such a thing. This is all nonsense.

The truth is, you were made to be amazingly fit and beautiful. It doesn't matter what you were born with. Nature doesn't make anyone ugly. People make themselves ugly through chronic self-neglect and persistent bad attitudes.

Usually, a fit and beautiful person is also very healthy. Great health enhances productivity and life expectancy. The longer you live, the longer you're on earth doing great things. Additionally, great physical health often enhances the strength and beauty of both mind and spirit. A beautiful mind and spirit is powerfully attractive, and powerful in itself.

The same goes for desiring wealth. It can be a noble thing to want, provided you're not harming others along the way. You can learn anything to help you achieve great wealth. There are many enjoyable ways to earn wealth while benefitting others. The more you earn, the more good you can do in the world. Achieving great wealth benefits both you and everyone around you.

Let's say you're looking for the perfect person to spend your life with. Or maybe you seek this incredible career, or amazing lifestyle. These are great to want and it's possible to have them. If you don't know how to get there, that's ok. We're not worried about the *how* right now, only the end result—what you ultimately want for yourself. Have you ever known where you wanted to go, didn't know how to get there, but somehow got there anyway? That's what's going to happen here but on a larger scale.

What's important is you're clear about what you want. This will take some thinking. Maybe in addition to being healthy and wealthy you want to be a world-renowned scientist, school teacher, artist, business executive, non-profit leader, athlete, author, engineer, doctor, attorney, spiritual leader, architect, florist, chef, nanny, or anything else that truly makes your heart sing. Any one of these things, anything you want to be, are truly beautiful and worthwhile. The potential for you to realize this dream *is* there. To do that, you must be clear about what you want. It's perfectly ok if it changes over time, and indeed you'll refine it as you grow and learn more about yourself.

The reason this clarity is so important is it establishes vision. With vision, there's direction. Where there's direction, your energy and efforts flow in that direction. It's in this directed flow where things happen.

If you could wake up one morning and live the life you always wanted, what would it look like?

If you could be anything you ever wanted, do whatever you wanted, impact whatever you wanted, what would it be?

No matter how "unrealistic" or grand, please capture your big dream for yourself right now and write it down.

It's ok if you update or refine it later. It's important to capture what's in your heart of hearts right now. This is your *Life Vision* statement.

Remember, status quo is *not* the goal. Living the life of your dreams is the goal. Your vision statement is hugely important and we will use it to reset your brain.

MY *LIFE VISION* STATEMENT

This space is offered for you to write your *Life Vision* statement. It can be as long or as short as you like. You can revise it at any time. If you could be anything you ever wanted, do whatever you wanted, impact whatever you wanted, what would that look like?

_____

_____

_____

_____

_____

_____

_____

_____

_____

_____

_____

_____

_____

_____

_____

_____

_____

_____

_____

_____

_____

_____

_____

_____

9 BE WHO YOU WANT, TODAY

Most people believe they must first *have* something before they can *do* the things they enjoy and then *be* the person they want to be.

For example, to be happy in life, one must first have a great life partner *before* one can do joyful things. Or, to be successful, one must first have money, education, and connections *before* they can run a business, travel the world, or write a book.

This belief system is called the Have-Do-Be principle. It looks and makes perfect sense.

But it doesn't work.

In fact, it's a trap. It's a trap because the Have-Do-Be principle puts you in a state of constant dependency. When you're dependent on others rather than on yourself, you operate out of desperation, as opposed to inspiration.

When you think you must *have* something in order to *do* or *be* something, you're trapped into chasing what you think you need rather than what inspires you. You'll struggle to reach your full potential with this mindset.

Let me fill you in on the mindset that does work.

Reverse the order to *Be, Do, Have.*

Simple, right? Here's how it works.

Think of the person you want to *be*. Exactly how would this person think, feel, and behave? Focus on the *thinking*, the *emotions*, and the *behaviors*. How does this happy, successful person who's living their dream think, feel, and behave? It could be a very different person than you are now, and that's ok.

When you embrace the mind of the "you" you aspire to be, *behaviors you did not have before will emerge*. You'll do things, both small and large, to bring you closer to your goals. You'll treat people differently. You'll spend your time and energy in different ways. You'll spend your resources in different ways. You'll attract help from unexpected places. People and opportunities will be drawn to you. Have you ever heard of "fake it 'til you make it"? Well, it's a lot like that.

I remember my first time acting in a play. The director, who took a huge risk selecting me for the lead role, asked me all sorts of pesky questions about the memories and history of the character I was playing. At first, I thought it was silly because all I had was the script. How was I supposed to know the life memories of this make-believe character?

But the director pressed me to go beyond the script, to make up a story, a life history, a whole head of memories about this character. I did as she instructed and tolerated her probing questions at every rehearsal. I adopted the thoughts and feelings of my character, and while I kept to the script in my words, I found my on-stage behavior changed dramatically. The tone in my voice, my gestures, and facial expressions—everything about my character *changed*. My character grew from boring and flat to captivating and real. The audience loved it, and I learned a powerful lesson in the Be-Do-Have principle. I figured, if this works in acting, it can work in real life.

Now is a great time to draft a short statement of the kind of person you want to *be*.

Choose to emphasize the life memories and thinking of this person and how he or she would respond to distressing situations or setbacks. Focus on the *positive* aspects of the past of this person (you), even embellish them if you want.

This will become your *Who I Am* statement. For example, "I am a person who keeps my commitments, thinks before speaking, finds the good in everything, sees opportunities in challenges, stays calm when angered, finds fun ways to stay healthy, listens sincerely, loves unconditionally, lives every moment joyfully, and…"

You might not know exactly how to define this person right now and that's ok. You can refine it over time.

MY *WHO I AM* STATEMENT

This space is offered for you to write your *Who I Am* statement. It can be as long or as short as you'd like. You can revise it at any time.

I am a person who:

_____

_____

_____

_____

_____

_____

_____

_____

_____

_____

_____

_____

_____

_____

_____

_____

_____

_____

_____

_____

_____

_____

10 ONLY ONE PERCENT OF PEOPLE DO THIS

Hopefully, by now you've drafted your *Life Vision* and *Who I Am* statements. If you haven't done that yet, it's ok. We can still progress for the time being. But it's important you draft them soon. If you have drafted your *Life Vision* and *Who I Am* statements, you're off to a fantastic start.

Do you know less than 10 percent of people in the world write any sort of goal for themselves in their entire lifetime? There's no shortage of books and studies indicating when you write down a vision for yourself, you're much more likely to achieve your goals in life. Consider yourself already in the top 10 percent of 7.5 billion people in the world. How awesome is that? It would be nice if we could stop there and let success magically happen. But it doesn't work that way.

While it's true only 10 percent of people write down any sort of goal for themselves, less than 10 percent of those people (1 percent of the total population) achieve them. Why is that?

The number one reason is their automatic mind was not on board. Maybe they encountered obstacles and gave up, and blamed it on the obstacles. Maybe their goals were unrealistic, like winning the mega lottery (that's just not realistic). Maybe they didn't think they were smart enough or capable of doing what they wanted. They might have allowed a false belief in their programming to hijack their dreams. With all that said, there's another important reason why most people fail to achieve their goals in life—they had the *wrong* goals to begin with.

How can a life goal be wrong?

Well, it can be wrong for you because it wasn't aligned with your true passions and values in life. A lot of people fall into the trap of creating goals that are simply an extension of what they're already doing, and they're not exactly thrilled about what they're doing to begin with. If you're happy with what you're doing right now, then this might not apply to you. But if the status quo does not excite you, then goals that simply glorify the status quo will likely not be met.

Another trap is creating goals based upon the expectations and values of other people rather than your own. Such goals will also end up in the graveyard at some point. Why? Because your heart isn't in it. Your goals aren't based on *your* passions and values as opposed to someone else's.

Remember, less than 1 percent of the world population achieves their dreams in life. To increase your chances of becoming a member of this exclusive club, it helps to learn your true passions and values. We're going to start this learning process now.

Start by completing this one, simple, wonderful little sentence:

"My life is ideal when I am... (complete the sentence)."

You're free to write down as many answers as you'd like. In fact, I want you to have at least five answers, but you can have as many as twenty or more. Take a quick moment to write them down because we're going to use these wonderful little statements to reset your brain.

It doesn't matter if you're not doing the "ideal" thing right now.

Maybe you have done the ideal thing in the past and enjoyed it so much you'd like to do it again. Or maybe the ideal thing is something you've only dreamed about. Either way, it doesn't matter. The ideal thing is what makes your heart sing. It's something that truly brings you joy.

Here are a few of my own statements. "My life is ideal when I am...connecting wonderfully with an audience, laughing with my husband, running on a cool morning at sunrise, having coffee with friends, surfing on a gorgeous day, in flow with writing a book, learning something interesting, traveling the world, being around like-minded people."

Like your *Life Vision* and *Who I Am* statements, your *Ideal Life* statements will add content to you Reality Show – your unique tool to resetting your brain.

MY *IDEAL LIFE* STATEMENTS

This space is offered for you to write your *Ideal Life* statements. You can have as many as you like, and you can revise them at any time. You don't have to fill up the space below, nor are you confined to it.

My Life is Ideal When I Am...

PEOPLE WHO MOVE YOU

There's an important connection between us and the people we admire most. When we admire others, usually the top two traits drawing us to them are *vision* and *grit*. Sure, there are other traits that draw admirers, but vision and grit are the top two. These traits speak to character, skill, creativity, perseverance, and a vigor for life. We are inspired by such people. They are our role models. We are connected to them through their passions and values.

The people we call our heroes have their faults, yet they're still admired. It goes to show perfection is not required. We can simultaneously learn from the qualities we admire *and* have empathy for their faults. After all, they're human too.

There's no shortage of admirable people in the world. Some are famous or well known, but the majority move about their daily lives (or once lived) without one shred of public recognition. You might know a few people in the latter category. Famous or not, their lives are truly incredible stories of trial and perseverance, love and sacrifice, hardship and determination.

We admire people not so much by how far they got in life, but by what they had to overcome to get there. They are our heroes, and none of them had it easy.

When you think about your heroes, what is it about them you admire?

Maybe they were good communicators, hard workers, or talented in their field of work. Maybe you admire their mastery of their chosen career or the products of their work. Maybe you admire how they made others feel good or how they solved problems. Maybe you identify with their personality and thinking. Maybe you like that they're bold or meek, creative or logical, outspoken or reserved, organized or merrily cluttered, serious or playful, energetic or calm.

Remember, we're connected to the people we admire through common passions and values. We can gain a great deal of insight about ourselves by examining the people who move us the most.

Think about some people you admire most. They can be living or non-living, real or imagined; it doesn't matter.

Take a moment to reflect on three people or characters with whom you connect. You might have some already in mind, or you might want to do a little searching. It's fine to take your time and give it some quality thought. What's important is to pick honestly according to *your* own values, not to someone else's. Once you have your three people in mind, write down their names.

Next, think of three to five traits about each person you admire most. Fantastic singer? Versatile athlete? Visionary leader? Innovative artist? Dedicated scientist? Motivating speaker? Nurturing mother? Attentive father? Humble winner? Gracious under fire? Well-dressed and poised? Loving father? Hard but fair? Encouraging coach? Write those traits under the names of each person.

For example, I admire my grandparents for their tremendous grit, perseverance, and for holding their heads high, even when they were utterly broke. I admire Abraham Lincoln for his incredible leadership, oratory skill, and tremendous resiliency. I admire Frederick Douglas, who overcame extraordinary adversity, educated himself, and sought to make a positive difference in this world without bitterness or thoughts of revenge. I admire many, people, not just these three.

Neither are you confined to just three people to admire, nor three to five traits. It's ok if multiple people have the same trait. In fact, if you notice several people have the same trait, then you know you're on to something. There's likely an important connection there revealing a passion or value you didn't realize before.

PEOPLE I ADMIRE

This space is offered for you to identify people you admire and the traits that make them special to you. At least three people and three traits each are recommended.

#1. A person I admire is:

_____

This person's special traits are:

_____

_____

_____

_____

_____

#2. A person I admire is:

_____

This person's special traits are:

_____

_____

_____

_____

#3. A person I admire is:

_____

This person's special traits are:

_____

_____

_____

_____

_____

12 YOUR MAGIC WORDS

Words have meaning and tremendous power. In the right context, words can produce strong emotions. Emotions are transmitted into the world as vibrational frequencies. Simultaneously, your emotions *govern* your behavior. The world responds to both your emotional vibe and your behavior. As a result, *things happen.*

When things happen, your life story unfolds.

In short, words trigger emotions and behaviors, causing an impact. Words are powerful.

Everyone has a unique combination of words that resonates deeply within them. These words capture their most treasured values. Not everyone knows their combination of words, but you're about to find out yours.

Learning your unique combination of words can reveal more about yourself than you might have ever guessed. Your combination is as unique to you as your DNA or fingerprints. No two people are alike. Are you ready to learn your unique combination? Here we go…

On the following page, you'll see a list of words. Take a deep breath, close your eyes, and visit your Happy Place for a moment. Then starting from the top, mark the words that *resonate* with you. There are no right or wrong answers. Don't try to be consistent or follow any sort of pattern or anything like that unless it comes to you naturally that way. No one is going to see your words (unless you share them), so feel completely free to mark whatever words you're gravitated toward. There's no minimum or maximum to the number of words you might select. If there's a word that resonates with you that is not on the list, write it down. You're not limited to this list. The list is there to help—not limit—you.

In the next lesson, I'll explain what to do with these words. For now, relax, choose your words, and we'll revisit them tomorrow.

Active	Daring	Graceful	Measured	Respectful
Achievement	Decisive	Gracious	Merciful	Responsible
Adventurous	Dedicated	Grateful	Methodical	Responsive
Affection	Deliberate	Grounded	Modest	Savvy
Analytical	Dependable	Growth	Morality	Security
Appreciative	Determined	Hardworking	Motivated	Sensible
Aristocratic	Devoted	Harmony	Neat	Serious
Articulate	Devout	Happn	Objective	Service
Artistic	Diplomatic	Happiness	Observant	Simplicity
Assertive	Discerning	Helpful	Optimistic	Sincere
Athletic	Disciplined	Honesty	Organized	Smart
Attentive	Diversity	Honorable	Outgoing	Solitude
Authentic	Driven	Hopeful	Patience	Sophisticated
Autonomy	Dynamic	Humble	Patriotic	Spirituality
Balanced	Educated	Humorous	Peaceful	Sprited
Beauty	Effective	Imaginative	Perservering	Stable
Boldness	Efficient	Impactful	Personable	Status
Brave	Eloquent	Independence	Pioneering	Strategic
Calm	Empathy	Industrious	Playful	Strength
Caring	Empowered	Informed	Pleasant	Successful
Certainty	Encouraging	Innovative	Polished	Supportive
Challenge	Energetic	Insightful	Popular	Sympathetic
Charismatic	Enterprising	Inspiring	Power	Tactful
Cheerful	Entrepreneurial	Instructive	Practical	Teamwork
Clever	Equality	Integrity	Pragmatic	Tempered
Collaborative	Exciting	Intelligence	Pretty	Tenacious
Comeraderie	Exemplary	Interesting	Productive	Thorough
Committed	Fairness	Introspective	Prosperity	Thoughtful
Communication	Faithful	Intuitive	Prudence	Tireless
Compassionate	Family	Inventive	Quality	Truth
Competetive	Famous	Joyful	Quiet	Trust
Competence	Fit	Judicious	Rational	Trustworthy
Considerate	Flexibility	Kind	Realistic	Understanding
Consistent	Focused	Knowledgable	Receptive	Unique
Constructive	Forgiving	Likeable	Recognition	Variety
Control	Freedom	Logical	Reflective	Versatile
Cooperative	Friendship	Loud	Relevance	Victorious
Courage	Fun	Love	Relaxed	Visionary
Courteous	Funny	Loving	Reliable	Wealth
Creative	Generous	Loyalty	Resilient	Well Spoken
Cultured	Gentle	Mature	Resourceful	Wisdom
Curious	Genuine	Meaningful	Respect	Witty

13 YOUR MAGIC WORDS – PART TWO

Welcome back!

We'll learn what to do with all those wonderful words you selected yesterday. These words capture a wide range of your values.

Now, return to your list with a calm, relaxed mind. Look at each word. Think about each one and then write a small #3 next to the words that are least important to you. It doesn't mean they're not important; it just means you don't feel as strongly about them.

Next, take a deep breath and have a look at your list again. This time, place a #2 next to the words that are more important than your #3 words, and a #1 next to the words that are *most* important to you. Again, there are no right or wrong answers—only the right answer for *you*.

We want to end up with five #1 words. If you have more than five, reflect on your words and see if you can move some words over to the #2 column to get yourself down to five words. If you have less than five #1 words, then have a look at your #2 words and see if there are any you can advance to the #1 column.

If you're torn on your words and can't get to five #1 words, don't worry. It's not that important to have exactly five. The reason for this exercise is to get you to *think* about your words because these words reflect your deepest values. Remember, no one is watching and no one is judging you on your words. More importantly, do not judge yourself on your words. Pick what's truly in your heart.

Once you have your five or so words, think about *why* you chose those words. This is an important exercise in self-reflection. There's likely a story or feeling or line of reasoning behind every word.

If you can't think of *why* the word is there then maybe the word doesn't belong there. If that happens, consider replacing it with a word from the 2 or 3 pile. In the end, you should be able to explain why each word is there. Your reason why each word is listed does *not* have to be articulate or logical or rational to anyone but *you*. The opinion or feelings of others matters not one wit here. Only *your* opinions and feelings matter here. Only *you* need be satisfied with your explanation.

Your final list of #1 words is your unique word combination. It's your own secret code to your unique values. When you abide by your values, you'll feel right. When you violate your values through thought or deed, you will *not* feel right. In fact, you'll sabotage yourself and go around in circles. That's not where you want to be, so it's important to know and understand your values.

Not only will we use your #1 words to reset your brain, they'll come up again in the AWARENESS series so don't lose them. In the AWARENESS series, you'll learn how these words reveal your hot buttons—the things that get under your skin. Then in the NEUROSCIENCE series, you'll get to see the connection between these words and the most primal part of your brain. It's fascinating stuff. But I digress…

Tomorrow, we'll start putting all this great stuff together to construct your Reality Show and reset your brain.

MY MAGIC WORDS

This space is offered for you to write down your magic words. We'll refer to them again in the AWARENESS series.

#1 Words	#2 Words	#3 Words

14 THE SECOND LAW OF THE AUTOMATIC MIND

You think in words and images. These words and images lie along your thought trails, leaving a visible mark. We call these marks *deposits*, and they become directional beacons for your thoughts in the future. They literally direct your thoughts, emotions, and behaviors. Deposits are extremely powerful.

Deposits in your programming form the essence of your automatic mind.

Deposits can be true or false. Your automatic mind thinks it's all *true*.

Deposits can be real or imagined. Your automatic mind thinks everything is *real*.

Remember when we talked about false beliefs becoming embedded into your automatic mind? Well, those false beliefs are what we call "ugly-lie deposits." They glow brightly on your thought trails and direct your thoughts, emotions, and behaviors the *wrong* way.

Our plan to get you on the right path involves creating fresh, healthy deposits and spreading them out on new trails. We'll get to that soon. But first, we need to introduce you to the Second Law of the automatic mind.

The Second Law of the automatic mind is:

All communication, whether thought or spoken aloud, no matter to whom or what, is reflected into the automatic mind.

In other words, your automatic mind takes everything you think or say *personally*. It doesn't matter whether you're thinking something to yourself or talking to your friend. Your automatic mind is taking it *all* in as though it were real, true, and personally directed.

When you give someone a compliment, you feel good because your automatic mind likes it. It thinks you're complimenting it.

When you condemn someone, you won't feel right. Why? Because your automatic mind thinks you're condemning yourself. Your *manual* (conscious) mind knows the difference, but your automatic mind does not.

Every time you communicate, whether you think or say what you're communicating, you're creating another deposit. You might be reinforcing old, ugly-lie deposits, or creating new, healthy ones. Your thoughts and word choices matter.

There's an entire series devoted to communication in which we'll explore this fascinating phenomenon in greater detail. We'll also share some tools and techniques to help you improve your communication.

In the meantime, have faith in this law because we're going to leverage it right now. We are going to deliberately create a series of wonderful, fresh deposits.

There are two key concepts to building your list deposits.

The first is you generate them from work you've already done: *Life Vision*, *Who I Am*, *Ideal Life* statements, your heroes (and their qualities), and your Magic Words. All this hard work represents the building materials for your deposits.

The second concept is to state your deposits in the *present* tense, as though the truth of the depositions has already arrived, in accordance with the Be-Do-Have paradigm. Most of them will start with "I am ..." or "I [action verb]."

We will build your deposits over the next few days, so we'll take it easy for now in preparation for this important activity.

Fortunately, most of the exercises are in in this series. So, you're getting it out of the way early. I promise you won't have as many exercises in the other series.

If you haven't completed your *Life Vision*, *Who I Am*, and *Ideal Life* statements, now is a good time to catch up on those. You'll also need to have your Magic Words ready. We'll use *all* this material to start building your deposits tomorrow. Remember, these deposits go into your programming. We want the contents of your program to be positive and empowering.

15 MAKING DEPOSITS INTO YOUR PROGRAM

Welcome back! Today we'll start building your list of wonderful, fresh, healthy deposits to help replace all those ugly-lie deposits causing havoc in your automatic mind.

The word *deposit* means we're putting something in, building upon it, and turning it into something awesome. Deposits are short, positive statements you repeat, either aloud or in thought, until they become embedded in the program of your automatic mind. To become embedded, they need to be accompanied by an emotion. The stronger the emotion, the more likely they'll stick.

It takes an active, *manual* effort to embed deposits. Any time you use the manual mind, it will "feel" like work. The good news is, once the deposits have taken root in the automatic mind, you need less manual energy to embed and nurture them, because once your deposits become embedded, the automatic mind *automatically* reinforces them for you. This is a nice feature.

But, you must put in the manual work up front for this to happen.

Now, some of you might think these deposits look a lot like "affirmations." There are similarities in that you're using short, positive-sounding statements and repeating them. *The similarities end there.* There are three important differences between affirmations and deposits.

First, deposits are specifically designed and tailored to your unique identity, life vision, and values. Sometimes affirmations are, too, but not always.

Secondly, deposits are accompanied by an emotion, preferably a strong one. Sometimes affirmations are too, but not always.

Thirdly, and most importantly, deposits are *actively* and *consciously* engaged with by the manual mind. Affirmations usually do not work this way. Affirmations are more *passive* in nature. They simply repeat in the background of music or some pleasant sound. Now, there's nothing wrong with that, and some people

35

find them useful. However, using passive affirmations is a lot like putting a book under your pillow, sleeping on it, and expecting the contents to enter your mind.

Deposits *require* you to *manually* and *actively* engage, which is like opening the book, reading it, and taking notes. You're much more likely to absorb the content that way than by passive measures. Deposits are more likely to produce real and lasting change in your automatic programming than passive affirmations.

Ok, back to building your deposits.

You'll want to generate about twenty to forty deposits, keeping each statement to about nine words or less. If your statements are too long then we sort of lose the "soundbiteness" of it all. Soundbites tend to stick better in the mind than longer statements. If you're over by a few words, it's no big deal. The nine-word limit is a guideline, not an absolute rule. If you want the *Declaration of Independence* as one of your deposits, you can; I just don't think it's optimal.

Starting below, you'll see a list of sample deposits. You're free to use them, but I encourage you to make your own based upon your unique *Life Vision*, *Who I Am*, *Ideal Life*, Admired People (and traits), and Magic Words. It's important your words come from the work you've done so far so that your passion and values show in your deposits.

Now, you don't have to draft these deposits all in one sitting. It's ok to take some time to reflect on your past work, refine it if you need to, and then come up with just the right words to create your deposits.

Your deposits are important because they'll form the primary content of your Reality Show. Remember, your Reality Show is the powerful tool we'll use to reset your brain. Once you create your Reality Show, the hard part is done, and your *real* journey begins.

EXAMPLE DEPOSITS

I am confident and poised in my demeanor	I am a victorious survivor (not a victim)
My habits are precise and productive	I am kind, even when I am hurting
I am organized and disciplined	I am happy, even if others are jealous
I renew my energy with every breath	I do good, even if it's forgotten the next day
My mind is sharp and ready for learning	I do the right thing, even if no one knows
I learn something new every day	I am grateful, even when things aren't going my way
I am a deep, sincere listener	I am flexible with my preferences
I avoid sugar because I love my brain	When I don't know something, I research it
I love trying new, healthy recipes	I enjoy spending my free time on my goals
I forgive everyone who has hurt me	I am responsible for my own mental state
I resonate with the world's positive energy	When my thoughts are negative, I am aware of them
I know when to rest and recharge myself	I reappraise negative situations in a more positive light

I am bold and make and impact

I know when to surge with my energy

I respond to setbacks with calm confidence

I see challenges as opportunities to learn

My hand-eye coordination is increasingly precise

I learn something new about my body every day

I learn something new about myself every day

I am grateful for the opporunity to train hard

I am mindful of my thoughts and emotions

I am keenly perceptive

I notice the best in people

I quick with appreciation and compliments

I am articulate and well spoken

I am curious about others

I seek to understand others

I am receptive to new ideas

I am aware of my emotions and how they impact me

I am aware of my emotions and how they impact others

I listen to the better side of myself

I enjoy celebrating every little win

I see trends and patterns that others don't see

The neurons in my brain get healthier every day

I find myself "in flow" often

I can learn anything, even if I struggled in the past

I see criticism as a chance to learn something new

I push through my fears with calm determination

I spend a little time daily to think quietly

I listen more than I speak

I seek to better connect to those I care about

I forgive myself for my own wrongs

No matter what anyone says, I am a good person

I have courage to engage in tough conversations

I am respectful of others even when they don't respect me

I am mindful of every muscle in my body

I continously challenge myself

I seek to eliminate unhelpful habits

I seek to improve the flow of my day

I walk with my shoulders back and my head held high

I walk deliberately and with purpose

I care, even if I don't take on the problem

I know how to quiet my mind

I am a world class athlete

I am a highly admired and respected executive

I am super fit and healthy

I am exceptionally creative

I do the little things that help me achieve my goals

I manage my time expertly

I move quickly from task to task

I stay on task and complete them quickly

I enjoy the present moment as though it were my last

I handle setbacks with grace and resiliency

I remain calm during upsetting situations

I persevere through challenges

I follow through in what I set out to do

I am balanced in all areas of my life

I have all the energy I need to do what I want

I live a wealthy life in _____.

I am strong, courageous, and bold

I enjoy vacations and lots of free time.

I enjoy tremendous success

Amazing opportunities flow to me constantly

I attract amazing, energetic talent to my business

I am a highly successful and sought after salesperson

I can easily get to my Happy Place

I am kind, wise, and gracious

I am a skilled and effective communicator

MY DEPOSITS

This space is offered for you to write your deposit statements. You can have as many as you'd like. You may revise them at any time. You don't have to fill up the space below, nor are you confined to it.

1. _____

2. _____

3. _____

4. _____

5. _____

6. _____

7. _____

8. _____

9. _____

10. _____

11. _____

12. _____

13. _____

14. _____

15. _____

16. _____

17. _____

18. _____

19. _____

20. _____

21. _____

22. _____

23. _____

24. _____

25. _____

26. _____

27. _____

28. _____

29. _____

30. _____

31. _____

32. _____

33. _____

34. _____

35. _____

36. _____

37. _____

38. _____

16 ★ LET'S PRODUCE YOUR REALITY SHOW

Remember, your automatic mind *believes* what you visualize and deposits these images in your programming. Your automatic mind then drives your thinking along certain thought trails based upon this programming. We're going to capitalize on this now.

You've done a great job creating your list of deposits. Now we're going to give them power by creating your Reality Show.

There are three ways to create a Reality Show. Each differs in its media form, technological tools, and cost. The form you choose is entirely your preference. All three of these methods work well. Low tech and free works just as well as high tech and costly.

This lesson will give you the step-by-step instructions on creating the *low tech*, low cost version. You might need a few days to get this done, and that's ok. You don't have to do it all at once. Whatever you do, please create your Reality Show. It is truly a critical tool for you.

You'll need these materials for the low-tech, low cost version of your Reality Show.

☆ A blank slate. This can by anything such as part of a large cardboard box, a big sheet of wrapping paper (using the blank side), back of an old poster, or a large piece of poster board. A good size is about three to four feet (90-120 centimeters) wide and about two to three feet (60-90 centimeters) tall. It doesn't have to be white, but is should be one solid color.

☆ Sticky notes (any color is fine), blank index cards, or blank paper. Lined cards are fine.

☆ Tape—clear or scotch is better.

☆ Marker pens. Any color or a variety of colors is fine.

☆ Access to photographs. Photos can come from magazines, books, advertisements, newspapers, your own collection, or you can print them from the Internet. We'll talk about this more later.

☆ Your list of deposits.

STEP-BY-STEP INSTRUCTIONS:

Step 1: Hang your blank slate in a visible location, preferably where you can sit comfortably and view it without distractions or obstructions for three minutes every day. This could be a bedroom, office, living room, dining room, den, or another home space.

Step 2: Write your deposits out, one by one, on its own sticky note, index card, or piece of paper. You're welcomed to write your deposits directly onto the blank slate instead, but you won't have the flexibility to move things around, especially if you make a mistake or want to refine your deposits. I recommend using bold marking pen. Using different colors is a good idea too. You can be as creative and artistic as you like in writing out your deposits.

Step 3: Stick your deposits on your blank slate. Try to space them out somewhat so your deposits cover your entire blank slate. Just remember we'll need room for photographs. That's next.

Step 4: Find photographs that are highly relevant to your deposits. For example, photographs of healthy foods, the lifestyle you seek, the body you want, are all good starts. More importantly, show photographs relevant to the *habits* you need to adopt to achieve what you want in life. Examples include, a person running hard, studying, doing research, meditating, hugging their loved one, and so on. Photographs can come from any source. You can cut them out of magazines or other publications, use your own collection of photographs, or find them on the Internet and print them out. Photographs need to be just large enough to see them clearly and commensurate with the size of the written deposit. They don't have to be huge.

Step 5: Stick your photographs next to their corresponding, relevant deposit. Your Reality Show is done. Remember, you can refine your Reality Show anytime you like.

Step 6: Display your Reality Show where you can comfortably reflect on it for three minutes daily. You may sit quietly, or play a favorite, motivating song. Playing a song is nice because most songs are about three minutes, and can evoke positive emotions to help anchor you to the contents of your Reality Show.

# EXAMPLE REALITY SHOWS

The low-tech version of your Reality Show is the oldest method in use, and is the easiest to create for those without a lot of resources. With that said, it's still tremendously powerful. It's been used by many famous people of old, and is still in use today. This format goes by many names, more commonly called a *vision board*. It's a collage of all your deposits and inspiring images in one place. Every day you focus on it quietly, without distractions, for three minutes. You'll want to visualize each deposit and image as current reality.

Here are a few stories from people who use Reality Shows to help them improve their lives. Their stories vary widely and the materials they used to build their Reality Show also vary. The purpose of sharing this with you is to show how anyone, from any walk of life, can assemble their own Reality Show.

THE FOOTBALL PLAYER WHO WANTS TO GO PRO

Jason made his Reality Show from the simplest materials: the side of a cardboard box, cut up pieces of paper, a black marker, and about a dozen photographs. Jason is a young man in college who wants to become a professional football player. He comes from a broken home and spent most of his childhood in foster care. Fortunately, he received a football scholarship to attend college, but he struggles in school and his football performance is inconsistent.

Right when Jason is performing his best, he tends to nosedive badly for a time before rising again. He tends to go through many girlfriends, which has created a lot of drama in his life. He knows he's sabotaging himself and wants to figure out how to stop doing so. He loves the feeling of accomplishment and camaraderie football gives him, but then there's a voice in his head saying says he is not deserving of those good things. He wants to make those voices stop, to be a good role model for younger kids (especially troubled kids), and be admired all the way around.

In his Reality Show, Jason puts a lot of effort into the good habits he needs to help him achieve his goals. Habits he focuses on include self-awareness of his negative self-talk, seeking help from mentors, getting enough rest, meditating, working out smartly, and eating a healthy diet. His tells himself "I am a professional football player" every day, so when he starts to think or behave in a way that is not in line with that identity, he catches himself and makes a change. As a result, he has reduced the drama in his life, has excellent nutrition and exercise habits, and surrounds himself with good people. His college performance has improved and remained consistently excellent. There is a lot of "buzz" about him in the upcoming NFL draft, and he feels ready to put on his new identity for real.

THE PROJECT MANAGER WHO WANTS CAREER PROGRESSION AND A FAMILY

Jeanne made her Reality Show from basic office supplies and printed images from the Internet. She is in her early-thirties and a construction project manager. Her degree is in architecture but she learned quickly after graduating from college she much preferred constructing buildings as opposed to designing them.

Breaking into a heavily male-dominated field was challenging for Jeanne. She sacrificed having much of a personal life to compete with her male counterparts, many of whom are married and seem to get further in their careers with less effort. She knows she is capable of much more and wants to become an executive in her firm to actuate her full potential. Additionally, she wants to get married and have children. Jeanne is single and has not dated for a long time due to the demands of her job.

Jeanne's years of sacrifice for her career has taken a toll on her body. She wants to lose weight and be more fit and healthy. She would like to achieve all this while enjoying the journey and without the constant difficulty.

Jeanne's Reality Show focuses on balance, setting reasonable boundaries, and staying true to commitments to *herself*. For example, if something comes up with work, friends, or family that disrupts her plans for herself, she has learned to politely decline and commit to her plans. In the past, she would drop everything and assist with other's needs, thereby leaving others with too much control over her life.

Interestingly, by setting boundaries at work instead of eagerly taking on every project she has found that others have more respect for her, not less. Also, the quality of her work has improved because she is not spread so thin.

She has taken an interest in healthy cooking and hiking the state parks. Her hiking activities serve as a perfect venue to date and chat with someone new. She has learned to be more vulnerable in allowing herself to become close to someone.

Because she is enjoying her job more, she is happier and more approachable at work. Her new personality has attracted the attention of the leadership who are thinking of promoting her. She is losing weight, and is dating someone consistently who also shares her desire to marry and have children.

THE ATTORNEY WHO WANTS TO BE A NOVELIST

Bryant created his Reality Show from fancier materials you might find at an arts & crafts store, and with nice, printed images. He's an attorney in his late forties who's married with two teenage sons. He hates his job but he needs the income to sustain his lifestyle and have enough money to send his boys to college. He dreams of someday writing a novel, maybe several, and teaching literature to middle school kids. Unfortunately, his law career takes up most of his time.

Long ago, Bryant sacrificed his health to serve his law firm. He is obese with growing health issues. He wants desperately to lose weight and improve his health so he can serve as a good example for his sons. He also wants to spend more time with them and his wife, and to no longer be a slave to the law firm.

Bryant's Reality Show is particularly interesting because it shows the path to follow his true passion and dreams, which is very different than what he's doing now. His Reality Show takes full advantage of the Be-Do-Have concept. He says *I AM* a fit and healthy novelist. He has learned to set boundaries at work and respect his own free time. While exercising, he listens to podcasts about healthy eating and writing novels.

In order to prepare for the transition from attorney to novelist, Bryant's family agreed to make some sacrifices and save more money. He has explained to his law firm that he can no longer sustain his past pace, and although they tried to bully and shame him into "keeping up," he stood his ground about not taking on more. The experience benefitted him because it gave him ideas for a future novel.

Bryant spends about two hours every evening working on his novel. He has experienced more quality conversations with his boys, who are more than eager to give him material for his stories. His wife has started going for walks with him in the morning, which is not only good exercise but gives them some alone time to chat. For the first time in a long time, he is losing weight and feeling much better about himself. He recently gave a book proposal to a major publisher who responded right away about their interest in possibly publishing him. He views his Reality Show every day and it inspires him deeply.

THE CALL CENTER WORKER WHO WANTS TO START A GLOBAL BUSINESS

Roxanne created her reality show by using the back of wrapping paper for the background, and cutting up pieces of paper for deposits. She used images she cut from several *Entrepreneur* magazines. Roxanne has limited resources, so the habits in her Reality Show encourage her to maximize the use of free resources from the Internet, Small Business Administration, and free workshops. Other habits include watching less TV and social media to spend more time studying business and getting good sleep. Her job of dealing with unhappy customers all day long, along with some family drama in her life often keep her awake at night, so learning to visit her Happy Place and relax so she can achieve healthy sleep is important.

Roxanne intends to leverage what she's learned in customer service in her future business. Roxanne grew up in a poor family, and she wants to be wealthy and successful. She knows deposits from her upbringing make it "wrong" for her to want success of this magnitude, so some of her Reality Show deposits address this matter specifically. Wisely, she included interim life goals to serve as steps to her ultimate life goal: to own a global business and travel around the world. She knows that won't happen overnight, so she focuses on the next little goal, and then the next. Her vision and emotional vibration are positive, which attracts quality people into her life who want to help her achieve her goals.

Roxanne's vision, hard work, and excellent attitude attracted the attention of a highly successful business woman who was interested in mentoring her. Roxanne's mentor also came from a disadvantaged background and was keen to help Roxanne navigate the fluid and mysterious world of business. The mentorship helped Roxanne tremendously and within a few months, she is now ready to launch her first product.

18 HIGH-TECH REALITY SHOWS

High-tech Reality Shows are convenient because of their mobility and accessibility. If you're not into hanging a vision board in your house, using one of the high-tech versions is a good alternative.

You will need a bit of technical ability to go this route. Fortunately, most of the programs and apps are user friendly and easy to learn.

The first high-tech method is a slideshow. You'll need slideshow software or an app. There are several slideshow apps dedicated to self-improvement. Some are free and some are a few dollars. As of this writing, a couple of apps I know of are Jack Canfield's Vision Success and Hay House's Vision Board. These apps both have a robust repository of images you can use to create your slide show, which is a nice feature. Deposits are typed in whatever font, size, and color you choose, accompanying a relevant image, or multiple images, on each slide; thereby, creating a series of slides. You can enhance the slideshow with music and animations.

A second high-tech method is at the top of the wiz-bang list. It's a video created using video making software or apps. Again, some are free and some are for purchase. The only video making software dedicated to self-improvement at the time of this writing (that I know of) is Natalie Ledwell's *MindMovies*, which is available for purchase. It has a lot of nice features and is easy to use. The resulting "movie" you create for yourself can be quite impressive.

All these methods are effective. None are necessarily better than another. It's all a matter of your delivery preference. There might be other products out there I'm not aware of and you're certainly free to explore and use them.

The high-tech versions usually allow you to put the slide show or movie to music. Most songs are about three minutes long, so if you observe the slide show or movie for the length of the song, you get your daily Reality Show viewing in. While viewing your show, ask yourself if you're doing the things in your show well. If you are, then congratulate yourself. Celebrating every little win is important to do.

If you're not doing those things well, ask yourself why. Maybe you have too much on your plate, need to work a little more on mindfulness, or just need to take a deep breath and keep working at it. Whatever you do, do *not* beat yourself up. That won't help one little bit.

You might do some things well and others a little less so. Any progress in the right direction is good news! It's not an all-or-nothing thing.

Remember, we call this your Reality Show because it's all *you*. It's one of the simplest yet most powerful tools to resetting your brain. By resetting your brain, we re-program your automatic mind to run the right program of thoughts. These thoughts then lead to emotions that vibrate into the world, whether you want them to or not. Your emotions, whether you realize it or not, drive your moment by moment behavior. Your behavior then leads to outcomes in your life.

Many famous and highly successful people have used vision boards. In fact, the concept of a vision board has been around for many decades. We're just improving upon it and giving it a modern name.

Not only is a Reality Show something you can do for yourself, you can teach it to others. It's a great tool to teach to kids. In fact, helping a child to create their own Reality Show and view it daily is one of the best gifts you can give them.

In the LEADERSHIP series, which is in volume two, we'll talk about the concept of a Group Reality Show. A Group Reality Show helps a family, work team, or sports team to understand the behaviors and habits they need to have to achieve their collective goals. It's a fascinating concept for group scenarios. If you're a leader of a small team—whether a manager at work, a sports coach, or parent—you'll find a Group Reality Show to be a valuable tool to help shape the mindset of the group. The biggest difference between a Group Reality Show and an individual Reality Show is the deposits usually start with *we* instead of *I*.

We'll talk a lot more about Group Reality Shows in the LEADERSHIP series.

19 REALITY CHECK YOUR REALITY SHOW

Your Reality Show is the vision of the life you want to have and the "you" you want to be. If you have deposits and images of mansions, gold medals, and the body of a superhero, that's fine. Just remember none of this is going to come out of a Cracker-Jack box.

I'm not saying don't dream it, but there is something you must do to bring it to reality.

More important than visualizing what you want is visualizing the *thinking, emoting,* and *behaving* you need to get you there. This is your primary focus area. Yes, goals are important because they give you a target, but your *habits* and behavior are what will get you there.

For example, if your target is to have an amazing body, you're not going to get it by wishing for it really hard. You get there by adjusting your mindset toward food, fitness, and health. You get there by understanding your mind, body, and spirit. You get there by learning what works for your body and what doesn't. *This* is the focus area.

The same goes for wanting a large income. If you visualize behaviors such as buying a lottery ticket or doing something illegal, you're on the wrong path. You receive a large income because you brought something of value to the world and marketed it well. You get there by learning from others and through prudence and perseverance.

Let's say you want to pass a difficult exam. Visualize how great it would feel to pass the exam. More importantly, visualize yourself studying hard and making smart decisions about your time and effort.

Let's say you want to be a champion athlete. Visualizing a gold medal is indeed important, but much more important is visualizing yourself training harder and more intelligently than the other athletes. *This* is your focus area.

Your brain programming drives your life. It does so by enabling the right energy and direction to go into your hard work and education. At the end of the day, hard word and education are still required for happiness and success.

You might say I just contradicted myself from an earlier lesson. Let me explain. Hard work and education alone can do a lot for you, but you won't achieve your true dreams unless your brain programming drives that train of hard work and education at the right speed and in the right direction. Otherwise, you simply derail over and over.

Take a good look at your Reality Show and make sure you included the thinking, emoting and behaviors that will help you achieve your goals. Deposits like "I can learn anything," "I make smart decisions on my time," "I see challenges as opportunities to learn," "I persevere through setbacks," "I relish difficult conversations," "I see criticism as a gift," "I'm constantly engaged in learning," "I wake up early to exercise," "I love trying new recipes with veggies," and others are the kind of deposits that will help you achieve your goals.

As you visualize what you want for your life, it's expected you won't know the technicalities of how to get there. You might not know all the rules yet, what resources are needed, or the tricks of the trade. What you *do* know are the thinking, emoting, and behaviors that will get you there. They include eliminating beliefs starting start with "I can't..." or "I don't..." and replacing them with beliefs starting start with "I am...," "I can...," and "I [action verb]..." For example, a limiting belief such as "I don't have the time" would be replaced by "I find time by managing my time well."

"I can't learn math" is replaced by "I can learn anything with enough effort."

"I don't know how" is replaced by "I research and ask questions to find out how."

Reframing your limiting beliefs into positive statements is an important technique to improving the quality and content of your Reality Show.

If you find making changes in your thinking, emoting and behaving is more difficult than you expected, you're normal. In this case, try breaking things down into smaller goals, smaller changes in habits, and smaller incremental changes over time. Be patient with yourself and keep things small and doable at first. If you try to do too much at once, you'll overwhelm yourself.

In fact, trying to do too much too soon could be a problem. We'll talk about that next.

THE THIRD LAW OF THE AUTOMATIC MIND

Many big lottery winners end up broke within just a few short years. Why?

Because the change in their life was too rapid for their brain programming to keep pace.

They might be hard workers and well educated, but if their brain programming is still operating in "broke" mode, it will continue to operate in broke mode even with millions of dollars in the bank. They spend all their money or give it away until they're broke again, in *obedience* to the programming in their automatic mind. If the automatic mind says "I'm broke," then broke is the reality you'll create for yourself no matter how much money is in the bank.

The same goes for rapid weight loss. I have personally known people who had surgery to staple their stomachs, lost a ton of weight, and then gained it all back in just a few short years. Why? Because their automatic mind was programmed for "I'm fat." With "I'm fat" programming still in place, they unknowingly *obey* their programming until they're fat once again.

We obey our automatic programming whether we like it or not, whether we *want* to or not. When you struggle to make positive changes in your life, the Third Law is behind the resistance.

The Third Law of the Automatic Mind is:

The automatic mind resists drastic change.

Now, don't think everything is hopeless because of this one silly law! What it means is we need to identify sabotaging beliefs embedded in the automatic mind causing this resistance. Your automatic mind doesn't mean to sabotage you, but it's programmed to. It's nothing personal.

50

Your *manual* mind must do the heavy lifting of understanding the automatic mind and keeping wide awake to its tricks. This takes real work and effort.

I will speak more about how using the manual mind feels like "work" in a later lesson. In the meantime, if you feel like you're overwhelmed by your goals or that you're slipping back into your old ways, then take notice of that important clue.

Feeling overwhelmed, burned out, or unmotivated means you need to take following three actions. These actions are super easy to do, which is great news. They're also very important.

ACTION #1: *Slow down.* Take a short break if you need to, just don't stop for too long or you lose momentum. It's easier to keep something going than it is to start moving from a full, long-term stop. By slowing down, you give your automatic mind a little time to catch up with reality. All you need for this action is *patience.*

ACTION #2: *Break down your goals into smaller chunks.* For example, if you want to publish a book (and you've never published anything before), maybe start with publishing a blog post, then a magazine article, then an e-book, then a hardcover book. Establish yourself as an author in easier arenas first before going into the hardcover world. Or let's say you want to lose weight permanently. Consider making one small change to your diet and exercise habits until you're *totally* comfortable and can do this new habit without having to think about it. Then make another small change. By breaking goals down into smaller, incremental chunks, the change doesn't feel so drastic to the automatic mind and it's less likely to resist. The automatic mind can accept many small changes over time to completely alter the programming it once had. However, if you try to change too much too fast, it *will* resist. All you need for this action is to identify your next, *small*, easily achievable victory, then focus on it.

ACTION #3: *Make it enjoyable.* If you don't truly enjoy what you're doing, you're going to stop doing it eventually. Period. The automatic mind will reprogram itself much faster if you truly enjoy what you're doing. All you need for this action is to add levity and fun. No need to be so serious!

☆ You've created your Reality Show. You've "reality-checked" your Reality Show. Now is a good time to identify the interim steps between where you are right now and where you want to be. Then get yourself excited and energized about achieving your next *little* step, knowing full well it's the first of many in your magnificent life's journey.

21 THE RIGHT WAY TO USE POSITIVE THINKING

Angela and Scott are college students in the same chemistry class and are about to take their final exams. Both have struggled with the subject in the past. Scott's friends say he has a negative attitude about chemistry and he should instead imagine a positive grade. Scott imagined making an A on his test and confidently spent his time playing video games to calm his nerves. When the exam came, he felt he did well, but when the scores came out, he was surprised to receive a C grade.

Angela's friends say she has a negative attitude about chemistry and she should instead imagine a positive grade. Angela ponders what is in the way of a good grade and realizes she doesn't understand the material. She sees a tutor and is excited about "finally" understanding the material. She nervously takes the exam, and is pleased to receive an A grade.

Both Scott and Angela leveraged positive thinking. So why did Scott perform poorly while Angela performed well?

The reason is there's a right way to use positive thinking, and there's a wrong way.

The wrong way is using *hope* as a course of action. Do not be confused; hope is *not* a course of action. Hope is nice, but without real and relevant action, it is a recipe for failure.

The right method of positive thinking is having an action plan. To help you with this, we'll introduce a popular mental strategy created by Dr. Gabriele Oettingen: *WOOP.* WOOP stands for *Wish, Outcome, Obstacle,* and *Plan.* Whenever you're using positive thinking to help you achieve your goals, you'll want to apply the WOOP concept to ensure you're on the right path.

WISH – Think of the challenge you wish to overcome. For example, maybe you wish to start running every morning, obtain a technical certification, or ask someone on a date.

OUTCOME – Imagine the outcome of what would happen if your wish came true. For example, an outcome of running every morning might be losing weight, looking more athletic, and fitting into your favorite pair of jeans. An outcome of obtaining your technical certification might be getting a better job you enjoy more and pays better. An outcome of asking someone on a date is having a wonderful person to spend time with.

OBSTACLE – This part is key! What is the *internal* obstacle getting in the way of your wish? You do not get to choose an external circumstance. You're looking for the obstacle within *yourself* keeping you from your wish.

For example, you don't run in the morning because you go to bed too late at night after watching all your TV shows. The obstacle is you watching your shows rather than committing yourself to going to bed earlier and getting up in the morning.

After pondering on why you haven't yet taken the certification exam, you realize you fear losing your relationship with your friends. You spend a lot of time with your friends on the weekends, leaving you little time to study. Moreover, you might get promoted over them, which could further strain your relationships with them.

You won't ask that special person on a date because you fear rejection. After contemplating your situation, you realize you don't know if the person likes you or not. The obstacle here is your lack of knowledge of how this person feels about you, which then feeds your fear.

PLAN – This is where you take real and relevant action. What is your plan for getting past the obstacle? We are not just *hoping* because hope is not a course of action. We are *doing* something highly focused on the obstacle.

For example, you might decide to sell your TV so you're not tempted to stay up late watching shows. This will help you get to bed earlier so you can run in the morning.

You might try asking your friends for support in getting your certification. If they support you, then they'll understand why you need to spend less time with them and more time studying. If they *don't* support you, then that's a red flag that maybe it's time to get some new friends anyway because these others are holding you back.

The person you like has never met you, so of course you have no idea if he or she likes you or not. You find an opportunity to work with this person on a project and spend some time forming a friendship. Once the friendship is in place, you know this person at least likes you as a friend, which gives you more courage to ask this person out on a date.

Now think of the goals and positive thinking messages in your Reality Show. You'll want to apply the WOOP methodology to your goals and refine your Reality Show accordingly. This effort could make a big difference in the outcome.

22 EVERY LITTLE WIN IS A CAUSE FOR CELEBRATION

Gratitude is good for your mind, body, and spirit. There's no shortage of evidence for this in scholarly articles or on the Internet. Nevertheless, gratitude takes a *manual* effort. If you leave gratitude up to your automatic mind, then your mind will still end up on the same old ugly pathways of negative lessons and beliefs. Gratitude helps us get off those ugly paths and create new ones. These new, more positive paths generate happier thoughts and emotions.

Let's say you're struggling with a behavioral problem. It's important to celebrate and congratulate yourself every time you do something right.

Let's say you had a pretty good day of visualizing your better "you" through your Reality Show. This is a cause for celebration.

Let's say you spent a whole week practicing a new habit to help you reach your goals. That is absolutely a cause for celebration.

You studied, learned something new, or exercised that morning. You deserve wonderful words of self-congratulations.

Celebrating every little win with gratitude and positive self-feedback is important to reinforce your healthy deposits and habits.

So, what if you didn't do so well?

To start, *don't* beat yourself up or put yourself down. Instead ask, "What can I *learn* from this?" Perhaps you were tired or had a human moment of not being in your best mind. What could have led to that? Perhaps you had too much on your plate and need some time for self-care. Maybe it's time to consider refining your schedule and activities. Or maybe you need to work a little more on self-awareness and how to *respond* instead of *react* to things.

Be careful to avoid blaming an external source. External stuff like a grouchy boss, an inconsiderate loved one, the dog chewing your good shoes, a flat tire, and so on is going to happen. You can pretty much count on that. What matters is what you decide to do about it. Could you respond to these types of external events in a better way? It takes time and effort to change. Don't worry. The gift of another day and another chance to get it right will come.

You can practice gratitude at any time. It's fun when you make a game of it. For example, if you and a partner go back and forth saying what you're grateful for, someone is bound to say something funny or ridiculous. The person who laughs first loses. Of course, you both end up laughing anyway, but the point is you're both laughing and feeling good. You can make yourself laugh by finding the most ridiculous thing to be grateful for. In this little game, you always win.

A popular way to practice gratitude is by writing down several things for which you're grateful in a daily journal. First thing in the morning is an ideal time for this. It helps to start your day right. Whatever time you choose, anytime is a good time to write in your journal or even visualize in your head.

Being grateful for even small things like a good meal, a friend's compliment, a productive work day, a running car, a fun puzzle, seeing the moon's eclipse, a cute little bird, a warm coat, a bed to sleep in, a gentle breeze, the sound of wind chimes, it's all good. Even if you're lacking in certain things, appreciate what you *do* have.

You might think you're "settling" for something less. That's not true. What you *are* doing is focusing on the positive, strengthening your mindset, improving your resiliency, and setting yourself up for greater things in life.

Sometimes when people start practicing gratitude, they feel better, and because they feel better they stop practicing. Afterward, they don't feel so great and wonder why. It's because gratitude is a mental lifestyle choice. You don't just do it for a little while. *You do it for life.*

23 STRENGTHENING THE MANUAL MIND

Whenever you engage your manual mind, it will *feel* like work.

The more you engage your manual mind, the more tired you'll feel because you are indeed burning more energy.

The manual mind is like a muscle; when you exercise it, you strengthen it. If you over exercise, you'll get tired. If you under exercise, your manual mind becomes weaker.

Whenever we're not using our manual mind, our automatic mind takes over. Our automatic mind can run on and on forever on its programming.

Whenever we're not using our manual mind, we're doing something called "cognitive ease."

Cognitive ease *feels* good because we're turning over all control to the automatic mind while the manual mind takes a break. When we're in cognitive ease, we're not *thinking*. Instead we're on autopilot while the automatic mind does all the work of running our lives. Just remember, the automatic mind does not *think*. It merely runs a program.

Using your manual mind is a lot like using a muscle. If you use it a lot, it gets stronger. But if you overuse it, it can get weaker for a time. For example, if you've been using your manual mind all day long at work, you'll be exhausted when you get home. That means when you are home, your manual mind is worn out and not paying attention to the shenanigans of the automatic mind.

I tell you this because you *will* have ups and downs in your journey to reprogram your automatic mind for success and happiness. Whatever you do, do not give up. Your downs will only be temporary.

After the initial rush of motivation and inspiration, usually two to four weeks of your Reality Show, you might start to lose momentum. Remember, we're re-programming your automatic mind from many years of unoptimized programming.

When we attempt to re-train our automatic minds, we will experience a *counteraction*. You might feel you're fighting with yourself. You might be more irritable or even a little depressed. You might feel the pull of your old thinking. You might feel a little bit lost and confused at times. This is your automatic mind resisting the change, and it's more important now than ever to stay the course. It's ok to give yourself some time and space to move a little more slowly if you need to; just don't stop or go backward.

Your thinking produces emotions that in turn elicit a *bio-chemical* and *hormonal* response. A different *bio-chemistry* is taking place inside your body and it will take some time to get used to it. You might start to feel a little weird. That's totally normal.

The Third Law states that the automatic mind resists *drastic* change, so to get around this pesky law, you'll want to make the changes gradually. But even gradual changes can make you feel a little off. Being a little off is ok as long as you don't feel overwhelmed. You'll want to reside in the land of "a little off" until you don't feel that way anymore, then you know it's time to move forward again. We'll talk more about the Third Law in the NEUROSCIENCE series. There's a lot of science behind this law.

The Third Law also applies to the *group* environment. If you're a leader in any capacity, you'll especially want to understand this law. The Third Law is usually the law behind a group's resistance to change. We'll go into it in the LEADERSHIP series as well, in volume two.

In the meantime, I'll encourage you along the way because I know you're going to hit your dips from time to time.

Keep in mind that transformation is a lifelong journey. You never fully "arrive", rather you continue to improve and grow into your higher purpose over the course of your entire life.

24 GROUND CONTROL TO THE RESCUE

Please let me be the first to warn you that you *will* have setbacks and disappointments. Of course, you've always had them, but now you'll handle them *differently*. Rather than feeling sorry for yourself, quitting, or blaming others, you're going to keep your cool, hold your head high, and persevere. At best, you'll find the lesson or opportunity within. At worst, you'll weather the storm with grace.

Challenges are an important part of your growth journey. Just because things don't fall into place right away doesn't mean they'll never happen.

When you think about the people you admire, remember they had their own challenges. Every hero struggles sometimes with situations that seemed hopeless. No matter how tough the situation, they kept fighting. The journey of their challenge only made them stronger, their story more interesting, and their admirable qualities more attractive.

You, too, are a hero. The challenges of your journey are all part of your story. Nothing in the past can hold you back unless you *let* it. The "you" in your *Who I Am* statement knows this. Everyday situations will tempt you out of your right mind. Driving on the freeway, a difficult co-worker, physical pain, a letter from the IRS. You might not feel like monitoring your thinking and emotions, visiting your Happy Place, watching your Reality Show, or practicing gratitude. That's precisely when they're most important. Think of how the person in your *Who I Am* statement would respond, and then try to do same.

When things are tough, it's important to be *aware* of your thoughts and feelings. When negative thoughts enter your mind or negative feelings enters your heart, the most important thing you can do right now is to *notice* them objectively without trying to control, justify, or judge them as good or bad. Sometimes you might not know if the thought is causing the feeling, or if they're independent of each other. That's fine. You don't have to *think* about it. All you must do is *notice* "I seem to be thinking this…" or "I seem to be feeling *x*."

Once you've *noticed* objectively, take a deep breath. This is important because it mentally positions you to step back and reset. It's like an objective "Ground Control" station pulling you back from the brink. Remember, we don't want to react or engage. You might find this difficult at first, but it's important to keep trying. It'll get easier in time.

If you've gotten this far, that's *huge*. Noticing your thoughts and feelings and taking a deep breath is probably something different than what you're used to doing. That's ok.

Once you're this far, you have several healthy choices on what to do next. None of them are necessarily better than the others. It all depends on the situation and what works best for you.

#1 *Be curious.* "What can I learn from this?" or "I wonder if there's an opportunity here?"

#2 *Reframe in a constructive or positive way.* For example, "I can't do pull-ups" is reframed with "I currently struggle with pull-ups."

#3 *Gratitude and appreciation* for anything, even small things.

#4 *Visit your Happy Place.* Take a mini vacation in your mind.

#5 *Let it float by.* If "thinking" is just too much to do right now, it's ok. Just continue to notice, stay detached, and let it float by like a passing cloud.

#6 *Secret Option Six.* We'll reveal this option to you until the WISDOM series of volume two. There's more you need to learn first in order to understand this option.

The process of noticing, breathing, and electing a healthy choice is called *Ground Control.* You'll want to do it whenever you need a mini rescue from a negative thought or feeling. Ground Control also helps you become more resilient. Remember, success is more a measure of the challenges you've overcome in life rather than any great achievement.

Whenever your thoughts or feelings are in a bad place, call Ground Control to the rescue.

☆ *Notice* the thought or feeling (without justification or judgment—do not *react*)

☆ Take a deep breath (you may take several if you'd like)

☆ Elect a healthy choice: Curiosity. Reframe. Gratitude. Happy Place. Let it float by. Secret Option Six (in the WISDOM series).

25 KEY WORDS

You might have noticed we use a number of key words and phrases in this book. This is intentional. You see, key words help to keep you on track. When a challenge emerges or a negative thought enters your mind, evoking the right words to re-orient your mind is critical.

For example, you just had a rough drive home from work and you're in a sour mood. Before walking through the front door to your family, a quick, mental "Ground Control" might queue you to the emotional frequency you're transmitting. From there you might evoke "Happy Place," spend a few seconds there, and dial into a nicer frequency. Top it off with a mini mental *celebration* for getting hope safely to your family. *Now* you're in your *right* mind and ready to walk through the door. All of this can take place in the span of a few seconds, yet the difference to your automatic mind and to your relationships is huge. All this benefit just for evoking a few easy-to-remember words. Maybe you're not into these particular words, and that's ok. If you have a phrase or technique to help bring you back to your *right* mind, that's what's important.

Another reason to have key words or phrases is they give you an instant thing to do, even if it's just to press pause. Generally, people become angry or distressed when they don't know what to do about a situation. When we don't know what to do, we automatically think the situation is a *threat*. If we think it's a threat then our primal "flight or fight" instincts kick in—usually fear or anger. While this instinct was useful in the stone-age, it's a significant handicap to us now.

Let's say you're confronted with a situation that makes you angry or fearful. You know you're not in your right mind and don't know what to do. You might *react* by doing something anyway, like lashing back, but rarely is that wise.

This is a great time to evoke your key words to help settle your mind and buy some time and space. Having a little time and space allows you to think through what you *should* do. In other words, it helps you to "table it" for a while. Knowing what to do when a tough situation arises is half the battle. Having key words at the ready gives you an instant response plan.

Remember, it's almost *never* good to decide on anything when you're not in your *right* mind. Better to delay the decision for when you *are* in your right mind.

Let's talk about the deposits in your Reality Show. Are there ways to make the phrases more catchy and memorable? Are there better, more fun, or emotionally captivating photos you could use? The more memorable, the more likely they are to stick and make and impact.

A good key word or phrase for you is a short version of your *Life Vision* statement. For example, for the young football player who wants to become a professional, he can think "go pro" whenever he's about to do something not in alignment with his life vision. That should hopefully change the course of his behavior.

For me it was "make leaders." I had so many interests and opportunities to do different things that this key phrase was critical for me to stay on track. To make leaders, I had to build products that could transform individuals and organizations into inspiring and productive leaders. This book series is the first of many products to come, and it will take some time to translate the best of my knowledge and experience into products and services distributable globally.

You *will* be tempted into unproductive behaviors or seemingly great opportunities that are not great for *you*. This is where your key words from your *Life Vision* statement will help.

Remember, you can revise your Reality Show at any time. You can watch it at any time. It's even better when your Reality Show plays automatically in the background of your mind when you're not watching it. When that starts to happen, you know program optimization is taking place. You're resetting your brain to become the person you were meant to be. You're transmitting frequencies out into the world that attract wonderful things to you. Your self-image improves. Your confidence improves. Your relationships improve. Your whole life improves. It's like a giant magnet of good things.

How does this giant magnet work? See the next lesson to find out.

26 YOU ATTRACT WHAT YOU TRANSMIT

Remember, every thought is an electrical current. If you pay attention to your thoughts, they will travel down the path *you* direct rather than the paths of the false beliefs of the past. As your thoughts travel down these new paths, they generate a vibrational frequency called *emotions*.

Different paths generate different frequencies, which is why we want to create paths that generate the right frequencies. The *right* frequencies will help you achieve your goals.

The wrong frequencies will keep you trapped.

Remember, you're constantly transmitting an emotional frequency, *whether you want to or not*. Those transmissions are sending signals out into the world. When the world gets your signal, it *responds*. The response might be subtle, but it responds nonetheless. Not only does the world respond, there's a corresponding response inside your automatic mind.

With all these new lessons you're depositing, your automatic mind is starting to *look* for signs of validation. Your automatic mind always has its antenna out. Even as the world responds ever so subtly to your frequencies, your automatic mind will still pick it up.

For example, you're in your right mind and you're feeling composed and confident at a social gathering. Your demeanor draws the attention of someone who strikes up a conversation with you. He or she hands you a business card before departing. The business card could be just a nice gesture or the opening of a great opportunity. Either way, *something just happened that would not have happened before* if you were not in your right mind, thinking in your old ways, and transmitting a different vibe.

Consciously, you might not think it's a big deal, but it *is* to your automatic mind. This little event just *validated* many deposits in your programing. The deposits behind your calm, confident demeanor were in play when a nice person, out of the blue, presented an opportunity for you. *Your new beliefs get reinforced.* Over time it becomes increasingly easier to think and feel in the way of the happy, successful person you envision yourself.

Emotions vibrating at the same frequency attract each other. When they interact, they create *resonance* and amplify each other. They become stronger.

Emotions vibrating at different frequencies repel one another. When they interact, they create *interference* and dampen each other. They become weaker.

Your vibrational frequency will attract opportunities of the *same* vibration. This is often referred to as the *Law of Attraction.* Over time, as you get used to the new programming, and the new ways of behaving, you'll become more and more of a magnet for what you're looking for in your life. In fact, the response can be a bit much at times.

You don't have to take every opportunity that comes your way. *Select your actions wisely.* A great opportunity does not always mean it's great for *you.* In fact, taking the wrong opportunity, however wonderful it is, could side track you for a long time from your true goals. So, think it through carefully. Don't worry. More opportunities, the right ones for you, will come your way. Just give it a little time.

In the meantime, enjoy what happens. Relish what you learn. Keep the antenna extended and pay attention to the subtleties of the world's response to you. The world not only responds; it sends you messages. Are you listening?

We'll talk about that in the next lesson.

27 MEETING OF THE MINDS

Every little thing in the world is *energy* because the molecules in them vibrate constantly. It's fun and interesting to think about molecules in rocks, dirt, water, trees, air, your house, your clock, this book, even your coffee cup constantly vibrating in their own way. The energy of every object, and every living thing, interacts with everything around it, connecting the world as one gigantic, inter-connected mass of energy. Everything is full of vibrating energy. And so are you.

There are many ways to think about and connect with this energy. Religion is one of the more popular means, while others prefer non-religious but spiritual means. Whether this energy is of intelligent design and origin is not the debate here. But most people find it helpful to give a *name* to this energy which indeed is the source of life and the source of you. Some people prefer *God*, others *Source*, and others still prefer something more fun like *General Manager of the Universe*.

Use whatever term you'd like.

The real point of this lesson is about listening and paying attention to the world's energy, because it *does* speak to you, just not in the way you would normally think or expect.

There are two ways to get messages from the energy around you. Both ways require the full extension of your *manual mind's* antenna but pointed in *different* directions.

The first way involves pointing your manual mind's antenna *toward your conscious thoughts*. As you perceive the world around you, do you notice things that validate your healthy deposits even in the slightest way? *What are you saying about them in your mind?*

Observing what you consciously say in your mind reveals your perception on what's going on in your external world. It might reveal more about your reality than you ever realized before.

The second way involves pointing your manual mind's antenna *toward your automatic mind*. A meeting of the manual and automatic mind creates a different perspective on things.

Remember, your automatic mind always has its antenna out, but extending the antenna of your manual mind and orienting it *toward your automatic mind* takes a *special effort*.

It starts by cutting off all stimuli to the manual mind. That means closing your eyes, being in a quiet place, and focusing on your breathing.

With nothing to do, your manual mind is forced to turn and face its neighbor, the automatic mind. When this happens, your brain waves change pattern. This is the pattern of the *meditative* state. While in this state, you're quietly listening to, and feeling, the energy around you and inside you. Your manual mind is quiet and still. It's not thinking, but it's not sleeping either. Rather, it's listening and sensing without judgment.

For those who have meditated before, you know exactly what I'm talking about. For those who have never done this sort of thing, it'll take some practice.

At first you might just get a lot of white noise, or no noise at all. With time and practice, you'll learn to quiet your mind and focus gently on the toughest questions in your life without "thinking" about them. It could take days, weeks, or months, but at some point, if you consistently have these little meetings between your manual and automatic mind, the answer to your questions will come. They might pop into your head, or formulate over time.

In both methods, you're listening and watching for helpful information from the energy outside and inside of you. In the first method, you're listening to your own interpretation of the external world. In the second method, you're listening to your inner world. You're training yourself to be aware of the help coming your way.

Whatever you wish to call the energy in and around you, your connection and conversation with this energy will help you stay focused on your higher purpose in life.

28 ✦ A CONQUEROR'S SMILE

There are two challenges you will certainly face during your transformation: *negative people* and *unfamiliar situations*. Be ready for them.

You're changing, you're dreaming big, and you're behaving differently. Those who knew how you used to be might not accept it. They might dump on your dreams, say you're unrealistic, or insist that your head is in the clouds. They might continue to treat you the same as before, labeling you according to your old self, and hold you to past mistakes. Some might even bully you, insisting you're being selfish, and demanding things from you to distract you from your goals. Then there are those who pretend to protect you by saying you're losing too much weight, working too hard, reading too much, spending too much time on such and such, and so on. There's just one thing to say about this:

Don't listen to them.

I realize that's easier said than done because some of these people might be your closest friends and relatives. There are ways to handle these situations.

First, *forgive them.* This is important because their negativity has nothing to do with you. Even though they're directing it at you in a personal way, it's *not* personal. I realize that's strange, but understand their negativity has everything to do with their own self-worth and mindset, not with you. They're not ready for the journey you're taking, and that's fine. That's their choice. Everyone has their own journey in their own time. *You stay on yours.*

Second, *surround yourself with like-minded people.* Join a club, chapter, organization, support group, online buddies, and get closer to like-minded friends and family. Not only will you get support to help stay on your journey, you're building an opportunity network. This network will prove valuable in the other challenge you'll certainly face: *unfamiliar situations.*

There's a lot of uncertainty in the land of "I know where I want to be but don't know how to get there." There's good reason why people stay out of this land—it's outside of their comfort zone.

Let me tell you something right now. You've got to *get comfortable with being uncomfortable.* People who never leave their comfort zone never improve. It's that simple. People abandon their dreams because when they try to pursue them, all sorts of unfamiliar situations pop up. Maybe there are legal issues, bureaucratic red tape, intense competition, or resource requirements. They freeze up, become intimidated, start listening to the inner critic, and then give up. Surrounding yourself with like-minded people and participating in support networks will help you tremendously with these challenges.

Remember, it's fine to take things slowly, to learn all you can before deciding, and to lean on the right people for support. With time and perseverance, you can *learn anything,* and you can *overcome anything.* The more you overcome challenges such as negative people and unfamiliar situations, the easier it becomes. These experiences build up resiliency, and are all part of your hero journey. Will you be anxious and even negative sometimes? Of course. But you'll think about why that's happening and work through it.

Conquerors have this certain smirk. When faced with an enormous challenge they smile with a confidence that gets them through the situation, knowing in the end they'll win.

When faced with a challenge, put on your Conqueror's Smile, nod your head approvingly, and drive on.

29 / WORSHIPING THE FUTURE

Please don't do this.

I realize that's a strange thing to ask, but worshiping the future is a common problem for many people. Worshipping the future is when you can't be happy until your ideal scenario of the future unfolds. *So, instead you hate the present.*

What happens when you hate the present is you put yourself right out of your right mind. You get impatient. You snap at people. You do and say mindless things. You get irritated easily. You might drive aggressively. You might be in a hurry all the time.

It's valuable to your growth to learn to love the present. Even if it's not so hot. Even if it's far from perfect. Even if things aren't going well. Find a reason, *any* reason, to *love* the present anyway.

I realize we've just gone through a major effort to write your vision statement, your life goals, and create an incredible Reality Show for you, so the points I make might seem contradictory. I realize your Reality Show might not be actual, physical reality just yet. It can be tempting to worship the future. Please don't.

You see, your future is *already* the present. Your future might not be actual reality *yet* but your automatic mind doesn't know the difference. Your future *will* eventually become reality if you keep up your good habits and make good decisions. So, don't worry about it. Give it time and stay with it. You don't have to wait for the reality of the future to arrive. You *can* be happy *now*.

If you won't be happy now, you likely won't be happy in the future.

I say "won't" because happiness is a matter of will. It is a *choice*.

Now, I know you won't be happy *all* the time because life has ups and downs. The golden retriever gets cancer, grandma dies, the car wrecks, the power outage causes all the food in the refrigerator to spoil, you don't get the job you want, the house won't sell, your blimp just fell out of the sky and now it's in a giant ball of flames. I get it.

Let me tell you something.

Hard times and calamities will happen now *and* they will happen in the future. So, if you won't be happy now—that is—you won't seek reasons to be happy anyway *despite* the calamities, then you surely won't be happy in the future, whatever it holds.

Trust me. It doesn't matter how much more money you make, how much more fit you become, or how much better your love life is. You will *still* have hard times and calamities. They just change in nature and scope to match your new life.

Think of your calamities as your valleys in life, and your happy moments as the mountain tops. The food you eat on the mountain tops (because you usually can't farm on a mountainside) is *grown* in the valleys. Your daily inconveniences, as well as your calamities, are opportunities to grow and learn. They'll make your happy times much sweeter.

You might not *feel* like "loving" the present when you're burying your dog, watching a loved one suffer, or getting a bad review from your boss. That's totally understandable. Just try not to dwell in the badlands too long. It's not good for you.

Now, if you find yourself worshipping the future, you are *not* going off the rails, a failure, or a rotten person. Worshipping the future is common and normal. That you're *aware* you're doing this and not loving the present is huge. Your awareness is something to celebrate. Just take a deep breath and return to loving the present. If this happens five, twenty, one hundred times a day, it's fine. It'll happen less often in time.

While you're working hard to make your dreams come true, also work hard to enjoy every minute of your life. You never know when your time is up. You never know when someone else's time is up.

Please do not hold your precious, present moments in contempt.

30 THE MIRACLE QUESTION

The challenges of life make it difficult to think about your dreams. Changing who you are to who you want to be is interrupted by challenges. Challenges such as being overweight, struggling with an addiction, difficulty with changing your behavior, being overstressed, or having too many distracting thoughts. There's a great little technique you can use to help you through some of these challenges and to make the changes you want. It's called the *Miracle Question* and it's a well-known technique used by psychologists and counselors.

The question goes like this. "If, by some miracle, you woke up one day and your problem was completely vanished, what signs or indicators would signal you the problem had indeed vanished?"

For example, let's say you're struggling with your weight. How would you know you no longer struggle with weight? Here's how a conversation with a counselor might go:

COUNSELOR: What might happen when you wake up?

YOU: Well, for one thing, I'd feel lighter and more energetic. I might even go out for a walk or exercise.

COUNSELOR: What would go through your mind?

YOU: I might be more focused on the day ahead instead of worrying about food. I just wouldn't obsess over food anymore. If I do think about food, I'd find ways to distract myself from the thought like listening to music, striking up a conversation, or going on a short walk.

COUNSELOR: What do your meals look like?

YOU: I think my meals would be more balanced and sensible overall, and the portions would be smaller.

COUNSELOR: What's your attitude toward sweets?

YOU: I'd probably just nibble on sweets from time to time instead of eating whole servings. I'd still enjoy sweets, I'd just do so in much smaller amounts.

COUNSELOR: How does a meal get in front of you? Where would it come from?

YOU: I'd probably eat out less and do most of the cooking myself. I sort of fancy myself as one of those healthy cooks that likes to use fresh and easy ingredients.

Now when you look at this conversation, notice the thinking and behavior changes you'd have if you woke up one morning and the miracle had happened. Are any of these behavior changes possible to do *right now*? If any *one* of these behaviors could be adopted right now, you're already better off. If after the behavior becomes a habit you adopt yet another, and then another, until all the behaviors are weaved into your daily life, you will have manifested your own miracle. You don't have to adopt them all at once.

In fact, you might not want to adopt too many new habits at once because of Law #3: The automatic mind resists drastic change. So, if you make the changes *incrementally* over time, your automatic mind is less likely to resist.

If by posing the Miracle Question to yourself, you realize new thinking and behaviors you want to turn into habits, then consider incorporating them into your Reality Show. The compounding effect of many good habits performed consistently over time is what will get you to your goals in life.

31 SUMMARY OF THE BRAIN RESET SERIES

Congratulations! You've finished the BRAIN RESET series. This is a tremendous achievement.

To sustain your momentum and keep you on the right track, there are six more series ahead (three in volume one and three in volume two). As we learn the upcoming material, you might want to refer to this summary of the BRAIN RESET series to refresh yourself on key concepts.

Manual mind = conscious mind. The user of the computer.

Automatic mind = subconscious mind. *Is* the computer.

Deposits are beliefs governing the programming of your automatic mind.

Resonance: similar emotions and vibrations attract and amplify each other.

Resonance, whether of positive or negative emotions, *feels* good.

Resonance of positive emotions is good for you; of negative emotions is unhealthy for you.

Interference: dissimilar emotions and vibrations repel and dampen each other.

Interference is welcomed when you want to change your mood.

Interference is unwelcomed when you prefer to remain in your current mood.

Cognitive ease = when our manual mind takes a break and lets the automatic mind run everything. This could be dangerous if the programming of the automatic mind is not optimized.

The three laws of the automatic mind are:

#1 Believes everything is real

#2 Directs all communication internally (whether thought or spoken)

#3 Resists drastic change

Acknowledge your icky emotions, decide to love yourself anyway, don't act out icky emotions.

Life skills: awareness of your emotions, gratitude, and getting to Happy Places.

Watch your Reality Show for three minutes every day.

Once goals are defined, focus on habits that will help you achieve them.

Have a key word or phrase to remind you of your Life Vision.

If something is not in line with your Life Vision, don't do it.

Strive to be the person you want to be now, regardless of what you have or don't have.

Technique to overcome mental resistance:

#1 Slow down (but don't stop)

#2 Set smaller, interim, achievable goals

#3 Make goals fun and enjoyable

Technique to return to your right mind – Ground Control:

#1 Notice the thought or feeling (without judging or justifying)

#2 Take a deep breath

#3 One or more of several healthy responses (next)

Healthy responses:

#1 Curiosity

#2 Reframe

#3 Gratitude

#4 Happy Place

#5 Let it float by

#6 Secret Option Six (volume two)

Listen to the universe: listen to your thoughts on outside world, and listen to your automatic mind (through meditation). Meditate for at least three minutes a day.

You will attract the emotional frequency you transmit.

Technique to use positive thinking correctly – Dr. Gabriele Oettingen WOOP model:

Wish: Challenge you want to overcome

Outcome: What will happen if you overcome the challenge

Obstacle: Internal factor inside yourself that's in the way

Plan: Your plan to overcome the obstacle. Hope is not a plan.

Two challenges you will always face: negative people and unfamiliar situations.

Negative People:

#1. Forgive them.

#2. Engage with like-minded people

Unfamiliar Situations:

#1. Embrace being uncomfortable.

#2. Be a voracious learner.

Don't worship the future. Cherish the present.

Put on your conqueror's smile

Miracle Question: If suddenly your problem was gone, how would you think and act?

PART 2
THE AWARENESS SERIES

1 LISTENING IS CRITICAL TO AWARENESS

Have you ever been in a conversation with someone in which you were afraid the conversation would not turn out the way you intended it? You're talking to a co-worker, spouse, or friend about something with which you two disagree, or about a difficult topic, or maybe you think they're being critical of you personally, so you're feeling anxious.

What happens when we're in this anxious state of mind is we tend to interrupt, think of our next response while the other person is talking, respond in an emotionally charged way, or shut down and not respond at all.

In other words, we're not listening.

When we're in this non-listening state, we're *not* in our right mind, and here's why.

Your higher order of cognitive thinking is hampered. Your scope of attention is narrowed. Your emotional centers are firing off louder than your rational centers, so you're less flexible and more reactive. Your ability to empathize is degraded. You tend to be negative. You're not learning anything.

When you're not learning, you're not growing. When you're not growing, you're not going anywhere. You're hampering your own growth and success.

This state of anxiety, particularly when we interact with others in any way, is so common and widespread you might not even notice it in yourself.

If you think we, as a society, tend to jump to conclusions and label people at the drop of a soundbite, you're not alone. The widespread problem of anxiety has led to an epidemic of non-listening. Few people truly listen and try to understand each other.

If you recognize yourself as a poor listener, don't feel bad or start beating yourself up. We're going to work on it (and by the way, this is a life-long effort). If you don't recognize yourself as among the crowd of non-listeners, you're either well advanced in mindful communication skills, or you're in denial. If you are in denial, that's a problem because it will get in the way of your *awareness skills.*

Awareness skills are so important to your success in life We've dedicated an entire series to it. It's important you snap out of your mental traps and open your mind to learning how to listen, learn, and understand.

In this series, we'll start off with a fun topic—personalities. Understanding what drives the different personalities in this world is an important part of building your empathy so you're a better listener, more *aware,* and improving your skills in interacting with the world.

Next, we'll go deeper by heading straight into the spooky, scary world of *emotions.* This is truly a fascinating topic, but a lot of people are afraid of any discussion pertaining to emotions.

I'm not going to have you dive into your childhood or dig up your deepest, darkest secrets. We're not doing any of that, so you can breathe a sigh of relief. What we *will* do is improve your *awareness* of how emotions drive human behavior—including yours.

Remember, emotions drive behavior, which in turn impacts everything in your life. "Everything" includes your relationships, appearance, happiness, resilience to setbacks, and career and personal success.

I think you'll find the topic of emotional awareness interesting and empowering.

If you notice people vary in their preferences regarding ethics and change, you're right.

We'll expose you to these preferences so you have a better understanding of them.

Finally, we'll reveal the categories of Hot Buttons that often lead to conflict. We'll also explore briefly some of the common reactions to Hot Buttons that don't help.

Communication works best on Hot Buttons. You'll learn more about that in the COMMUNICATION series. In the meantime, let's get started with building a critical life skill – *awareness.*

WELCOME TO PERSONALITY SCHOOL

When it comes to measuring and assessing personality, there are several schools of thought. The most popular by far used worldwide is the Myers-Briggs Type Indicator (MBTI). There are many opinions as to why this is the case. I believe it is the most pragmatic and least judgmental of all the personality assessment models in use today.

Other schools of thought tend to be less useful to non-psychologists and surprisingly judgmental. For example, if you're a person of faith (that is you believe in God in any way) you'll tend to score lower in "Openness to New Experiences," as though you were closed minded and prefer to live under a rock. Or, if you have strong feelings about certain things that get your passions fired up (maybe you feel strongly about the environment or another cause) then you'll score high in the area of "Neuroticism" labeling you a *neurotic*. I don't think anyone likes to be labeled *closed minded* or a *neurotic* by anyone, no matter how "scientific" the assessment.

This brings me to my next point. The primary charge often levied against MBTI by some scientists is it's "not scientific." The MBTI model was built upon observation, and given most science is based on observation, I'm not sure why this is a problem.

Case in point: if you observe a beautiful bird gliding in the air and a PhD graduate in ornithology (bird studies) sees the *same* bird, does that mean your observation of this creature is any less relevant or meaningful than that of the "scientist"? Of course not. I think the charge that MBTI is "unscientific" is a little unfair. The world seems to agree, which is why MBTI is used to assess personality more than any other system. It's pragmatic and doesn't resort to negative labels.

So, what is MBTI?

MBTI consists of four personality areas, each with a polar opposite—neither of which are right or wrong, better or worse. Most people have traits from both sides with a slight to strong preference toward one of the poles.

The four areas and their respective poles are:

Extroversion and Introversion

Sensing and Intuition

Thinking and Feeling

Judging and Perceiving

What MBTI does is help you determine your preferences among these four groups. There are no character judgments implied whatsoever, so you're free to reside near any pole to your heart's content. In fact, you might find your pole preferences change over time, or even in various situations. For example, you might have different pole preferences when you're at work then when you're on vacation with your family. That's ok.

Understanding yourself and your preferences is useful to building your skills in self-awareness. Understanding others and their preferences is useful to building social awareness.

Building your awareness of personality preferences is why we are going to take a little journey into MBTI.

The following four lessons provide an overview into these four personality areas. They're far from comprehensive, but they serve our purposes for now.

Should your curiosity about MBTI require greater fulfillment, check out the resource section at the end of this book.

For now, let our journey into personality types begin.

3 INTROVERTS AND EXTROVERTS

R on keeps a candy dish on his office table. His office is decorated with nice, visually appealing art and work-related content. The door is always open, and there's always a place for visitors to have a seat. Usually it's easy to start a conversation with Ron. He'd much rather speak in person to someone than over email. In fact, he loves when someone comes to his office to brainstorm ideas. In conversation, his eye contact is so direct it's almost unnerving. At work, he's at his best doing multiple projects at once. On the weekends, Ron prefers social engagements with his many friends or entertaining at his home.

Ron is an *Extrovert*.

Chris's office has four completely blank walls except for a pictureless calendar. There's no candy dish and no chair available for visitors. Chris prefers to keep his office door closed. Walking into his office feels like committing some sort of violation. When talking to Chris, he might seem distracted. Chris interacts best through email. His responses aren't quick, but they're always thorough and well thought out. He prefers to work on one major project at a time and devote all his time and energy to it. On the weekends, Chris would much rather take a hike with a close friend or sit alone on his patio listening to the birds and reading a good book.

Chris is an *Introvert*.

There are slightly more Extroverts (E) than Introverts (I) in the world, which places more suffering on I's[1] who just want a little more peace and quiet. There's nothing wrong with that, but E's sometimes just don't understand.

---

1   For the sake of readability, I will use an apostrophe on these letters although they are plural and not possessive.

I's are not shy or anti-social; they simply process the world differently than E's.

I's process the world deep inside their minds.

E's process the world by talking to others or interacting with the environment.

E's conduct their most brilliant thinking through *external* processes (talking).

I's conduct their most brilliant thinking through *internal* processes (thinking).

When E's speak, they're thinking out loud and it's generally best *not* to take them at their word until later when they've clearly made up their mind.

When I's speak, they've already thought everything through.

Here's a classic conversation between an I and an E:

E *Speaking*: What do you think of this plan? You're so quiet! I don't know what you're thinking. Why aren't you talking?

I *Thinking*: I'm still on your first question. Please be quiet so I can think.

E *Speaking*: Did I say something to upset you? What did I do wrong?

I *Thinking*: For God's sake, please be quiet! I cannot *think* under these conditions!

Do you recognize yourself in any of this?

Silence tends to drive an E crazy, while silence to an I is golden.

To add a twist, sometimes E's might behave in an introverted way and sometimes I's might behave in an extroverted way.

For example, an E who is under a lot of stress might become quiet and reclusive, preferring less interaction than usual. An I who is knowledgeable and passionate about a topic might appear gregarious and chatty whenever that topic comes up.

E's *need* interaction while I's *need* space. A healthy compromise is necessary for the two to get along. That compromise begins with *awareness* of your own personality and that of others. From there, you can better understand each other's needs, respect each other's limits, and foster a great relationship.

4 SENSORS AND INTUITIVES

Sisters Megan and Wanda are going to college together. Each ordered herself a new desk online. The two desks arrived at their apartment at the same time.

Megan opened her box and diligently read the directions before touching any pieces. While assembling her desk, she enjoyed admiring the design cuts in the wood, the feel of the tools and hardware in her hands, putting all the right parts in all the right places, and the practical application of her skills. When the desk was assembled, every part was used and the desk was perfectly built to detail. The desk was placed exactly where she planned to put it. She immediately began to populate the desk with her computer, school books, and office supplies. She Facetimed her parents and gave them a detailed account of the experience, noting the directions were clear and logical, and she was proud how every part was used. After the call, she sat at her desk and began her studies.

Wanda opened her box and started assembling the pieces right away, completely ignoring the directions. While assembling her desk, she admired the wood, wondered if it was grown in Indonesia, if the government there had fair labor laws, and maybe she should become an attorney. When the desk was completed, there were a few pieces of hardware still left but she wasn't concerned. The desk wobbled but worked well enough. She examined the desk and her room and decided to move the desk closer to the window instead of her original planned location. She Facetimed her parents, told them she bought and assembled a desk, and then explained how the experience was like trying to put together some crazy puzzle. She populated the desk with her Siamese Betta fish in a bowl, some books, and her favorite coffee mug. Then, she opened her books and began her studies.

What's the difference between Megan and Wanda?

Megan is what the MBTI would call a *Sensor*, and Wanda an *Intuitive*.

Neither is right nor wrong, better nor worse. They are simply different, and we need *both* types of people in the world.

Sensors (S) prefer to process information through the five senses (sight, sound, touch, taste, and smell). What they detect through their five senses is their total reality, and that's that. They prefer details and facts over theories and concepts. They prefer to focus on what's immediately in front of them instead of on possibilities or the future. They like logic and clear sequences, and aren't too keen on change unless the benefit of the change is clear and unambiguous. Without S's, we wouldn't get much done in the world. You want an S packing your parachute, doing your taxes, or performing your neck surgery.

Intuitives (N) prefer to process information through their gut, hunch, or sixth sense. They appreciate their five senses but don't heavily rely on them like S's do. They find details and facts boring and prefer to focus on the big picture. They like to explore the future possibilities of things, quickly moving on from the reality in front of them. They're open to change because change represents a new possibility to examine. Without N's, we would not have light bulbs, cars, mobile phones, or Harry Potter novels. N's are good at spotting trends, seeing patterns, and exploiting them. They make excellent strategists. You want an N as a commanding general or CEO because they'll come up with the strategy no one thought of, and win.

S's and N's can conflict. N's think S's are too stuck in the weeds and S's think N's have their head in the clouds. This kind of thinking isn't helpful. The best approach is patience and appreciation of others' gifts.

Do you recognize yourself or others in any of these descriptions? If so, consider how you can better leverage and appreciate your own gifts, and those of others.

5 THINKERS AND FEELERS

Sarah and John have two little boys and are struggling to make ends meet. The boys long for a puppy. John has tried many times to convince Sarah to adopt a puppy, but she won't hear it. If they get a dog, they'll have to pay more in rent. The cost of food, licensing, vet bills, and other pet expenses are simply more than the family budget will allow. Much time will be required to train and care for the dog. Both parents work and both boys are in school. Who will take care of the dog, and when? For John or Sarah to get better-paying jobs, they might have to move to another city, which is costly. They must save now for this eventuality. Sarah's arguments are clearly rational, logical, and based on facts.

John, on the other hand, does not see it that way. He had a dog when he was growing up. Although he grew up poor, his most treasured memories were with his dog. He wants his two boys to have the same experience. John believes a dog can teach his growing boys valuable lessons in life: commitment, responsibility, and unconditional love. These are lessons no amount of money can buy. Even though they don't have a lot of money and time, he believes the value of having a family dog is well worth the cost. They'll get by somehow. John's arguments are clearly emotional based on values and worth.

Whose side are you on?

Neither is right nor wrong.

Difficult, huh?

Sarah is what the MBTI calls the *Thinker*, while John is the *Feeler*.

Thinking (T) and Feeling (F) speaks to how you prefer to base your decisions. Do you prefer to use facts and logic? Or do you prefer to use relative worth and value?

You might find you're not always consistent with your preferences, and neither are others. If something of value to you is much stronger than facts and figures, then even if you're a T, you'll make the value decision.

For example, maybe you choose to take time off work to care for your dying parent, even though you're losing money or promotion opportunities by doing so.

The reverse is also true. Let's say you finally land an interview with a prospective employer after eleven months of unemployment, but you must miss your daughter's championship softball game to do it. The F might go for the interview because the pressure to have a paying job to care for the family is strong.

There's also a degree of relativity. You might be a weak T while someone else is a strong T (they're heavier on the Thinking side). A weak T might *look* like an F relative to a strong T. The same goes on the other side. A weak F might *look* like a T relative to a strong F.

T's and F's communicate differently. T's believe they're most helpful when they offer *critique*. T's are happy to receive constructive criticism because they view it as helpful. Offering the same to an F requires much greater tact because F's are more likely to be put off by criticism.

On the other hand, F's believe they're most helpful when they offer *praise*. F's tend to respond and perform better with praise.

If you offer praise to a T, don't be surprised if there's little or no reaction. They generally have less need for praise than F's do.

F's might view T's as cold-hearted and impersonal and not without reason. T's who don't actively work on their empathy are at risk of developing a blind spot in their relationships and leadership.

On the other hand, T's might view F's as overly emotional and illogical. This, too, is not without cause. F's who routinely ignore facts and logic are bound to make some poor decisions impacting their relationships and successes in life.

We need both T's and F's in the world, but we don't need either of the extremes. T's help us *think* clearly so we can make good decisions, while F's help us *live* fully so we can enjoy life.

JUDGERS AND PERCEIVERS

A lex is a project manager at a construction company. He runs an orderly shop with meetings that start on time, to-do lists, and detailed schedules. His office is impeccably organized. His meetings always include an agenda. He identifies the outcomes he wants to achieve at every meeting. He quickly starts on all new tasks, writing them down, and placing a little open check box next to each one. He loves to check off his tasks, often completing them well ahead of their due date.

At home, Alex schedules his weekends so he can accomplish his personal goals. When shopping, he'll either have a list, or know exactly what he wants, and purchase to it with little deviation. Alex is married to Maria, whom he dated for only six months. He knew what he wanted in a wife, so after meeting her and realizing she was "it", he relentlessly sought her hand in marriage. To ensure quality time with her, he makes every Friday night their "date" night.

Once, Alex and Maria went car shopping. When Alex found a car he liked he bought it right away, against Maria's protests. Maria argued there were better cars available at a lower price, but Alex just wanted to get it over with. A few months later, Alex learned the hard way Maria was right. He saw an advertisement for a much nicer car for thousands less than he paid. Buyer's remorse set in and Alex regretted not listening to Maria.

Nigel is a senior biologist at a government facility. He runs a fluid work place with meetings that are often rescheduled to a non-routine time, and vague goals (if any). There are books, papers, and folders stacked high in his office in no organized way, but Nigel knows exactly where everything is. If you asked Nigel for a document, he'll sift through his enormous mess and find it for you in seconds.

When Nigel holds meetings, there's rarely an agenda. There's often a lot of open ended discussion and outcomes. He keeps his task list and calendar in his head, rarely writing anything down. He usually does not start on a task until it is nearly a crisis or near the deadline. Most of the time, he pulls off a miracle, but sometimes he's a little late.

Nigel is married to Sabrina whom he dated for nearly ten years, on and off, before finally settling down with her. He wanted to "keep his options open" and did not want to be tied down before he was ready. On the weekends, Nigel and Sabrina might spontaneously take off for a little unplanned trip or attend a local event out of the blue. When Nigel shops, it can be an all-day affair. He'll go to nearly every store in town to compare products and find the best deal. He almost always finds the best deal possible.

The MBTI identifies Alex as a Judger, and Nigel as a Perceiver. (I think there are better terms but we're stuck with these for now).

Judgers (J) prefer "git-r-done," an orderly world, and finality.

Perceivers (P) prefer to take in *all* the information before committing to something, a more flexible world, and open-endedness.

Some of you might find yourself squarely at one of these two poles, while others see themselves on both sides at different times.

P's generally learn to behave like J's while at work because the business environment is largely a J world. Their personal lives, however, will remain P.

J's can look like P's when they're in a mid-life crisis of sorts, or burned out. They'll suddenly become indecisive and averse to task lists and schedules for a time. J's would do well to learn how to slow down their decision making and take in more information, like P's are good at doing.

P's would do well by learning to be more organized and tidy.

Both J's and P's have pluses and minuses. The best course of action is to try to adopt the best of both worlds, even if you're solidly on one side or the other. To do that takes awareness of yourself.

Getting along with others in a J versus P world requires an awareness of others and compromise.

J's can trust P's will get the job done—not early, but just in time.

P's can please the J's in their life by being a just little more decisive.

We need both J's and P's in the world. J's help us get things done while P's help us not get stuck into something we don't want.

7 WHAT'S YOUR PREFERENCE

Are you right or left handed? If you're left handed, does it mean you're unable to use your right hand ever? Of course not. Same thing goes for right handers. You can certainly use your left hand, you just prefer your right. You gravitate toward it. If you want to use your non-dominant hand, you must *work* at it because it's a little harder to coordinate and control. This same concept applies with the four personality areas.

In the last four lessons, you might have felt you were more of an Extrovert (E) than an Introvert (I), or the other way around. If you saw yourself more on one side than another, then that's probably where you land because you're your own best judge.

When you learned about Sensors (S) and Intuitives (N), did you relate more to the "here and now" part? Or, the "future possibilities" part? Many people get a little torn on this one, and you might have elements of both, but you'll have a preference of one over the other.

What did you think of the Thinker (T) and Feeler (F) description? If your head rules over your heart, then you're more likely a T. If your heart rules over your head, then you're more likely an F.

How about the Judger (J) and Perceiver (P) dynamic? You just might be a J if your garage is as organized as a library. You might be a P if things would fall out of your garage if you dared to open the door.

Chances are, you have an idea of where you land within these four areas.

You can search the Web for "free MBTI test" and find several of them. You might want to take one of these tests to see where you are.

Now if the test comes out differently than what you think you are, then *you* are likely right, and not the test. There are so many factors behind personality such as environment, stressors, and even health; no test can possibly nail what your true preferences are every time.

For example, if you take the test while on vacation you'll likely have a different outcome than if you took the test while at work. If you take the test with a migraine headache, you won't get the same answers as when you feel great.

There's another factor, too, and that's how *far* you land in each of the four personality areas. For example, are you a strong J or a weak J with some P tendencies? You can have a lot of P qualities and still lean toward J. J is your more dominant side while P is your non-dominant side. Being a J means you have *preference* for J, much like you prefer a lot of other things in life. Some of those preferences can be weak, and some can be strong. The same goes for the other three personality areas. You'll prefer one side or the other in each of the remaining areas. Sometimes the preference will be strong and sometimes weak.

Population distributions show slightly more E's than I's, and slightly more J's than P's.

The bigger differences lay in the other two dichotomies. The population is roughly 60 percent F and 40 percent T. So, if you feel like the world is more emotional than logical, you're right.

S's form the largest group, 70 percent; while N's form the smallest group, 30 percent. N's are truly the loneliest lot. N's like to go from A straight to Z, as opposed to going through all the letters in between like S's do. S's just aren't comfortable with leaps like that.

Awareness of where your preferences lay can help you understand yourself and others better. Adopting a *curiosity* about your preferences and those of others will help to build your awareness and understanding. When you have this understanding, you're more in tune with your thinking and emotions, and that of others. You're also more empowered to navigate the people in the world around you.

Differences in preferences often generate differences in opinion, thinking, and behaving. These differences are often the source of conflict in different personality types. We'll talk about this phenomenon in the next lesson.

WHEN PERSONALITIES CLASH

O ne of the more sure-fire ways you know you're dealing with a person whose personality type is different from yours is if that person irritates you.

Let's say there's a manager with an Intuitive (N) dominance and she decides to change the format of her weekly team meetings. In the past, she simply went around the room and let everyone report on their work. Now she would like everyone to send her a slide the day before the meeting detailing their accomplishments and anything else they plan to brief. They will then conduct the meeting using the combined slideshow presentation. This change should help better focus the meetings and keep the discussions more relevant. She announced this change, and immediately gets a surprising level of pushback from several people. They complain her idea is "more work" for them, so they need to understand better the value of this additional time commitment. Also, what was wrong with the old format? Chances are, these people are pre-dominantly Sensors (S). Now both the N manager and the S staff are annoyed with each other. The N views the S's as obstructing a great idea that "obviously" makes things better. The S's are annoyed because she jumped to this change without including them in the conversation, considering their work load, and giving them a clear reason for the change.

N's need to learn what is "obvious" to them is not obvious to an S. Don't get me wrong, S's can be extremely smart people, they just don't see things the way N's do. N's have a true gift for seeing things others can't see. If you're an S, understand that just because you don't see the connection right away doesn't mean it's not there.

N's should fully include S's in the conversation and truly *consider their input*. N's might not think they need the input of an S, but trust me, they do. An S's input will often help calibrate the N idea into something much better, and help the N avoid pitfalls and traps.

S's should choose their battles wisely when it comes to dealing with N's. If an S challenges every little thing, he'll indeed look like an obstructionist. Even so, S's should still talk with N's about what needs more thinking through. N's need S's to do that. S's have a gift for finding chinks in the armor of the best, most well intended plans.

Now let's talk about J's and P's.

Mike and Tonya are preparing for vacation. Mike gets home from work, excited about his upcoming vacation, wondering what kind of spontaneous adventures they'll have. At dinner, Tonya announces she booked activities for every single day of the vacation. Mike swells with frustration and snaps, "I don't want to do any of that!" Tonya is hurt and doesn't understand Mike's outburst.

In this instance, can you guess who's the Judger (J) and who's the Perceiver (P)?

Tonya is eager to make decisive plans and have closure with those plans. Mike wants to leave his options open so he can enjoy whatever adventure opportunity comes along.

Like the situation with the N and S's, communication could have prevented this misunderstanding. Tonya (J) should have consulted Mike (P) before making plans.

Mike could have responded better by calmly expressing he'd like to leave a few days of their vacation open to relax or enjoy other opportunities.

Both J's and P's have something to contribute. It's probably a good idea to have some high-level plan for any big vacation so there's a measure of safety and predictability. It's also a good idea to leave some open space in those plans to allow for flexibility.

We didn't get a chance to talk about Thinkers (T) and Feelers (F), or Extroverts (E) and Introverts (I), but you get the point. Communication and understanding each other is critical to getting along.

In our next lesson, you'll learn what happens when you or others are under tremendous stress, and your non-dominant side takes over. I think you'll find this fascinating to learn.

Different personality types do indeed respond to stress and set-backs in different ways. Understanding personality types is useful. It's also useful to understand their *dark* side.

That's next!

9 THE *GRIP*—OUR OWN LITTLE HORROR MOVIE

Get out the popcorn; we've got some real drama ahead.

When under a *moderate* amount of stress, people will often exaggerate their dominant function. For example, a Thinker (T) might appear more severely focused on logic, and less considerate of values or other's feelings when under a moderate degree of stress.

If we turn up the heat and put the same T under an *extreme* amount of stress, the inferior function (Feeling (F)) might erupt in an ugly way. The dominant T steps aside and the worst side of F comes out. T will show a sudden, and surprisingly strong emotional outburst, and they *still* won't consider other's feelings. Our once highly-rational Thinker, who is now temporarily F, will be completely irrational, engrossed in their own emotional hell, and bring you down with them. When something like this happens, we're in the grip of our non-dominant function, and it's not pretty.

So as not to pick on the T's, let's look at F's. F's under moderate stress might appear overly considerate and generous to others. Turn up the stressors and these super nice people can become shockingly rude, hyper-critical, and even vicious in their verbal assaults on others. Some might even become violent. They temporarily become the dark side of T, pointing out every little perceived flaw, bringing up past matters and re-arguing them, and hurting everyone in their path. We've seen that on more than a few soap-operas.

How about Extroverts (E) and Introverts (I)? An E under stress might annoy everyone by being even more outgoing, chatty, and sociable. An E under *extreme* stress, however, is nothing like that. Instead, they retract into a dark, sad state devoid of interaction with the outside world. I say *sad* because they're usually depressed. If you know an E who has suddenly gone quiet, you might consider intervening because they might be fixing to jump off a bridge. They have taken on their "I" side in the worst possible way, and it's not good at all.

An Introvert (I) will become more reclusive and withdrawn with stress. When in a pressure cooker, however, I's might be prone to near terrifying outbursts. They become vocal, loud, and not at all in a nice way. The worst of their "E" side will come out, and it's not to say "hello."

How does this happen to us?

It's because we rely too heavily on our dominant side and don't exercise our non-dominant side enough. Everyone has *both* sides to them. Which side you choose to exercise, and to what degree, is entirely up to you. It's a mental choice you make when you're aware of your dominant sides. If you *never* exercise your non-dominant side, well then at some point it will exercise *you*. And we don't want that.

People are generally uncomfortable exercising their non-dominant side, just as they are uncomfortable with using their non-dominant hand. You must get comfortable with being uncomfortable if you want to improve your relationships, your resiliency to set-backs, and your life overall.

Understanding your own personality type is half the battle. The other half of the battle is understanding the *emotional* realm. We're going to go into that realm next, and you're going to *love* it!

Why?

Because it's just so darn interesting and *useful*!

The emotional realm gives your personality true dimension. In other words, it makes it 3D. So, put on your 3D goggles, and stay tuned...

# 10 EMOTIONAL INTELLIGENCE

All human beings, except those who are *dead*, have emotions.

If you're reading this right now then you're very much alive. So, yes, you have emotions, along with everyone else who is currently living. No amount of "toughness" on your or anyone else's part can ignore that.

You can either be *intelligent* about emotions and live a happy life, or you can be ignorant about emotions and be unhappy.

Awareness and knowledge about emotions is a real science that has gained a lot of attention in recent decades. It's called *Emotional Intelligence*, a concept created and popularized by Dr. Daniel Goleman. It's the latest and greatest in personal development, leadership, and psychology, and for good reason—it works.

The study of Emotional Intelligence (EI) has been around for a while, and keeps getting better with age. As such, it's getting more attention by corporations, government, school teachers, family counselors, coaches, and more. EI is so helpful to personal development that I enthusiastically encourage you to discover more on your own when you're able.

Ok, so what is it?

EI is *awareness* and *management* of emotions within yourself and others. To be clear, management is not about bottling up your feelings or shutting down the feelings of others. Such a management style can cause a lot of problems, bigger than you had before. We'll talk about this more later. Management is about healthy responses.

There's a level of *intelligence* when it comes to emotions.

Most people improve their EI over time, as life experiences shape them. In ordinary language, EI is a wisdom or maturity factor.

Do you know anyone who is off the charts in terms of his technical knowledge and abilities, but has terrible relationships and can't lead a group of people? This person is Exhibit A, and they have a low level of EI. Just because you're book smart does *not* make you people smart too.

In contrast, do you know anyone who doesn't understand how to use a screwdriver (let alone anything more complicated) but has great relationships with nearly everyone and inspires the best from people? He encourages and leverages the "smart" people around him to make things happen—and they're more than glad to help. This person is Exhibit B. He might not be technically smart, but his EI is high. He's great with people.

Who do you think is more likely to *succeed* in life?

How about happier?

Studies consistently show people with higher EI are more successful and happier in life. If you improve your EI, you'll improve a lot about your life.

To be clear, EI is not about Extroversion or Introversion. You don't have to be a social butterfly to have great relationships or great people skills.

EI is *completely* different from your MBTI, but it does add substantial dimension to it.

For example, someone who is an ENTJ with low EI will appear a *very* different person than an ENTJ with high EI, even though they have the same personality dominances.

There's a lot of ground to cover on EI, and we're just getting started.

11 THE FOUR REALMS OF THE EMOTING UNIVERSE

As we mentioned in the last lesson, Emotional Intelligence (EI) is awareness and management of emotions in yourself and others. Because the definition is so dense, we'll unpack it a little further for you.

There are several different ways EI is broken down. The most popular way is the four-realm model. We'll introduce the four realms here and then go into each one further in future lessons.

The first realm is *Self-Awareness*, which is how well you recognize your own emotions. We often don't know what we're feeling because we're not paying attention. This can be problematic because if you aren't aware of what your emotions are doing, they'll play you in ways you might not like.

For example, if you're sad about your cat passing away, you might go to work in a depressed state. Because you're depressed, you're not watching your social manners and might not say good morning, or your tone might be cold when you answer the phone. As a result, people might form an unfair poor opinion of you because of your bad week at work. You might think you're behaving normally, but you're not, and it's effecting your life.

This brings us to the next realm: *Self-Management*. If you *are* aware of your emotions and understand you're not your best when you're sad, then you can mitigate the negative effects. So, your cat died and you're sad. You're going to work knowing your sadness could affect your behavior. You mitigate this situation by making a conscious effort to watch your social manners, say good morning, smile, and answer the phone nicely. You go further by telling a couple of co-workers with whom you have a great relationship that your cat died and you're sad, and apologize if you're not your best self, and you'll be better soon. You'll likely have a great response to this little outreach, and people will be much more forgiving of your forlorn behavior.

Now let's say you're at work and you notice Dan is a little off today. He seems rather aloof and unfriendly. A few people complain Dan is being a grouch, but you have keen *Social Awareness* skills, the third realm. This means you're better able to pick up on the feelings of others. You know Dan is normally a pretty out-going guy and his dour mood is out of the ordinary. Because of your awareness, you decide to employ the final realm of EI…

Social Management. You find a reason to talk to Dan about a work matter, and you say, "Hey, Dan, what's up? You don't seem yourself today." Dan shrugs his shoulders and won't look at you. You say, "So there *is* something wrong." Dan is silent for a moment. You give him his space and don't say anything. Then quietly, Dan says, "My cat died." Now you enter consolation mode with Dan. You've leveraged your Social Management skills to help Dan through the healing process. His mood lifts and he's not as grouchy as before.

No matter where you are in life, not matter your age, you *can* improve your EI. Building your Emotional Intelligence will help immensely to reinforce the reset of your brain, especially if you're still watching your Reality Show, practicing gratitude, and using Ground Control.

With better EI, you can better understand the *thinking* behind emotions. When you understand the thinking, you'll know if it stems from a *false* belief, or an *empowering* belief you created in your automatic mind from your daily deposits.

If you notice your thinking is negative or unproductive, it probably stems from a false belief. This is why Ground Control is such a useful tool. Ground Control can help you escape this trap and refocus your thoughts in a healthier, more productive direction.

As a quick reminder, here's how Ground Control works to rescue you from negative thoughts and emotions.

☆ Notice the thought or feeling (without justification or judgment, or *reacting*).

☆ Take several deep breaths.

☆ Exercise one or more wonderful Option Items (Be Curious. Reframe. Gratitude. Happy Place. Let it float. Secret Option Six *coming in the WISDOM series*).

12 ⭐ SELF-AWARENESS

Emotions don't just arise spontaneously. They come from beliefs and values. Think about the exercises you did to build your Reality Show.

Do you remember your Magic Words? Do you remember *why* you picked the words you did? You chose those words because you had an *emotional* connection to them.

Do you remember your list of people you admire and their traits? You admire them because they share many of your own values, so there's an emotional connection there.

Your emotions come from *your* values. When your values are embraced, you feel positive emotions. When your values are violated, you don't feel so good. If you know and understand your values, then you possess the master key to your emotions. When you understand your emotions, you have what the experts call *Self-Awareness*. It's ground zero for building your Emotional Intelligence.

Remember when I asked you to think about how you feel about things, and to try to identify your feelings? It's an important reason for doing this is to identify the values triggering the emotional response.

For example, if you feel content and happy when reading a good book on the patio and hearing the birds chirp, then what do you think your values are? Maybe you value control; that is, being able to do what you want, when you want, on your terms. There's nothing wrong with that. You might also value peace, solitude, and nature. So, you're feeling content and happy because all these values are positively in play right now. Hence, your positive emotions are up.

Let's say you're driving home from work. The traffic is heavy, people are honking and being aggressive, and there's litter on the side of the road. If your values are control, peace, solitude, and nature, then every single one of these values is being violated. When your values are violated, your emotions become negative.

When your emotions are negative, your communication and behavior *can be* negative *if* you're not aware of your emotions and managing them. Negative behavior is not a recipe for happiness and success.

Are you connecting the dots now? If you're not willing to become familiar with your own emotions, their underlying values, and the situations triggering your "wrong" mind, then it'll be difficult for you to reach your *authentic self* in terms of happiness and success. So, if you weren't tracking your feelings before, you need to start now.

Some people are utterly terrified of Self-Awareness. Why?

Because of deeply ingrained false beliefs. The automatic mind innately knows Self-Awareness is the first step toward unlocking your authenticity—the key to happiness and success. Those ugly false beliefs are screaming, "No! You don't deserve to be happy and successful!"

Another ugly false belief is thinking that understanding your feelings is somehow weak and fragile minded. Who wants to think of themselves as weak and fragile minded? So, sadly we sabotage ourselves. Of course, Self-Awareness is *not* weak or fragile minded at all. It's empowering.

Now is the critical time. Will you forever sabotage yourself? Or will you persevere to replace those false beliefs with healthy ones that work? I hope you persevere because the world is counting on you.

Now, why in the world would I say that? Because when you're striving to improve yourself (perfection not required) people look up to you as a role model. The world desperately needs good role models. So yes, the world needs you to be your best *you*. To do that you must have self-awareness first.

13 SELF-MANAGEMENT

What do you do when your emotions go negative?

If you said Ground Control, that is a cause for celebration. Good job!

Often, people are unaware of their negative emotions. They're also unaware of the impact these negative emotions have on others and on their own lives.

When you're unaware of your emotions, you're not in control of yourself. You might *think* you are, but you're decidedly *not*.

It's a whole lot better for you to be in control as opposed to your emotions running the show. Letting your emotions be in charge rarely leads to ideal outcomes. Control starts with Self-Awareness, which we just talked about. When you practice Self-Awareness, you can better enter the next realm Emotional Intelligence experts call *Self-Management*. It's in *this* realm where you exercise control.

Let's say you've become aware your emotions are heading toward the badlands. What do you do? First, congratulate yourself because you've become aware! Second, you must act. To do nothing is tantamount to self-sabotage.

So, you've noticed your thoughts and feelings, and you've taken several deep breaths. Now you just have the third and final step of Ground Control—one of the option items.

The final step is both simple and hard. It's simple because at the least, all you must do is find something, anything, to be grateful for, and visit your Happy Places.

For example, let's say your loved one just said or did something to annoy you. It's easy to let that event trigger a series of negative thoughts and emotions leading you to behave in a cold, angry, or passive aggressive way. This behavior doesn't help your relationship one little bit. To snap out of it, think of some of the wonderful, sweet, kind things this person did for you. I bet there are lots of them.

102

Later in the COMMUNICATION and WISDOM series we'll talk more about how to communicate in relationships, and how to manage your thinking within them. For now, it's more important for you to learn how to snap out of your bad spells. This is a critical skill to learn first.

Another example is getting rejected for a date. Your mind might start to conjure up all sorts of silly ideas about yourself worth. This is terribly toxic to yourself and you can't let this happen. Instead, take a deep breath, and enter your Happy Place—preferably one where everyone is smiling and cheering for you, or where you feel unconditionally loved. This will help you snap out of your self-defeating state of mind and build your confidence back up.

Gratitude and visiting your Happy Places (among other options in Ground Control) are simple techniques in Self-Management. At the same time, these seemingly simple techniques can be hard to do. Why?

Because negative emotions can be *addictive.*

How can negative emotions be addictive?

It's because of *neurochemistry.* Just as drugs cause a neurochemical effect, so do negative emotions. How and why this happens is way beyond the scope of this topic. Experts in neuroscience say so and it's widely accepted.

For example, if you find yourself seeking things that upset you or make you angry, or you create drama when nothing is wrong, then you might have a negative emotion addiction problem. Don't beat yourself up if you do because a lot of people have this problem.

The great news is it's possible to heal and totally reverse this addiction in a positive direction. *Positive emotions are also addictive.* It just takes a little more work to cultivate. That work begins in the form of vigilant Self-Awareness, Gratitude, and visiting your Happy Places.

Your best friend is Ground Control. It provides you with lots of wonderful Option Items to help you back into you right mind. The more you practice, the easier it gets. I promise. Just stay with it.

14 SOCIAL AWARENESS

Just as your emotional frequencies vibrate into the world, so do those of the people around you. The stronger vibrations of happiness, anger, or sadness are easy to spot because of clear behaviors such as laughing, shouting, or crying. What's harder to spot are the subtle emotional vibes. Correctly interpreting these vibes require more advanced skills Emotional Intelligence experts call *Social Awareness*.

Social Awareness is the ability to correctly pick up on the emotions of others.

For example, let's say over the past few days your boss has become increasingly less approachable, distant, and irritable when normally he's easy to work with. Everything between the two of you was great, but his mood is just a little darker lately. Most people might not notice this change because they're not paying attention, but you do.

At first, you might be tempted to think the boss is unhappy with you. Given everything was fine before, and you know you've done nothing wrong, this would be a hasty conclusion. Chances are, what's going on is he's feeling overwhelmed. He might have too much on his plate and can't take all the pressure. He might have received bad news from his own boss. Perhaps something suddenly changed in his home life to create an added burden. He's probably completely unaware of his changed behavior. Often when people feel overwhelmed they respond by decreasing their interactions with others and becoming grouchy. Chances are, this is what's going on with your boss.

Do you see the difference between the two interpretations? The hasty, and likely incorrect version is he's angry at you. The more thought out, and more likely correct version is he's overwhelmed, and it has nothing to do with you.

Getting it right is important because it directly feeds into how you respond to this vibe. If you respond incorrectly you could make matters worse. We'll get into responding in the next lesson. For now, it's important to know how to correctly pick up on the emotions of others. To start, you must have your own emotional house in order first before you can correctly interpret the emotions of others. In other words, you must be in your *right* mind.

Being in your right mind is important because you must be able to put yourself into someone else's shoes, and you can't do it if your mind is focused on your own emotional baggage. Remember, being in your right mind means your mind is open, objective, loving, and at peace. It's hard to empathize (see things from other's perspective) if you're closed off, judgmental, angry, or depressed.

To get in your right mind you must have Self-Awareness (understanding your own emotions) and exercise Self-Management (Ground Control). From your right mind, you're better able to empathize. When you empathize, you build your skills and abilities in Social Awareness.

Let's go back to your boss for a moment. Can you put yourself into his shoes? Can you sense the pressure of all his responsibilities in his job? Do you know anything about his personal life?

Perhaps some time ago he shared with you in confidence he and his wife were having marital trouble. Under these conditions, can you sense the pressure cooker he might feel, particularly if he hasn't learned to manage his stress through Self-Awareness and Self-Management?

How do you think his *personality type* plays into this (Extrovert or Introvert, Thinker or Feeler)? Have you thought all that through? I know it's a lot to think about. You might not be used to thinking about all that stuff so it might be hard at first. You'll want to think it through carefully to ensure the best *response.*

At the end of the day, your response to a situation like this and many others will determine a cascade of outcomes. Those outcomes impact *you.*

We'll talk about responding in the next lesson.

15 SOCIAL MANAGEMENT

Remember when we talked about *you* being in control as opposed to your emotions being in control? That will be important right here and now.

The ability to get into and stay in your right mind is a critical skill because it's a key enabler to your ability to *empathize*. Empathy is crucial to your Social Awareness skills. Social Awareness enables you to correctly interpret the emotions of others. Once you've done that, you can *respond* to those people and their emotions. This response is what Emotional Intelligence experts call *Social Management*. It's the pinnacle realm of Emotional Intelligence and requires strong skills in the three other realms to perform it well.

As promised, we'll go back to how to respond to your boss who's been distant and grouchy in the past few days. You figured out he's not angry at you, rather he's feeling overwhelmed and stressed. What should you do?

The best thing is to make things easier on him and give him his space. At some point, you'll get a chance to talk to him and that's when you can casually say he doesn't seem like himself lately and see if there's anything you can do to help. If he doesn't open up right away, then you know it's probably something personal to him that he's not ready to talk about. Perhaps his marital problems have turned for the worse. Give him his space and continue to be helpful and supportive in the tasks at work. If he does open up to you, then this is your chance to understand him better and build your relationship further.

If you were not in your right mind, do you think you could have responded in this way?

Chances are, you would have responded in kind—that is, acting distant and grouchy yourself. This response would have made matters worse.

If you had misinterpreted his vibe as being angry at you instead of being overwhelmed, you might have behaved in a more closed or defensive manner, or you might have crowded him by confronting him with the question of whether he's angry with you. That response would have been less than ideal as well. You see, your ability to respond optimally (Social Management) hinges on your being in your right mind (Self-Awareness and Self-Management) and on your ability to empathize (Social Awareness).

Do you see now how all these realms are related?

Of course, there's way more to life than a grouchy boss. There are spouses, siblings, parents, friends, co-workers, perfect strangers, and more. It's impossible to make a "how to" book for every conceivable situation. What *is* possible is to give you knowledge and tools to help you navigate the emotional realm of life more optimally.

We'll cover many of these tools in the COMMUNICATION and WISDOM series. For now, continue the important work of building your awareness. That's what this series is about.

We covered the four MBTI personality areas and four Emotional Intelligence realms. We barely scratched the surface of these topics, but you know enough now to appreciate other people's differences and to understand yourself and others a little better.

When you understand yourself and others, you're enabled to respond deliberately as opposed to react rashly to the speed bumps of life.

Situations such as criticism, rejection, rudeness, failure, threats, and setbacks generally do not bring out the best outcomes because people tend to *react*.

If you're aware of personality type differences, your emotions, and the emotions of others, you're much better prepared to take a deep breath and *respond* smartly and in a healthy way. This leads us to our next topic: dealing with every day conflict. You can run, hide, or fight, but you'll have much better outcomes if you *manage*.

Stay tuned.

16 RESPONDING VS REACTING

We've all been there. Someone says something rude or does something to make your blood boil. The urge to lash out can be strong, and for good reason: *your deepest held values were violated.*

When your values are violated, emotions such as fear, anger, anxiety, and frustration can arise. This is the stuff of conflict.

Regardless of our differences, most human beings value three things the most:

1. Survival and safety
2. Identity and belonging
3. Self-actualization

For example, if your life or livelihood is under threat, there will likely be an emotional reaction. If you're expelled from an organization or prevented from doing something you love, there will likely be an emotional reaction. If you experience these misfortunes in life with absolutely no emotional response at all, then you just might be a robot.

Since you're not a robot, chances are you're going to feel angry, anxious, fearful, or frustrated. When these feelings take hold inside you, a powerful neurochemistry takes place that can profoundly affect your decision making and behavior. This neurochemistry happens in a tiny part of the brain called the *amygdala*.

If you let this neurochemistry run wild (meaning you make no effort at self-management) then you get what psychologists call an *amygdala hijacking*. During an amygdala hijacking, the primitive fight, flight, or freeze (F3) response is triggered. This automatic reaction served us well a million years ago, but doesn't work too well in humans anymore except in truly extreme life or death circumstances. Giving in to our primitive F3 response almost always makes matters worse. Since we aren't reptiles but civilized creatures, an uncontrolled amygdala hijacking can get one arrested, fired, divorced, or dead.

Clearly, this is not the outcome we envision for ourselves. As such, it's important to recognize when your F3 response is being triggered, and to manage it.

The most important thing you can do when you sense a trigger is to slow down.

Now if you're getting shot at, that won't work too well, but we're not talking about extreme circumstances. We're talking about the everyday things that push your buttons.

These buttons are embedded in your Magic Words. Remember those words? These are your most treasured values. Even the other words that didn't make it to your top five can sometimes show up as buttons that when pushed, can trigger a reaction. Knowing these other value words is useful too.

Let's say some of your value words are: *respect, status, convenience, freedom*, and *money*. If you're driving a little too fast to work and get pulled over by a cop, then every single one of these values could get violated. The cop might be curt with you (disrespect), he might treat you like a criminal (lost status as a "good" citizen), you're late for work (inconvenient), you can't ignore him and drive off (no freedom), and you're likely to pay a big fine (lose money). In the span of just one minute, five of your buttons just got pushed. Your amygdala is going off, you're not in your right mind, and the F3 response compels you to do or say something unwise. Things could get a lot worse for you from there.

The best thing to do is to slow down and stay in the present moment. Your heart will pound. Let it pound. Take slow, deep breaths. Speak slowly, and take a moment to think before speaking. Move slowly (it might feel like slow motion). Doing this might seem a little awkward. That's ok. An awkward *response* is better than a thoughtless *reaction* you'll later regret. It'll keep you out of trouble, and possibly jail.

This technique not only works on cops, it works on spouses, bosses, and others.

Responding vs reacting is easier said than done. That is why slowing down and giving yourself some time and space helps.

17 HOT BUTTONS

Hot Buttons are behaviors or situations with the potential to derail you from your right mind. Hot Buttons are a source of conflict, both external with others and internal within yourself. It's helpful to your growth to know what your different Hot Buttons are.

There are a lot of experts of *conflict* (imagine that!) Opinions vary on how to categorize or define specific Hot Buttons, and I have my own. In consideration of several great sources of information on the subject, I narrowed down dozens of potential Hot Buttons to ten categories.

Each category holds multiple Hot Button behaviors or situations. That's a lot of Hot Buttons.

No wonder it's so easy for us to slump into a negative state of mind.

Hot Buttons affect different people in different ways. Some people might respond strongly to some Hot Buttons, and not much at all to others.

The hotheads of the population might react to many Hot Buttons, while the cool cucumbers among us don't let much of these things sweat them.

The acronym I created for these Hot Buttons is U-HIDE-CUPID. Now you don't have to memorize this acronym or the Hot Buttons within them. What's important is to think about how much of a trigger these Hot Buttons are for you. Do you respond strongly, somewhat, or not much at all? What do you tend to do?

Please take a quick moment to think about the strength of your response, and how you respond. Writing it down is even better. This information will prove useful to you later. You don't have to share it with anyone. You just must be honest with yourself.

#1 UNFAIR: Situations and people that seem inequitable or unjust.

#2 HOSTILE: Behavior toward you or others (verbally, psychologically, economically, socially, physically, or other) that is clearly threatening. It's more than just inconsiderate, it's a conflict where something bad could happen.

#3 INCONSIDERATE: Behavior that to you appears abrasive, curt, cold, rude, aloof, condescending, dismissive, or other manner that seems inconsiderate of you or someone else as a person. It does not rise to the level of a threat like in HOSTILE, but it still gets under your skin.

#4 DISRUPTIVE: Or inconvenient. Situations that slow you down, create more work for you, or adversely impact your goals or interests.

#5 EMBARRASSING: A situation that seems to showcase you in a way do you not want.

#6 CONTROLLING: People who are over-demanding or micromanaging,

#7 UNRELIABLE or UNTRUSTWORTHY: People who have demonstrated themselves to be unreliable, undependable, or cannot be trusted.

#8 PAINFUL: Physical pain, illness, or incapacitation.

#9 INDECISIVE: Or uncertainty. People who are indecisive or over-analytical. Situations lending to uncertainty so that decision making is difficult.

#10 DISAPPOINTMENT: Situations in which expectations are unmet.

Some Hot Buttons can arguably fall into more than one category, and that's fine. What matters is that it's a Hot Button for you.

Awareness of your Hot Buttons helps you understand yourself better. Some Hot Buttons are hard-wired triggers that we'll talk about in more detail in the NEURO-SCIENCE series. With that said, just because certain Hot Buttons are hard wired doesn't mean you can't control them.

In the next lesson, we'll examine further the Hot Buttons that affect you and what you can do about them.

18 THE STRENGTH OF MY HOT BUTTONS

This space is for you to reflect and identify the Hot Button categories that affect you the most. To help you, a range of responses are offered. Circle the response that fits you best. If there's a range of likely responses for you, feel free to circle more than one response.

UNFAIR: Situations and people that seem inequitable or unjust.

Mostly calm   A little annoyed   Very annoyed   Angry outburst

HOSTILE: Behavior toward you or others (verbally, psychologically, economically, socially, physically, or other) that is clearly a threat.

Mostly calm   A little annoyed   Very annoyed   Angry outburst

INCONSIDERATE: Behavior that to you appears abrasive, curt, cold, rude, aloof, dismissive, condescending, or other manner that seems inconsiderate of you or someone else as a person. It does not rise to the level of a threat, but it still gets under your skin.

Mostly calm   A little annoyed   Very annoyed   Angry outburst

DISRUPTIVE: Or, inconvenient. Situations that slow you down, create more work for you, or adversely impact your goals or interests.

Mostly calm   A little annoyed   Very annoyed   Angry outburst

EMBARRASSING: A situation that seems to showcase you in a way do you not want.

Mostly calm   A little annoyed   Very annoyed   Angry outburst

CONTROLLING: People who are over demanding or micromanaging.

Mostly calm   A little annoyed   Very annoyed   Angry outburst

UNRELIABLE or UNTRUSTWORTHY: People who have demonstrated to you to be unreliable, undependable, or cannot be trusted.

Mostly calm   A little annoyed   Very annoyed   Angry outburst

PAINFUL: Physical pain, illness, or incapacitation.

Mostly calm   A little annoyed   Very annoyed   Angry outburst

INDECISIVE: Or uncertainty. People who are indecisive or over-analytical. Situations lending to uncertainty so that decision making is difficult.

Mostly calm   A little annoyed   Very annoyed   Angry outburst

DISAPPOINTMENT: Situations in which expectations are unmet.

Mostly calm   A little annoyed   Very annoyed   Angry outburst

Now have a look at your responses. Are you more of a cool cucumber, a hothead, or somewhere in between?

Cool cucumbers generally have the advantage. It's not that they don't care or are apathetic. They've just learned to not let these things get to them. Cool cucumbers are better able to *choose* a more positive emotional state for themselves rather than allow others to determine their emotional state.

For the hotheads out there, your tendency to get triggered into a negative state is a good thing to know about. By knowing about it, you can *do* something about it. You see, being easily triggered does not bode well for success in many areas of your life. You will want to do what you can to tone it down and be more like the cool cucumbers.

19 YOUR RESPONSE TO HOT BUTTONS

When you look at all the Hot Buttons from the last lesson, it's no wonder we have so much strife in the world. There's no shortage of unfairness, inconsiderate behavior, hostile acts, pain, inconvenience, and disappointment.

A vicious cycle can start when we react to Hot Buttons *with* Hot Buttons.

They demean, we shout a nasty name. They shout a nasty name, we start a fight. We win the fight, causing both physical pain and emotional pain for them and their loved ones. They seek revenge, and it just keeps going. It's war.

Passive Hot Buttons might look peaceful, but they're still toxic.

Passive Hot Buttons are things like the silent treatment, avoidance, discreet undermining, and poisoning the well, so to speak. They perpetuate a reaction-in-kind cycle that can turn active. It's a cold war.

When someone pushes your buttons in either an active or passive way, what's your typical reaction? When one or more of your Hot Buttons are pushed, do you put others down? Use sarcasm? Accuse? Threaten? Give them the silent treatment? Dismiss them? Say bad things about them behind their backs? Use a crude gesture or call names? Lash out? Seek to win at all costs? Find opportunities to get even?

If you *know* you react to Hot Buttons *with* Hot Buttons (active or passive, it doesn't matter) then congratulate yourself because you're ahead of a lot of people. You're ahead because you're *aware*. A lot of people are not aware of this shortcoming in their emoting and behaving.

Now, some people might be perfectly aware they react to Hot Buttons with Hot Buttons but think it's ok. In other words, it's a form of revenge and revenge is ok.

Let me tell you something right now. It's *not* ok! Revenge is *extremely* poisonous. You might have been taught growing that revenge is ok. You were taught *wrong*.

The good news is you *can* change. You want to change if you want to succeed in your goals.

For example, let's say you've had a tough day at work. You're hungry and want to go out to dinner. You ask your spouse where she'd like to go and she can't decide. You get testy, she gets defensive, and you get testier. Now there's a fight. The Hot Button categories at play here are:

DISRUPTIVE because her indecisiveness created a delay in eating, creating an inconvenience and perhaps even a certain amount of pain because of your ongoing hunger.

INCONSIDERATE because you might not have considered she had a tough day too and was not able to think clearly enough to decide on something as simple as dinner. Your testy behavior was perceived as inconsiderate by her. Her defensiveness is perceived as inconsiderate by you, and so on.

Here's another example. Your boss tells an embarrassing joke about you at a meeting. You react by avoiding him, carbon copying his peers on your emails to make a point, and giving him incomplete information so he looks bad at his briefings in front of his boss. The Hot Button categories at play here are:

EMBARRASSING because your boss told a joke about you at the meeting (also viewed as inconsiderate.) You're also embarrassing your boss by carbon copying his peers and setting him up to look bad at his briefings.

UNRELIABLE and untrustworthy because you are demonstrating to your boss he cannot trust you.

The best way to respond to Hot Buttons is with healthy and effective *communication*. We have an entire series dedicated to communication so we won't get into it here. What's important right now is to build your awareness on *your* Hot Buttons.

What's equally important is to learn *not* to react to Hot Buttons with a Hot Button. You will only make matters worse and lose respect in the process. If you remain in your right mind in the face of a Hot Button, people will notice and respect you for it.

# 20 THE SEVEN EVIL DWARVES

Sometimes people will say things you don't want to hear. That does not always mean they're negative. In fact, they could offer valuable information.

People are often unaware of their own shortcomings, or they *are* aware but either don't care or mistakenly believe it's an asset. They're very much mistaken.

If anyone tells you you're exhibiting one of the following seven behaviors, consider it a gift. It takes courage to deliver uncomfortable news and they had the courage to tell you. Thank them, and do not take offense. Then take some quiet time to reflect on their input.

Here are what I call the Seven Evil Dwarves. They are not nice and they *will* sabotage you.

#1 *Bullying or aggression.* Coaches, parents, and managers sometimes mistake their aggressive ways as "necessary" to get what they want from their subordinates, kids, or customer service. It often works, but there are serious consequences. Bullying and aggression leaves a substantial wreckage of resentment, anger, and thoughts of revenge in its wake. *Never* underestimate someone who is angry at you. Most people will get over it, but some will not. It's truly not necessary to bully people to get your way. That's a false belief that's better purged. It's possible to get your way through *considerate* assertion. If sometimes that doesn't work, then it's probably high time you learned to take "no" for an answer. Taking no graciously earns you respect, and *that* is what you want to retain.

#2 *Over-controlling.* The false belief driving this problem is "I must control..." whatever it is. Most of the time, it's not the case. It doesn't mean abdicate your responsibilities, not follow up, or fail to ask thoughtful questions. It means don't helicopter over people, insist on perfection, or give little autonomy. When you deny people their autonomy it's a surefire way to cause resentment. Remember, it's a bad idea to make people resentful.

#3 *Mocking or putting down others.* This is a big no-no! But it happens so often we think it's ok. It's *not.* It reveals your poor opinion of others in a public way. It's understandable when you're frustrated with someone and you might mock them or put them down. I've done it myself and I'm not proud of it. When people see you do this, they become fearful and distrustful of you. Why? Because they fear if they upset you that you'll mock or put them down too. That's not how you inspire people. It's how you scare them away.

#4 *Defensiveness.* This is probably the most widespread blind spot, and some people have it really bad. The false belief at play here is "all criticism is bad." That is simply not true. It's exactly the opposite. Criticism is often a gift. Constructive criticism can help us grow. I promise you'll be just fine. Go through Ground Control to settle your initial reaction to be defensive, then thank people for their input. Give the matter serious reflective thought. Defensiveness is a form of aggression. You don't want to go there. Humility is much more likely to earn you respect and admiration from others as opposed to defensiveness.

#5 *Grandiose.* People talk and act big when they feel small. It's a subtle form of bullying in that you're trying to make others feel small. People behaving in a grandiose way rarely see it, but others see it and it makes them uncomfortable to be around you.

#6 *Blaming or making excuses.* This is one of the biggest red flags you're not responsible, accountable, or dependable. Blaming is a fast way to shut down a conversation. Making excuses just plain makes you look incompetent. It's better to wear the mistake and own it. You're not only more likely to do something constructive as opposed to crying victim, owning a problem will earn you a whole lot more respect. Blaming and excuses makes you look weak.

#7 *Inconsistent behavior.* When people don't know what to expect from you, it makes them uncomfortable around you. That's not the vibe you want around your being. If someone asks you why you act differently around someone, or why you act differently when something happens, you should pay attention. Don't become defensive. Don't give excuses or blame. Examine the thoughts and feelings behind the behaviors. Reflect and reframe, then resolve to think, emote, and behave in a more consistent way.

While the Seven Evil Dwarves are shortcomings, you are *not* an evil, rotten, no good person if you have or ever had any of them. Everyone has shortcomings in one or more areas, and awareness of your shortcomings is truly a gift because then you can do something about them. Shortcomings limit you, and you don't have time for limitations in your life.

21 CHANGE HAPPENS AT THE SPEED OF TRUST

In general, there are four types of people when it comes to change:

EXPLORERS: Thrive on constant change; seek novelty, challenges and adventure; tend to initiate and follow through on change easily.

HOMESTEADERS: Prefer the status quo and are stressed by change; like routine, constancy, and stability; tend to resist change.

FLOATIES: Flow with change. They don't say much and just try to get along when change happens. They neither resist nor initiate change.

ADAPTERS: Some people accept change if it's orderly and makes sense. They understand change is a part of life. They might even help implement the change to ensure it is on their terms and they have a say in it.

Do you see yourself in any of these descriptions? Experts identify these four characteristics as *Change Types*. Depending upon the situation, you might present any one of these four behaviors. With that said, you'll likely show one of these behaviors more often than the others. This is your Change Type *preference*.

Change Type is strongly influenced by a person's need for security. Some people prefer a steady job, a roof over their head, and certainty as to when they'll eat next. Others could care less about these matters. Neither is right nor wrong. They just are.

People with a greater need for security will either want a slow and orderly change, or no change at all. If there's low trust in the relationship, then resistance is more likely. If the change threatens security or deeply held values, then resistance is more likely.

Remember, security (safety and well-being) is one of the strongest values held by most people, even if it's not in your Magic Words. Some measure of security is everyone's common denominator.

People with less need for security will either lead the way with their flag flying high, or merely allow themselves to be swept up by the change riptide. It's not that they don't care about security, they just have more faith everything will be ok. These people tend to be more driven by curiosity for newness and novelty. Such characteristics make them more open to change. As you can see, change is easy for some people and hard for others.

If change tends to be easy for you, then your transformation in this program might come more quickly.

If change isn't easy for you, then your transformation will *still* come; just take your time and go at your own pace.

The more you trust yourself, the easier it will be. The less you trust yourself (indicating there are still false beliefs lurking in the programming of your automatic mind) the more effort you'll need to build trust in yourself. Trust in yourself is critical for your transformation to take place.

If you're resisting your own good change, even sabotaging yourself, then consider going a little more slowly, adopting new habits more incrementally, and revising some of your deposits to focus on building trust in yourself.

Something else to consider if you find yourself resisting your own transformation is whether or not the change is aligned with your values. If the change you seek is not aligned with your values, then you may need to re-consider the change.

When your values are truly represented in the change you seek, there's more trust in yourself. With trust in yourself, your transformation will happen more quickly.

If you're struggling to trust yourself, take it slowly, add new habits over time, and stay consistent. Remember, the compounding effect of good habits done consistently will pay off for you in time.

Just give yourself a good fighting chance and don't give up on yourself!

Like trust in yourself, people will be more open to change if they trust the change, and the people proposing or implementing the change.

Taking the time and energy to earn and build trust creates an environment where change is easier.

22 THE GOLDEN RING OF POWER—USE IT FOR GOOD

By now, you've been exposed to a few years' worth of psychological studies in the span of an hour (broken down into three minute sessions). That's a *lot* of information to absorb, and you're probably wondering how to remember it all.

Well, here's some good news: you don't. The point of the AWARENESS series was to increase your awareness. It was never meant to turn you into the local shrink. You don't have to memorize the MBTI poles, the Emotional Intelligence realms, Ethical and Change Types, or anything like that.

Think of opening a door to see a fantastic view of the mountains and city below. Take in all that's there. You don't have to memorize everything you saw in the scene. That would be missing the point.

In fact, if you went to work one day and said to a co-worker, "I think we have conflict because you're a Feeler and I'm a Thinker," you'd probably get a funny look back. If you told your spouse, "Your Social Awareness skills are poor and you should learn to read my emotions better," it's probably not going to end well. Imagine if you told your aging mother, "You're insecure, which is why you're resistant to change."

Do you see the problem in any of these statements? Rather than using your knowledge to better understand yourself and others, you're using your knowledge to *judge* others. That's a big no-no! There's a danger in having shared all this great information with you in that you just might leverage it to judge others. If you do that, you set yourself backward.

When you judge others, you're not listening. You're not learning or under-standing. You set yourself up to be judged as well. What happens if those judgements are unfavorable? Ugly lie-deposits land right back into your programming and start driving your thinking, emoting, and behaving in the wrong direction.

What was shared with you in the AWARENESS series is like the Golden Ring of power. Use it for good, not for evil. At the end of the day, the most important thing you can do to build and maintain your awareness is to *listen*. That means listening to the internal conversation happening in your head, and listening to the conversation of others.

Let's start with the conversation in your head. Are you repeating the words of ugly lie deposits, or are you repeating your new, healthy deposits?

When you're under stress, feeling down, or upset, you might find your mind repeating ugly lies to itself such as, "I'm not good enough," "They're rotten people," "I don't have the connections," "The system is rigged against me," "He or she doesn't care about me," and more. It's important to catch this so you can intervene with an antidote. Remember, Ground Control. That will help you tremendously.

Alternatively, when things are going well, do you actively reinforce positive thoughts?

It's important to reinforce your positive thoughts to build momentum in your transformation. Reinforcing positive, productive thinking will help build resiliency for when things don't go your way. You can use Ground Control for this too, except you elect Option Three: Gratitude.

Let's talk about listening to others. Are you thinking of something else or of your next response? Are you taking anything they say personally? Are you interrupting them, or completing their sentences? Have you already judged them?

These are all indicators of a great opportunity to improve your listening skills, and to *respond mindfully* (as opposed to reacting.) By clearing your mind, directing your focus toward *them*, and staying objective, you can better hear what they're saying and understand what's driving their behavior. Try this first with people who don't push your buttons too much. This will give you practice. Later, you can challenge yourself to listen to people with whom you've struggled to get along. It takes time and perseverance. Listening skills don't happen overnight, but if you become a great listener, you'll be pleasantly surprised at how much this greatly increases your likability.

And that's a good thing.

23 SUMMARY OF THE AWARENESS SERIES

Congratulations! You have completed the AWARENESS Series.
As mentioned in the BRAIN RESET Series, awareness of one's emotional state is a critical life skill. It is the foundational skill by which all awareness builds. It is also a critical first step to having empathy.

Awareness is empowering. The better your awareness skills, the more you're empowered to think, emote, and behave in healthy, productive ways. Awareness impacts your communication, your leadership abilities, and even your health. This link between awareness and these other areas of your life will become more apparent as we progress through the remaining series.

Below is a summary of the AWARENESS Series. You might want to refer to this summary section to remind yourself of the concepts presented here.

Listening is crucial to awareness.

MBTI = Myers Briggs Type Indicator. Profiles four different personality dichotomies.

#1 Extrovert (E) and Introvert (I)

Extroverts process information externally, while introverts process information inside their mind.

#2 Intuitive (N) and Sensing (S)

Intuitives think big picture and possibilities, while Sensors think details and "here and now."

#3 Thinking (T) and Feeling (S)

Thinkers use logic to make decisions, while Feelers use values to make decisions.

#4 Judging (J) and Perceiving (P)

Judgers need certainty and closure, while Perceivers need open-endedness and flexibility.

Personality dichotomies present a range, and not absolutes. One's preference can change.

The Grip: when the non-dominant side emerges in an ugly way due to high stress.

Emotional Intelligence (EI) is awareness and management one's emotions and that of others. Dr. Daniel Goleman.

Self-Awareness is the skill of being aware of one's own emotional state.

Self-Management is the skill of managing one's own emotional state in a healthy way.

Social Awareness is the skill of correctly assessing the emotional state of others.

Social Management is the skill of responding appropriately to others.

F3 = Fight, flight, or freeze response.

Hot Buttons = UHIDECUPID

#1 UNFAIR: Situations and people that seem inequitable or unjust.

#2 HOSTILE: Behavior toward you or others that is clearly threatening.

#3 INCONSIDERATE: Behavior that to you seems inconsiderate of you or someone else.

#4 DISRUPTIVE: Or inconvenient. Situations that slow you down, or create more work for you.

#5 EMBARRASSING: A situation that seems to showcase you in a way do you not want.

#6 CONTROLLING: People who are over-demanding or micromanaging,

#7 UNRELIABLE or UNTRUSTWORTHY: People who have demonstrated to be this.

#8 PAINFUL: Physical pain, illness, or incapacitation.

#9 INDECISIVE: Or uncertainty. People who are indecisive or over-analytical.

#10 DISAPPOINTMENT: Situations in which expectations are unmet.

Unhealthy responses to Hot Buttons = Demean. Sarcasm. Accuse. Threaten. Silent treatment. Dismiss. Gossip. Crude gestures. Name call. Lash out. Seek to win at all costs. Revenge.

The Seven Evil Dwarves are:

#1 *Bullying or aggression.*

#2 *Over-controlling.*

#3 *Mocking or putting down others.*

#4 *Defensiveness.*

#5 *Grandiose.*

#6 *Blaming or making excuses.*

#7 *Inconsistent behavior.*

Four Change Types are:

EXPLORERS: Seek novelty, challenges and adventure; tend to initiate change.

HOMESTEADERS: Prefer the status quo and are stressed by change; tend to resist change.

FLOATIES: Flow with change. They neither resist nor initiate change.

ADAPTERS: Accept and support change if it's orderly and makes sense.

PART 3
THE COMMUNICATION SERIES

 # 1 COMMUNICATION MATTERS

Communication is much more than the words you say and hear. Communication occurs in the forms of tone, gestures, symbols, flags, pictures, sounds, music, and actions.

Every time communication takes place, there is *influence*.

If the communication is *positive*, then a positive influence will likely occur.

If the communication is *negative*, then a negative influence will likely occur.

There's a well-known verse in the Bible: "A gentle answer turns away wrath, but a harsh word stirs up anger" (Proverbs 15:1). Sometimes, a single communication delivered in a certain way can trigger a profound decision in someone else.

Here's a story that makes the point.

Two young Catholic boys grew up in Europe around the same time. Both were altar boys in their churches. Both experienced an incident in which they spilled the ceremonial wine as they passed the cup to their respective priest. One boy was publicly rebuked by his priest in a loud and harsh manner. Embarrassed and angry, he never returned to church again. The other boy was kindly reassured by his priest and forgiven on the spot. He chose to remain with his church for the rest of his life. The first boy grew up to become Slobodan Milosevic, the genocidal leader of Serbia. The second boy grew up to become Pope John Paul II. Two different communication styles resulted in two different decisions.

Now, there were probably many other factors influencing the outcomes of these two boys, but it makes the point. A single communication can influence a profound decision to remain with or leave your religion, family, job, marriage, town, organization, friendship, and more. Such a decision will indeed have a significant impact on the future of your life, and sometimes the lives of others as well.

Your word choice, tone, and timing *matter*.

Your gestures *matter*.

Your eye contact and facial expressions *matter*.

The symbols and pictures you choose to display *matter*.

Your social media, text messages, and emails *matter*.

Your actions *matter*.

Every single one of these communication mediums matter because they *influence* the thinking, emoting, and behavior of others. The behavior of others will help, hurt, or make no difference to you, your interests, or your goals in life.

Ideally, you want to influence the behavior of others in a *positive* way. Doing that well takes advanced skills in communication. That is what this series is about.

In this series, you'll learn the dynamic taking place every time a communication exchange takes place.

We'll reveal how different personality types communicate in different ways.

You'll learn techniques for engaging in difficult conversations, traps to avoid, and tools to leverage.

Finally, I'll explain what it will take for you to truly transform your communication skills for the better. It doesn't come easily.

Lessons learned in the BRAIN RESET Series and AWARENESS Series will help you. You might want to refer to those lessons periodically.

If you exercise excellent communication skills, you exercise *influence*.

When you exercise influence, you have *power*.

When you have power, you can better manage outcomes in your favor, whether you're working on a relationship you hope will turn into marriage, implementing unpopular changes at work, or coaching a soccer team.

It doesn't matter if you're talking to a stranger on an airplane, calming your three-year-old child, or negotiating a high stakes business deal. In small matters and in large, the power to influence outcomes to your advantage can result in profound differences not only in your life, but in the lives of others.

THE SECOND MOST POWERFUL FORM OF COMMUNICATION

L istening.

We all want to be heard. More importantly, we want to be heard *sincerely*. This might sound counterintuitive, but your ability to empathetically listen to others is the second most powerful form of communication you can exercise. The *most* powerful form of communication are your *actions*. We'll talk about that in the LEADERSHIP series.

Here's why listening is so powerful.

Sincere, empathetic listening positively influences others. People who are truly heard usually become calmer, less defensive, and more cooperative. When people are afforded the opportunity to express their ideas to an empathetic listener, they tend to be more open minded to other ideas.

People who can tell their side of the story, and when that story is not just heard but *understood* (not necessarily agreed to), they tend to be more accepting of outcomes even if those outcomes are not entirely in their favor.

Empathetic listeners often enjoy more trust from others because they are perceived as *fair*. When people sense fairness, they are less likely to feel threatened.

When people feel less threatened, they are more trusting, and less emotional. When emotions are more level, there is more rational thinking.

With more rational thinking, there's more productive communication, which usually leads to better outcomes overall.

Listening with empathy when emotions are running high is much easier said than done. In situations where others communicate at you in a toxic way, you might feel threatened. When you feel threatened, your brain is hard-wired to become defensive, turning off your objectivity and ability to listen with empathy.

What's worse is if your emotions truly take over, you might be seduced to communicate in a toxic way yourself, making everything *worse*. This is precisely what we want to avoid.

In the NEURO-SCIENCE series, you'll learn about the hard-wired triggers in the brain that tend to bring out our unflattering side. Understanding the neuro-science behind your response to perceived threats is useful in helping you exercise better control when your emotions are fired up. If you can manage your emotions, you'll be much more effective in your communication.

For the purposes of this series, we'll assume normal, everyday communications that might sometimes get our feathers a little ruffled, but far below the point of velociraptor, Tasmanian Devil madness. You'll need the benefit of the knowledge of the NEURO-SCIENCE series to do that, and even then, you'll still use the same tools and techniques presented here.

Now back to listening.

Listening is the number one most valuable tool in your communication tool box. The happiest, most successful, most admired, most well-liked, and influential people are fantastic listeners.

Of course, the whole purpose of you engaging in this process is to become that happy, successful, admired, well-liked, and influential person you want to be, so this is another one of those critical life skills to learn.

The topic of listening will come up repeatedly in this series. That said, we'll introduce you to someone who is *always* listening in on your conversations, whether *you* are listening or not.

That's in the next lesson.

3 MEET FIFI

In every single communication, there's a presence.

I'm not talking about God, Source, the General Manager of the Universe, or some other deity-like entity. *This* presence is part of the conversation, no matter who you're talking to. Sometimes the presence is small, and sometimes it's large. Sadly, it's invisible to nearly everyone, but fortunately it is now visible to *you*.

Ladies and gentlemen, meet FIFI.

FIFI is an acronym for *Facts, Identity, Feelings*, and *Impact*.

Every single time there's a communication, these four factors are in play. The weight and influence of these factors on your conversations vary from extremely small to extremely large. We'll introduce each factor, and then expand upon them individually in upcoming lessons.

FACTS: Each of us have different facts. It's normal human behavior to notice facts that support our values and disregard facts that contradict them. A great example of this phenomenon is when two people have different opinions about the same movie, news article, or event. Our facts lead us to different perspectives, opinions, and conclusions. When we engage each other in communication, we do so from the foundation of *our own* facts. The tricky part is, no two people have the same foundation of facts. When our foundation of facts doesn't jive (which is often the case), there's potential for miscommunication and conflict.

IDENTITY: Every time you speak, you're doing so as a parent, child, friend, co-worker, boss, subordinate, sibling, male, female, and so on. Every time someone communicates with you, their own identity is out there too. Identity is a huge factor in any conversation because it often challenges everyone's sense of being a "good" person. It also feeds directly into a hard-wired, neuro-threat trigger: *status*.

We'll save the discussion of neuro-threats for the NEURO-SCIENCE series. For now, it's sufficient to speak of identity in terms of our own perception of being a good or bad person whenever we're engaged in communication.

FEELINGS: Unless you're dead, you have emotions. Emotions influence what you communicate and how. If you feel relaxed and happy, your emotions will reflect this and you'll likely communicate in a positive way. If you feel sad, angry, anxious, or threatened, your emotions will reflect this and you might find yourself communicating in a negative way.

IMPACT: For every message sent, there's an impact. Sometimes the impact is negligible. Other times, war or peace breaks out. With every communication, there's an impact on the other three elements. Fact foundations might alter. Identities might be threatened or re-affirmed. Feelings might be aroused or quelled. There's a response in thinking, emoting, and behaving. That response might involve yet more communication, and so the cycle of impacts continues.

FIFI is no small matter.

FIFI is present even when you're alone with your thoughts. The conversations in your head involve your own foundation of Facts, your Identity, Feelings, and the Impact of your thoughts on those three things.

In the BRAIN RESET series, where you were encouraged to focus on things supporting your passions and values (Facts), to visit your Happy Places (Feelings), and to watch your Reality Show (reconfirm your Identity as a fantastic person) to achieve a certain Impact: a positive, happier, healthier, much better you.

FIFI was present there all along, and she will always be present until the day you die.

FACTS

Why does it often seem so difficult to give "just the facts"?

Because at the end of the day, all facts are interpreted *subjectively*.

A fact is either relevant or irrelevant, damning evidence or just a coincidence, a major clue or a distraction, a big deal or nothing at all. Such interpretations determine the weight and relative importance of facts in the formation of our opinions and conclusions.

There are facts (*Webster's Dictionary*) and then there are *Facts* (FIFI). Your values heavily impact your personal foundation of Facts.

For example, consider these three brothers. One is a chef, one a musician, and the third a mechanic with a taste for classic cars. They all attend the wedding of their sister, who is meticulous about her dress and flowers.

Weeks later, the family got together for dinner and talked about the wedding. The chef spoke about the food quality and its presentation. The musician spoke about how the bass player was out of tune and how well the drummer kept everyone on tempo. The mechanic spoke about seeing his cousin's 1973 Mustang and his uncle's 1969 Chevy truck. Little sister was wondering if any of her brothers had seen the wedding at all since they made no mention of her dress or flowers.

The fact is everyone went to the same wedding, yet none of them present the same views. The paradox is while all their perspectives are different, *everyone is right*.

Another major impact on your foundation of facts are your *assumptions*. While our values are neither right nor wrong, often our assumptions are wrong.

Our assumptions about the intentions of others are often wrong.

Our attributions about other people are often wrong.

These assumptions are at the root of most bias to include race, gender, culture, and such.

For now, let's briefly return to the wedding story above.

Little sister might assume *incorrectly* her brothers had no interest in her wedding because they didn't mention her dress or flowers. She might attribute them as selfish men who don't care about her, when the reality is all three men made substantial personal sacrifices in terms of time and money to make the wedding because they love her dearly.

The brothers might assume her silence at the family dinner means she's just exhausted from the wedding, moving to her new home, and adapting to married life. The reality is she's unhappy with her brothers for not mentioning her dress and flowers.

Everyone has made the wrong assumptions about each other. These assumptions feed into each individual foundation of Facts.

We often make assumptions about others when we don't have all the information. When this happens, the programming in our automatic mind fills the void with its *own* story according to beliefs already deposited. If any of those beliefs are false, or worse, ugly lies, then we end up with the wrong story.

Once it's done this little bit of mischief, it then drives your manual mind with the story it just invented.

When we have the wrong story, we behave and communicate in less than ideal ways.

What's more is we're often not aware this is happening to us.

We're not aware because the automatic mind works in the background without our realizing it.

This is why building your awareness of the conversations going on in your head is so important. By having this awareness, you can catch yourself. Awareness that you're making assumptions and attributions to fill the story is the first step to correcting this problem.

The second step is to *ask thoughtful questions*. Doing that well takes a healthy dose of genuine curiosity. We'll talk more about how to maintain your curiosity and how to ask good, thoughtful questions in a later lesson.

5 IDENTITY

There are many facets to one's identity.

The good person—bad person facet is at the top of everyone's list. Other important facets include being male or female, an expert in your field, a certain socio-economic or ethnic background, a conformist or rebel, a parent or other relative, a victim or survivor, and a whole lot more.

The invisible, unspoken questions that come up in *every* conversation are, *are any facets of my identity being challenged? Am I competent? Am I good? Am I worthy?*

The question of our identity comes up no matter if the communication is verbal, non-verbal, a conversation in our head or a conversation with others, whether we're reading a news article or watching a movie. This phenomenon is perfectly normal, and there's nothing wrong with it *except* for one thing: If our automatic mind's programming holds a shred of uncertainty about our identity, then challenges to identity could trigger an unfavorable F3 response, resulting in unfavorable behavior such as defensiveness or hostility. In other words, we could potentially sabotage ourselves.

For example, Harold is a vegan, an activist for animal rights, and a volunteer at the local animal shelter. We can imagine Harold believes he is a good person who cares deeply about the welfare of other living creatures. This is indeed the reality, even if others do not see it that way.

Harold has a dog whom he takes with him everywhere, even when it's probably not wise. At the post office, he left his dog in his truck with the air conditioning on while he ran in to post some mail. The line was long and the task took longer to complete than he anticipated. When he returned to his truck a police officer confronted him, saying he received an anonymous call of someone "abusing" their dog by leaving it alone in a vehicle. Harold felt his identity as a good person who cares deeply about his dog was under public challenge by the police officer. Additionally, his identity was under challenge by the anonymous caller who reported the alleged "abuse."

Is Harold now a bad person who abuses animals? Of course not. Maybe he doesn't have the best judgment sometimes, but he's still a good person who loves animals.

Now, there are two ways this could play out.

In the first scenario, Harold feels a threat to his identity and his F3 response is triggered. He might be inclined to get angry and argue back. The problem with this kind of response is it can make him look guilty even though he's innocent. If the programming in the automatic mind holds any uncertainty about one's identity as a "good" person, then threats to identity will trigger an F3 response, and defensive behavior will result. Generally, defensive behavior is self-sabotaging. We want to avoid this whenever possible.

In the second scenario, Harold feels no threat to his identity. The allegations are so ridiculous that he is actually amused. He smiles politely as he listens to the police officer's lecture, and apologizes for having his dog in an air-conditioned vehicle. Of course, he's already taking excellent care of his dog, as well as scores of other animals, so the comment would be ironic.

If the programming in the automatic mind is 100% confident in one's identity as a "good" person, then threats to identity simply float by, and calm, confident behavior will result. Generally, calm, confident behavior soothes a tense situation and makes a person look more trustworthy.

The point of this lesson is that questions of one's identity come up in every conversation. So, whenever you're talking to someone, remember that just like you, their identity is out there too, on the stage of their automatic mind, being judged.

As you can see, perceived challenges to identity can arouse strong feelings. We'll talk about the Feelings part of FIFI in the next lesson.

6 FEELINGS

Of all the FIFI components, *Feelings* is the undisputed drama queen.

Feelings get involved in every aspect of *everything*, including the other three FIFI components: Facts, Identity, and Impact.

In the Facts lesson, you saw Feelings at work regarding how each of the three brothers viewed their sister's wedding, and to how the sister responded to her brothers' views.

In the Identity lesson, you saw Feelings jump in to play the role of anger or amusement in the case of a challenge to Harold's identity.

In the upcoming Impact lesson, you'll see Feelings engaged in no less visible way. In fact, it's here Feelings become even more dynamic.

You can ignore Feelings, but Feelings will not ignore you! In fact, the more you attempt to ignore Feelings, the more Feelings will become a nasty problem for you. We'll talk about how to acknowledge and manage your feelings in a healthy, respectable way in the NEURO-SCIENCE series. For now, it's sufficient to talk about Feelings in FIFI so you understand the concept.

Remember, our values have emotional hooks in them. Our feelings about values are exactly what make our values our *values*. It's why we spent so much time identifying your values through your *Ideal Life* statements and Magic Words, in the BRAIN RESET series. When our values are supported, we feel good.

When our values are not supported, we don't like that so much. What's more is the emotional hooks we have with our values drive us to seek information that validate and support our values, and ignore information that contradict or is out of line with our values.

This filtering can work both for and against us.

It can work for us when we try to validate all our good deposits, reprogram our automatic mind in a healthier way and achieve a worthy goal.

It can work against us when we *over-filter* and ignore important information critical to a healthy world view and to our relationships.

Our values, and our feelings about those values, form our foundation of Facts, the first element in FIFI. If there's any missing information, our automatic mind gladly fills the gap with assumptions. These assumptions (good, bad, or indifferent) lead to *conclusions*, and then we quickly decide how we *feel* about those conclusions. Feelings will then automatically jump in and play the role. No questions asked.

Our sense of identity has a strong emotional element. For this reason, we constructed your *Who I Am* statement and advocated use of the Be-Do-Have principle in the BRAIN RESET series. We identify positively who you are, and then we say you *are* that person *now*. It takes time and persistence to reprogram your automatic mind of its new, better identity. Your Reality Show is a powerful tool to achieve this outcome.

While in conversation you perceive other individuals becoming angry, sad, or laughing, you're going to have a feeling about that. You respond to the emotions of others, and they respond to your emotions. Generally, in any communication, the strongest emotion usually prevails, *especially* from leaders. Whether you're watching a funny movie, consoling your three-year-old child, or receiving a presentation at a board meeting, you'll have some sort of emotional response to the feelings expressed.

Feelings don't die until you do. Until then, Feelings will make its impact felt for as long as you live.

In the next lesson, we'll talk about the last FIFI component, *Impact*.

 **IMPACT**

Every communication has an Impact. Even the most minor communications with seemingly negligible impacts can accumulate over time, leading to much bigger consequences later.

On one hand, there's the case of the "straw that broke the camel's back." One too many inconsiderate communications can lead to an outcome of a child running away, a divorce, a decision to leave one's job, or other unfortunate consequence.

One the other hand, there's the case of "many small stones build a bridge." Considerate communications delivered consistently can lead to an outcome of a child making good decisions, a healthy marriage, great job satisfaction, or other happy outcome.

Sometimes, the impacts of your words go beyond your immediate family, friends, and work life. Strangers are impacted too. A customer's curt tone at a barista, even if she was in the wrong, can lower her already sad mood and degrade her work quality even more. A police officer giving a young man a stern warning as opposed to arresting him could impact that young man's decision to clean up his life. A complement from a stranger can become a happy topic of conversation later at a family dinner.

Our words, tone, and delivery *matter*.

People who are aware of this important fact tend to be more mindful and considerate in their communications. People who are mindful of the impact of their communications tend to have better relationships and better outcomes in their personal lives.

People who are unaware or disregard the impact of their communications on others tend to be less mindful. Chances are you've run into more than a few of these types. They tend to communicate in a more toxic manner, particularly when they're emotionally aroused. When they're considerate, it's only when they're in a good mood. Otherwise they're caustic, curt, or just plain rude. These same, unmindful people then wonder why their relationships fall apart, or why they seem to have so much trouble at nearly every job they have.

Sometimes we're so deafened by the conversation in our own heads, and blinded by our own feelings, that we cannot anticipate the consequences of our words. When this happens, we are not in our right minds, and we are more likely to communicate in an unhealthy way. We hurt others with our mindless words and cause undesirable impacts.

If you find this describes you even in a small way, then there's room to improve. To start, do *not* beat yourself up about it. Rather, *congratulate* yourself for having the courage to admit a difficult truth. This is a cause for celebration because you have become *aware*, a critical first step.

Communication begins deep in the recesses of your automatic mind. That's why we started with the BRAIN RESET series and the AWARENESS series, to help prepare you to get the most out of the COMMUNICATION series. It's impossible to achieve real, lasting change in the way you communicate without addressing what's happening in your automatic mind.

In the upcoming lessons, we'll present numerous techniques to help improve mindful communication. We'll also cover some of the advantages and challenges that different personality types have with communication. Some communication techniques are easier for some personality types to adopt, while other techniques are more challenging.

Improving your communication will require a change in your mindset, so get ready. Throughout this series, you might want to update some of the deposits in your Reality Show to help you with this effort.

# 8 TALKING IS SUCH A HASSLE

Many people have a hard time talking.

If you get anxious at the idea of talking to a stranger, you're not alone.

If the thought of confronting someone with upsetting information makes your heart and mind race, you're in a bigger crowd.

If you'd rather be on a plane headed anywhere as opposed to talking to someone about your own shortcomings, you are normal.

A lot of people avoid talking if there's perceived *risk* involved. We might experience rejection, cause distress, or endure pain at the exposure of our weaknesses. Most people are uncomfortable with these risks. The people who *are* comfortable with these risks are usually happier and more successful. Why?

Because talking *is* power.

For those who leverage this power well, relationships are smoother, improvements are made, deals are struck, and things *happen*.

Those who avoid talking because of perceived risks wield little power. Things do not go as well for them.

Talking *well* is a life skill. Your ability to engage in and navigate the most difficult conversations is a strong indicator of your happiness and success.

It's not so much you're speaking the King's English. It's your word choice, tone, delivery, and timing. It's the questions you ask. It's your ability to defuse the perceived sense of threat others have of *you*. It's how well you *listen*. It's how well you navigate the emotional terrain. It's your mindfulness overall.

If you improve your ability to converse just enough to reduce toxic talk, improve understanding, and assert yourself appropriately, *much* about your life will improve. *Much* about your *leadership* will improve. In fact, as a responsible adult who *is* a leader in one form or another, you have a *duty* to improve your skills. You don't have to become the grand master of talk radio or high stakes negotiations, but you must learn how to communicate in a healthy way.

To start, let's face some hard realities.

If you initiate a conversation with a stranger, there *is* a real possibility he or she could be rude or reject you outright. Count on that happening from time to time.

Delivering an unfavorable message to someone *is* likely to generate an unpleasant response. Expect this to happen *most* of the time.

Talking to anyone, especially someone close to you, about your shortcomings *is* going to generate a certain level of anxiety within you. You can take that to the bank.

Why does any of this scare us? It's so *irrational* to be afraid of any of this! Yes, it is irrational.

No, it's not your fault. There's some hard-wired stuff going on in your brain that pre-disposes you to fear these things. We'll talk about that in the NEURO-SCIENCE series. For now, we'll accept the fact these things are scary and continue with the current topic.

Now, I debated whether to put NEURO-SCIENCE ahead of COMMUNICATION, but in the end, I thought delivering the techniques first, and *then* the science, would prove more useful to you. Why communication can be so scary to many people will make more sense later.

For now, hang on tight, and be properly warned: the next two lessons present a subject squarely in your *scary* zone.

9 NO ONE WINS THE BLAME GAME

If you knew the seemingly inconsiderate attendant at the gas station just lost his mother to cancer, would you feel differently about the poor treatment?

If you knew your boss was under threat of being fired if he didn't meet a deadline, would you be more tolerant of his pushy ways?

If you knew your husband's friend was promoted over him, would you understand his forgetting your wedding anniversary?

When we encounter objectionable behavior we're often quick to lay blame—*they* are the problem. We zero in on their faults and forget about our own.

When we blame, we immediately put others on the defense, and they're less likely to listen. When *you* are blamed, you might be inclined to go on the defense and stop listening. This is normal, as well as unhelpful. We want to change this.

Blame hampers our ability to learn and see things from another perspective. If we shift our focus to our own contribution to the problem, we begin a more productive conversation. If you stop to think of how you could have contributed to a problem, then admit it, there's usually a disarming effect.

Admitting your own faults is not what people expect, and it usually catches them off guard. When they're guard is down, they're more likely to hear what you say next. This is when you ask them non-accusatory, non-confrontational questions (we'll discuss techniques for asking questions in a later lesson). By asking questions, you invite them to give their perspective.

At this point, you'll generally get one of three responses, with a range or blend of responses along these three lines.

The first type of response is they, too, admit their own contribution to the problem, and apologize. This is ideal and the best you can hope for.

The second type of response is they vent all sorts of things, giving you an understanding of what's really going on inside their mind. From here you can make better decisions about a more refined response. This isn't so bad either.

The third type of response is what terrifies us. They might pounce on your "confession" and continue to dig. The risk of this happening is precisely why we often avoid admitting any fault. Fortunately, there are ways to deal with this scenario that we'll cover in a later lesson. So, have faith. We'll get there.

What's important to understand right now is there's a *greater* chance of a positive outcome when you approach a problem from the perspective of *contribution* as opposed to blame. Blame is tantamount to *judging*. It focuses on who's at fault. It reinforces the problem. It harms relationships.

Contribution is *learning*. It asks, how can we improve? It solves problems. It builds relationships.

The point of *this* lesson is that focusing *first* on *your* contribution gets the conversation going in a more productive direction. Starting with your contribution first is more likely to put others in a less emotional state and into a more rational mindset. When both of you are more rational, you're both more empathetic. When you're both more empathetic, there's more cooperation, a better relationship, and better outcomes. *That* is the point.

Sometimes you might not know how you contributed to a problem. That's ok because I'm about to tell you in the next lesson.

10 FOUR WAYS *YOU* CONTRIBUTE TO PROBLEMS

G et ready for another acronym.

You learned how FIFI (Facts, Identity, Feeling, and Impact) is part of every conversation. While I invented the acronym, the concepts behind them are not new. There are entire books and dissertations written about the concepts of FIFI. It's a lot easier to remember complex concepts when there's a useful acronym available.

So, here's another useful acronym: AMUM.

AMUM stands for *Avoid, Misunderstand, Unapproachable,* and *Mindless*. These are the four ways *you* contribute to communication problems. Here they are in order.

AVOID is when you deliberately avoid talking to someone. You're afraid of the conversation so you don't engage. Going out of your way to avoid someone so as not to converse with them about a difficult matter is passive-aggressive behavior. Such behavior communicates in a toxic way. It's hurtful and arouses assumptions about you in the other person's mind. You add fuel to the fire when you avoid.

MISUNDERSTAND is when you don't fully understand the other person's perspective (their Facts and Feelings). You might not have asked enough questions, placed yourself in their position, or heard enough from them. Your misunderstanding is something only you can correct. The best way to correct this problem is to admit you don't understand and make a sincere effort to learn.

UNAPPROACHABLE is when you're exactly that. If you're in a foul mood, overly negative, or complain a lot, people will not find it easy to approach you. If you tend to bully, condescend, intimidate, or put down others consistently (especially when the news is bad), people will go out of their way to avoid you. You can try to spin this as though *they* are the problem for avoiding you, but that is missing the point. We're talking about *your* contribution to communication problems right now, not the contribution of others.

MINDLESS is when you're either absent minded, or worse, not in your right mind. Absent mindedness is simply not paying attention to the situation at hand and you forget your manners or say something less than appropriate. Not being in your right mind is when you're sad, angry, frustrated, anxious, or in any negative mindset. When you're in this state, your words, gestures, and tone will reflect this negativity. The Impact of this negativity is usually less than ideal outcomes.

Now, if you've ever Avoided someone, been Unapproachable, Misunderstood another, or was Mindless, you're *not* a mean, bad, selfish, narcissistic, no-good, rotten, awful person. Don't go there.

You're a wonderful, fantastic, loving, empathetic, kind, generous, and worthy *human* being who has his or her moments and is learning from them. You're growing. Stress and life's challenges don't always bring out our best selves. This is normal.

Admitting your contribution to a problem opens the door to more productive conversations with better outcomes. It helps tremendously if you're genuine and honest about your contribution (you're AMUM).

Something as simple as saying, "I'm sorry I forgot my manners," or "I shouldn't have been so grouchy to you," or "It seems I might have misunderstood you," are powerful door openers. Some people might find this hard to do because we feel we're relinquishing being "right"." In the WISDOM series, we'll talk about how being right isn't all that. In fact, being right can sometimes be *harmful*. More on that in volume two.

In our next lesson, we'll return to FIFI and how you can leverage it to your advantage.

11 WHEN FIFI IS YOUR ALLY

FIFI plays a huge role in our conversations, yet most people aren't even aware of it. We simply sense unknown forces beyond our control are at play, adding to our anxiety levels. This added anxiety only adds to the difficulty of the situation.

On the other hand, if you're aware and mindful of FIFI, you're much better able to manage the forces of FIFI to your advantage. You have greater control and can steer difficult discussions toward a more favorable direction. In this case, FIFI can be your best friend.

Listening is powerful in communication because you become aware of the other person's FIFI. By staying objective, admitting your AMUM, and listening to their story open mindedly, you learn *their* FIFI.

Learning another person's FIFI is like having secret intelligence. It's power. With that said, your own FIFI can get in the way of obtaining this powerful intelligence.

Starting with *your* Facts, you'll need to set them aside while you listen and attempt to understand *their* Facts. Taking a third person view helps in this regard.

Your Identity might sense a challenge to itself when you admit your contribution (AMUM). You might also sense a challenge to your Identity in other ways. This sense helps you retain control because if you start to feel anxious about your Identity, you'll know, "Oh, that's my Identity feeling challenged—no worries—I'm ok."

Your automatic mind, however, might *not* be on board, at least not yet. It my still trigger an ever so slight F3 response. That's why it's important for your manual mind to be on the alert and *notice* it.

Each time you notice even the slightest F3 response, you can settle yourself so you don't behave unfavorably. You'll also know you have more work to do in re-programming your automatic mind. Your Reality Show is a valuable tool to do this. No matter the challenge to your Identity, you're going to be just fine. Over time, your automatic mind will begin to accept the truth of your goodness unconditionally. When this happens, you won't have to commit so much manual energy and it becomes easier.

At some point, your growing ability to humble yourself appropriately, admit your shortcomings, and remain resolute in your positive identity will become, in and of itself, a *positive* part of your identity. Instead of feeling challenged, you'll feel like your *growing*. The feeling of growth is positive, and it becomes reinforcing.

You will have a spectrum of Feelings—some related to your Facts, some to your Identity, and some related to Impacts of recent communications.

We have spoken at length already in both the BRAIN RESET and AWARE-NESS series about the importance of your own emotional awareness. This awareness helps you tremendously in identifying your Feelings when it comes to FIFI. Identifying your Feelings with simple, honest labels gives you an immediate sense of control. A single label in your mind, such as "angry" when you're feeling angry, alerts you to your mental state. A series of labels in your mind such as "anxious, sad, confused, scared" alerts you to the spectrum of emotions going on inside you.

Given your own Facts, Identity, and Feelings, as well as input from the external world (words, gestures, actions, and such) there's a resulting Impact inside you. This Impact adds to the churn.

Altogether, this is *your* FIFI. Awareness of your own FIFI is like having top secret intelligence on yourself. Knowing yourself, honestly and thoroughly, is a huge advantage going into any conversation. When you understand the whole FIFI (yours and others) you're empowered in your communications. You have the advantage.

12 ★ HOW TO NOT SHUT PEOPLE DOWN

In the last lesson, I mentioned it helps to take a third-person perspective when asking questions to learn the perspective of others. This is important, especially if their Facts are different from yours. Remember, Facts include values and interests, not just "the facts."

When individual Facts differ, everyone's inclination is to judge others as wrong and disregard their Facts. This reaction is unhelpful in communication.

What *is* helpful is taking on a third-person perspective to give you some space from your own Facts. Getting space from your own Facts helps you to listen objectively. This is important because if you're not objective or sincere about learning *their* Facts, your insincerity will reveal itself. When your lack of sincerity is apparent, you can make matters worse.

For example, let's use the example of an accusation disguised as a question. "Why are you so stubborn?" or, "Is there a reason why you're so lazy?" and other such questions are more likely to put people on the defense and shut them down.

Accusations challenge Identity. When someone's Identity is challenged, the response is usually unfavorable.

More useful questions could look like, "It seems you prefer_____. Can you tell me what you like about it?" or, "I'm curious to understand your decision to _____. Can you share with me your thought process?" or, "I sense there's something preventing you from performing at your full potential. What are your thoughts?"

Sometimes, even with indirect questions like these, there might still be a defensive response. Follow with something like, "I'm not trying to put you on the defensive; I want to understand your perspective." That angle will usually settle them down and they'll start to open up. As they do, continue to show your interest with thoughtful follow up questions—and without hidden accusations.

Another way to shut someone down is disguising an assertion as a question.

When you assert something disguised as a question, they know you're not sincere. When they know you're not sincere then it's tantamount to disregarding their FIFI. If you disregard someone's FIFI, they're likely to shut down.

For example, a question like "Why would you vote for ____ when that person is clearly (negative description)." Or, "Don't you think that's a stupid thing to do?"

A better way to approach these questions might be, "I'm curious to know why you feel ____ is the better candidate. Will you share with me your insights?" Or, "I'm curious to learn more about this idea you have about ____. Will you tell me more about it?"

Remember, Facts are not always *facts*. Facts are what is experienced from someone else's perspective, whether they are realistically true or not. Everyone has a filter, and people tend to allow only the information that supports their values and interests. Values and interests are an important part of Facts. Getting to know the underlying values and interests at play in their world of Facts will help you understand how they perceive reality. When you better understand their reality, you can better empathize. When they sense your empathy, even if you don't agree with them (empathy is not the same as sympathy), they're more likely to trust you and to communicate with you in a more productive and rational manner.

Replacing your certainty of "rightness" with *curiosity* goes a long way toward demonstrating sincerity, building trust, and fostering better relationships.

Questions starting with, "Can you help me understand...", "I wonder if it's possible...", "It seems we have different perspectives about...", "I wonder if it would make sense to..." helps to open others to you.

Finally, make your empathy known with something like, "I can understand why you might feel or see it that way." It does *not* mean you agree, it means you *understand*.

13 HAVING YOUR SAY

I know, I know! You're thinking, "When do I get to have *my* say?"

I'm not suggesting you become the village doormat. Certainly, you may assert yourself, and you *should* assert yourself. It's just that assertion usually isn't the problem for most people. Listening and understanding is the problem. That's why we focused on listening and understanding first. But now we'll talk about *you* having your say.

To start, if the person you're communicating with is a bit toxic, you don't want to wreck everything by reacting to them in kind and stooping to their level. You'll want to assert yourself *mindfully*, and with precise language. We'll talk about using precise language and how to avoid common communication traps in later lessons. For now, we'll continue to focus on the remaining elements of FIFI.

You heard their perspective.

You asked thoughtful questions.

You exercised your best listening skills.

You repeated back what you heard to show understanding.

You acknowledged their feelings ("I understand you're feeling such and such about this").

You admitted your contribution to the problem (AMUM).

By now, they're more at ease and in a more receptive mode to hear your perspective.

A great way to introduce your perspective is to simply state you have a different perspective on the matter. Then go on to explain your view of the Facts to include your interests and values. Your interests and values are important too. Remember, just because we're talking about "facts" doesn't mean you can't talk about your values and interests. Values and interests are part of your world of Facts, even if they aren't Webster's definition of "facts." (There's a great technique for presenting your view while demonstrating you still remember their view in the next lesson.)

Along with presenting your Facts, you'll want to express your Feelings.

When expressing your Feelings, there's often an Identity and Impact element built into them. A triple score happens when you communicate your Feelings, Identity, and Impact all in one statement.

For example, "I felt belittled and intimidated by ____'s behavior." Such a statement conveys the challenge to your Identity, your Feelings, and the Impact of someone else's communication on you.

Another triple score can look like, "Your comment about my work made me feel good." Or, "I appreciate you took the time to listen, even if we don't agree. I feel valued." Or, "I feel under-appreciated in your unwillingness to hear my view. I'm not asking for you to agree. I'm just asking that you listen."

"I felt such and such when such and such occurred," or, "I feel such and such about the way this is going," conveys your feelings without judging them.

It's possible you might have a spectrum of emotions going on, meaning you have different feelings about different things happening at the same time. "I'm happy you're getting married, and scared and sad I might lose a friend to your new married life."

Immediate feedback about the Impact of their words on you is a healthy way to assert yourself. For example, "I felt hurt by your comment; is that what you intended?" or "Thank you for noticing my hard work. I enjoyed hearing what you said about it."

You might notice I gave positive examples right along with the negative examples. While it's important to assert yourself when someone is unmindful of you, noticing and commenting on the healthy and mindful communication of others reinforces desirable behavior in them.

As your communication skills improve, others will automatically learn how to better communicate with you. As the best person you can be, reinforcing healthy, mindful behavior in everyone you encounter is both free and priceless.

# 14 THE "AND" TECHNIQUE

The "And" technique is nothing new. Communication experts have used it for a long time now, and it's a fantastic technique. It's also underutilized because to use it effectively, you must leverage your listening and empathy skills first.

It's the listening and empathy part that people tend to struggle with. The reason listening and empathy are essential to using the "And" technique is you're conveying the FIFI of others at the same time you're conveying yours.

To convey the FIFI of others *convincingly*, you must truly understand it. To truly understand it, you must listen objectively and put yourself in their shoes—that is, listen with empathy.

These skills are critical enablers to communication and leadership. It's why we've emphasized listening with empathy so much throughout this program.

In addition to listening and empathy, there's another skill to introduce: *navigating paradox*.

Paradox is a situation in which both sides are right, both arguments have their flaws, and both sides have value and worth. At the same time, both sides are different, perhaps even totally incompatible with each other.

There's more to the topic of paradox covered in detail in the WISDOM and LEADERSHIP series (volume two). In the meantime, we introduce it here because when you use the "And" technique, paradox is often present. You'll want to navigate this carefully.

Let's take the perspective of a college football coach informing his top player he might get kicked off the team. The conversation might go like this:

"I think you're a fantastic player, *and* I'm disappointed about your drinking. I know you work hard in school, *and* you're under a lot of stress from your mother being sick. I'm concerned your drinking is hampering your best performance *and* setting a bad example for the other players. I don't want to lose you *and* I cannot allow you to negatively impact this team. I understand you might feel this is harsh *and* you know this team has high standards. I know how much you love football *and* I know getting kicked off the team would devastate you. I hope you commit to staying sober *and* seek help. I prefer to keep you on the team *and* I will not hesitate to let you go."

In a few concise sentences, the coach represented the FIFI from both sides. He recognized the student's Facts of working hard, being under stress, and having a sick mother. He preserved the student's Identity by confirming he's a fantastic player, and hard worker. He acknowledged the student's Feelings that the coach was harsh, and that the student loved football. He also acknowledged the Impact on the student should he get kicked off the team.

Simultaneously, the coach presented his own FIFI and asserted himself. He stated his Facts plainly—a good, hard-working player, under stress, with an alcohol problem, who's performance is declining, and will be kicked off the team if he doesn't sober up fast. He did not speak directly to his own Identity, yet it's clear he's speaking from an Identity of a firm and fair coach who's considerate, yet not afraid to make tough decisions. He expressed his Feelings for the player of both care and concern, as well as disappointment. The Impact is implied. The coach doesn't feel good about the prospect of letting his top player go, and yet he will do exactly that if he must.

If the coach had only asserted his own perspective without acknowledging the student's FIFI, the student is much more likely to shut down, as opposed to turning the corner. By using the "And" technique and recognizing FIFI on both sides, mutual respect is sustained.

The "And" technique allows you to keep the tether of empathy alive while also asserting your views. When you keep the tether of empathy alive, others are more likely to hear what you have to say, even if it's not what they want to hear.

15 ACCEPT YOU CAN'T CONTROL EVERYTHING

B ad news does not get better with age.

Sometimes, you must bear the burden of delivering bad news.

You can contemplate FIFI. You can listen with empathy. You can assert yourself in a healthy, mindful way. You can use the "And" technique. In the end, there's going to be an Impact.

In communication, you can *influence* the Impact, but you can't *control* it.

We know this instinctively. It's why we avoid breaking up with people, admitting a terrible mistake, or telling someone their performance was poor.

We know the reaction is likely to be anger, fear, sadness, or disappointment. We fear we might be implicated as a "bad" person for delivering this news, especially if *we* are the news!

Let's say you want to break up with your current steady, but are afraid you'll make this person cry. The reality is this person will become distressed at the news, and you'll feel bad about this. This doesn't mean you coldly blurt goodbye and walk away. If you do, not only will they cry, but you'll also lose mutual respect. This is less than ideal.

A better way is to deliver the news in a considerate, honest way, using the "And" technique. "You're a great person, *and* it's just not working for me. I need to break up with you *and* I know it's not what you want to hear." Don't ramble on forever and do get to the point fairly quickly. Yes, they will cry, but you're more likely to retain respect for each other. This is a little better.

How about giving a poor performance evaluation? First, a poor performance evaluation should not be a surprise. If someone has been performing poorly at work, then each instance of poor performance (as well as desirable performance) should have been communicated.

154

Nevertheless, a poor performance evaluation is difficult to give. You can either deliver the news with both honesty and consideration (using the "And" technique) or merely hand them their evaluation and walk away. Either way, there will be disappointment. In the first case, a better outcome of hope and mutual respect will result. In the second case, there is no hope, and no mutual respect.

One of the hardest things to do is to tell someone bad news, especially about a death, or when *you* are part of the bad news.

I'm not talking about AMUM; I'm talking about something serious, such as a DUI, losing your job, or being a victim of a terrible crime. Your parents, boss, spouse, whoever is closest to you will likely respond unfavorably to the news.

In this case, there's no point using the "And" technique. Bad news of *this* magnitude cannot be softened up with preludes. It's better to ask for a private place to talk, and simply say what happened in one short sentence.

You *will* be scared, anxious, nervous—all of that. There is absolutely no way to control the reaction you'll get. This is a fact of life.

Even in less serious matters you cannot control the response. All you can do is communicate in a way that best preserves mutual respect.

It's not so much that *they* continue to respect *you*, because they might or might not. Rather, it's that you continue to respect them, and you continue to respect yourself.

You'll feel much better about yourself if you know you communicated in a healthy, mindful way than if you lowered yourself to their level or communicated in less than your best effort.

When you communicate, you reinforce the deposits in the programming of your automatic mind. That's why it's important to communicate to your best ability.

Even if you can't control all the outcomes, you can still influence them in tremendous ways.

16 LEVERAGE CLEAR AND SPECIFIC LANGUAGE

When we use clear and specific language, we're more likely to be understood, and outcomes are more likely to go our way. When we use vague and general language, there's a greater chance of being misunderstood, and less ideal outcomes are likely.

If your words leave questions about what you mean, then people will fill in the blanks with their own interpretation. Remember, the automatic mind will gladly fill in the blanks of any unknown information with its own assumptions. Often those assumptions are wrong.

For example, something as simple as "stop acting that way" can be interpreted as personal criticism, as opposed to a request to alter behavior. The good person/bad person Identity is immediately challenged with whom you're speaking.

When Identity is challenged, Feelings of anger and resentment are common, usually leading to an Impact of defensive behavior. When someone is defensive toward you, they're *less* likely to hear what you say.

"Stop acting that way" is too vague and general, leaving the listener unsure of what you mean to convey.

Instead of "Stop acting that way," consider leveraging more clear and specific language such as, "Please lower your voice and sit still so I can concentrate on driving."

Or, "Please help me understand what you're feeling. When you don't talk, it worries me."

Or, "Please use a more respectful tone when talking to your grandmother."

In these examples, there's less room to misinterpret the request as a personal attack.

Identity is less likely to perceive a challenge, and Feelings are less likely to become aroused.

The resulting Impact is less defensiveness and a greater likelihood your request will at least be heard, if not honored.

Adopting the habit of using more clear and specific language takes time and practice. In fact, adopting this habit can be a sizable challenge for some people. There are three reasons for this.

First, it takes a greater amount of brain energy. When we're trying to come up with better words to say what we mean, our brains must process more information. This extra processing uses up more brain energy until it gets used to thinking in this way. Once the habit is adopted, less brain energy is required.

The second reason is when we're emotionally aroused, our brains tend to cut straight to our old bad habits of speaking. Exercising awareness and slowing yourself down will help you through these rough patches. Do your best not to resort to your old ways of communicating. When you finally *do* master keeping your emotions in check as you find the right, clear, and respectful words to say, you'll command a great deal more respect and admiration than people who have not taken the time and energy to master this incredibly important skill.

Finally, the third reason speaking with greater clarity is difficult is because of the strong link between communication and the automatic mind. To change communication habits, you must reprogram the automatic mind, which is exactly what we're trying to do. We'll talk more about the impact of the automatic mind on communication later in this series.

For now, it's helpful to know that using more clear and specific language might not be as easy as you'd like, and to not beat yourself up if you're not good at it right away. Keep trying. Working at clear and specific communication is a lifelong effort and important skill. Even excellent communicators must work at this.

Below are some examples of commonly used, vague statements with suggested alternatives. You'll want to refine these suggestions based on the specific situation.

VAGUE STATEMENT	ALTERNATIVE
Stop that!	Please don't hit the dog with the fly swatter.
Why do you always do that!	I noticed you tend to drive on people's bumper.
You don't do anything around here.	Can you help me wash the dishes after dinner?
Don't talk that way!	Please use a more respectful tone with your father.
Make yourself useful.	Please keep the place clean when between tasks.
You rat bastard!	I am disappointed in your decision/behavior.
Why do you talk like that?	I noticed you have a negative view on the matter.
Stop bugging me!	I need my space for the moment. Can we set a time to chat about this when I'm more rested?
I hate that stuff!	I prefer a different…cuisine, art, style, music, etc.
What an idiot!	It appears that person is behaving irrationally.
You can't do anything right!	I've noticed several times in the past week you've forgotten instructions. Can we talk?

# NEGATIVE PEOPLE DO EXIST

17

Why are some people negative?

Is it because they're "bad" people?

Is it because they're out to push your buttons?

It's easy to make assumptions about seemingly negative people because we don't have all the information. We don't understand them, so we rush to judgment with our own assumptions. Remember, most of the time, our assumptions are wrong. So, when we judge people as "bad," it doesn't help our communication at all.

There are people who will criticize you unfairly, accuse you unjustly, make unreasonable demands of you, put down your dreams, say hurtful words to you, and spin your best intentions into something nefarious.

And yet, we're not supposed to believe these people are bad?

For the most part, yes. Here's why.

Everyone has their own unique journey. You're on a journey to cleanse your automatic mind, mature your thinking and emoting, and sophisticate your communication and behavior. You have chosen this journey. They have not yet made such a choice.

The heavy baggage of their poorly programmed automatic minds, and the fears surrounding their identity and feelings often sabotage their better selves and pollute their communication. These people are out there, and some might be close to you. You're going to have to deal with them.

There are two ways to deal with negative people.

The first is to try to understand them. Your effort to understand can sometimes indirectly help them through their issues so they aren't so negative. This isn't always easy when they've just implied you're bad, mean, incompetent, or deficient in some way; your identity is under challenge; and your emotions are aroused. When you feel threatened in this way, it's difficult not to become defensive.

To avoid becoming defensive, it's best to step aside yourself and take a third-person view. From this viewpoint, ask questions to try to get inside their mind.

For example, let's say someone calls you a name or unfairly accuses you. Try responding with something like, "Tell me more about why you think that way," and hear them out. Re-state their perspective and get confirmation. If you learn through their view you've contributed to the problem through AMUM, this is usually a good time to admit your contribution.

With that said, they have a contribution to the problem too. Start with, "I have a different perspective," and present your perspective without blame or accusation. If they interrupt, let them know they've had their say and now it's time for yours. Let them know how they made you feel when they said certain things such as, "When you said ___, I felt ___. I'm sure that's not what you intended. What was really going through your mind?"

Let's say you need to start a conversation with a difficult person. A good way to start is by saying, "I want to talk to you about ____. It appears we have different perspectives about the matter. I wanted to hear your perspective and share mine with you."

The second way to deal with negative people is to avoid them when you can.

Negative people can interfere with your high emotional vibration and set you back. You don't need that. You've been through so much already and are working hard to better yourself.

Instead, surround yourself with positive, optimistic, more like-minded people. People who want to learn and grow.

With that said, do not confuse people who merely disagree with you as being negative.

One of the biggest mistakes people make in their communication and relationships is believing disagreement is all bad. Not true. Disagreement can be a valuable opportunity to learn and grow. It is important to know the difference.

Negativity happens when conversations involve put downs, name calling, labeling, blaming, and disrespect. Negativity happens when someone puts down your dreams or tries to stop you from changing into a better person. These are the people you can try to understand better, or if that is too hard or impossible, avoid them as much as you can.

18 PERSONALITY TYPE AND COMMUNICATION

In the AWARENESS series, we covered different personality types. We examined how different personality types have different preferences on how they interact with the world. These preferences are neither right nor wrong, they just are.

It turns out different personality types have preferences in how they communicate. Here are some examples.

Extroverts (E's)[2] prefer to process information externally and Introverts (I's) prefer to process information in their heads. E's tend to think "out loud" and need discussion to help them think. I's often find talking distracting.

The problem with this scenario is I's can appear like they're Avoiding (AMUM). On the other hand, E's can appear like they're Mindless (AMUM) because they might say a lot of things they don't mean until they reach their conclusion.

E's have more trouble saying what they mean the first time around because they haven't thought it through yet. I's, on the other hand, have a little bit of an advantage in that they think things through before they speak. I's usually mean what they say when they speak.

When it comes to using clear and specific language, iNtuitives (N's) and Sensors (S's) have their differences. S's prefer details, facts, and the here and now, while N's prefer generalities, implication of facts, and the future.

N's usually have more trouble with clear and specific language than S's. The reason is N's tend to move on from facts to generalities quickly, forgetting about the facts that brought them to the generality in the first place. S's aren't so quick to move on like this and are a lot better at sticking to the facts.

---

2   For the sake of readability, I'm using an apostrophe on these letters although they're plural and not possessive.

S's prefer to communicate in terms of clear specifics. As such, S's have a little advantage when it comes to leveraging clear and specific language.

N's on the other hand, have an advantage in that they tend to be more curious than S's. N's are more likely to ask questions to satisfy this curiosity.

Feelers (F's) and Thinkers (T's) have their differences too.

T's prefer to focus on the logical aspect (Facts), while F's prefer to focus on the values aspect (Feelings). Neither is right or wrong; they just are.

F's can and *should* state when they sense their Feelings are being ignored by a T, without overdoing it, of course.

T's can and *should* state when they sense their Facts are being ignored by an F; again, without overdoing it.

Judgers (J's) prefer certainty and closure. Perceivers (P's) are more comfortable with open ended matters.

When it comes to situations of paradox and using the "And" technique to present multiple viewpoints, P's are more likely to excel here.

The open-endedness of a paradox and presenting of multiple viewpoints is a little outside the typical J comfort zone. J's will have an easier time if the multiple viewpoints are made clearly and are well supported.

J's would do well to learn paradox is reality, and navigating this reality is an opportunity, not a threat. Paradox is an opportunity because you're presented with more information and more choices than you otherwise would have with the certainty of just one perspective. P's instinctively know this.

Next, we'll talk about words to avoid, and words to leverage.

This is a lesson all personality types can learn from!

19 WORDS TO AVOID AND WORDS TO LEVERAGE

"We liked your presentation, *but...*"

"The house was nice, *but...*"

"That was a great kick, *but...*"

Doubtless, you've heard many statements start with what seems encouraging, only to be followed with *but*. What happens when we get to *but*?

We erase everything that came before it.

Experts in communication tell us *but* is the *great eraser*. It matters not one little bit what nice thing you said before the *but*. Only the words after *but* are heard.

There are three ways to communicate without using *but*.

The first is by using the "And" technique. Remember, the "And" technique is great for telling both sides of a story. You can use this technique to tell both the good and the not-so-good of what you want to convey.

For example, "We liked your presentation, *and* we were hoping to see more financial detail." Or, "The house was nice, *and* we'd like to see other houses." Or, "That was a great kick, *and* I'm sorry you missed the goal."

Now there *are* times when "And" is awkward to use, particularly when you need to convey a contrasting view. Some people prefer to use words such as *however* and *yet*. While they avoid the word *but*, they're so close in meaning they're viewed as one in the same.

Another technique is to break the sentence in two. Let the positive sentence stand on its own and then present the contrasting view in its own sentence.

For example, "We liked your presentation. We feel more financial detail is needed." Or, "The house was nice. We'd like to view other homes for comparison." Or, "That was a great kick. Let's work a little more on your accuracy."

A third way to avoid using *but* is to reframe.

For example, "One way to polish your already excellent presentation is to add more financial details." Or, "We'd like to see if there are other houses out there as nice as this one so we can compare options." Or, "With that strong kick, I thought for sure you'd have made the goal."

Personally, reframing is my favorite method to avoid using *but*.

Other words to avoid are absolutes. Absolutes are words such as *never, always, all, every*, and so on. These words entrap you, so avoid them. It takes only *one* instance of an exception to the absolute to null and void your statement. When your statement is null and void, you lose credibility.

For example, "We *always* follow the rules." Or, "*Everyone* is against this measure." Or, "There's *no evidence* to support…" A simple internet search into such statements like these can turn up numerous exceptions. It's the use of such absolutes that lose credibility for many people, especially people in leadership positions.

There are many ways around using absolutes. While the methods are more verbose, the outcome is you avoid lost credibility.

For example, a better way to express "We always follow the rules" could be, "We try hard to follow the rules, and we know how important it is to follow them strictly, which is why we have measures in place to help ensure compliance. Compliance is a high priority for us."

A better to way express "Everyone is against this measure" could be, "It would appear a significant majority of people are opposed to this measure." In both instances, you communicate in a more credible way. Even if opposing facts are presented, you can continue to fully assert your original statement. You avoid getting trapped.

In the next lesson, we'll talk about three more communication traps that can harm your credibility and your power to influence.

20 COMMUNICATION TRAPS

Communication Traps impair learning and thinking.

When learning and thinking are impaired, you're not your best self, and your emoting and behaving sabotage you. It's hard to be authentic, inspiring, or convincing when you're not your best self. It's harder to achieve your goals in life when you self-sabotage.

The three Communication Brain traps, according to neural-linguistic experts, are Generalizing, Deleting, and Distorting.

Generalizing is forming a universal opinion from limited information. For example, you read in the paper about a couple of dog bite incidents and decide all dogs are bad. You then go about telling everyone how bad dogs are because they bite. Generalizing can bring you to unfair conclusions because you fill in the missing information with assumptions that are usually wrong. We generalize more often than we realize, and often out of necessity.

For example, if you had a bad experience with a certain business, you might simply move on to another business. Fair or unfair, your time and energy matters and sometimes you must make the best of your decisions whether you have all the information or not. The point is to ensure generalizing does not become so prevalent in your thinking and communication as to hamper your learning.

Deleting is over filtering information to conform to your preferences. This is a classic case of focusing on a specific phrase and then applying our *own* meaning to that phrase. We delete everything around the phrase clarifying its intended meaning. We hear only what we want to hear, and read only what we want to read. When we delete information, we close our minds to possibilities and hamper our learning.

There's a reasonable limit to this concept as well.

For example, if you know illicit drug use is bad news, then no amount of information purporting the merits of drug use around children is going to open your mind to that. Fair enough. The point is to ensure you're not over deleting in situations when there's an opportunity for you to listen, learn, and grow.

Distorting is a mix of Generalizing and Deleting, and then spinning the outcome into something out of step with reality. This is often an outcome of a pre-existing bias or agenda.

Let's say your ex-wife just remarried and her new husband is dropping off some clothes for the kids who are staying with you. Without knowing this person, you could assume he "stole" your wife, forget the many favors he's done for your family, and choose to believe he's only stopping by to add salt to your wounds and spy on you. You have a bias against your ex-wife, so pretty much anything or anyone pertaining to her will be viewed in a negative way.

We not only distort reality in our personal lives, it happens in the big world too. We see Distortions often in political messages. I'll refrain from giving examples because that could get touchy!

The point is to be aware of Distortions, and when Distortion takes place in your own mind. If it does so, it will come out in your communication and you could lose credibility. You don't want this.

Ideally, you want a reputation as someone who listens, processes information logically and fairly, and then speaks calmly and assertively from that mindset. If you're not aware of your own generalizing, deleting, or distorting, chances are others *are*. If anyone notices this out loud, *thank them*, and then reflect on how you can balance your thinking to resolve the problem.

21 WHAT MESSAGES ARE ALLOWED IN YOUR MIND

More than at any time in human history, our brains are bombarded with content. Before the information age, we enjoyed more time to think and meditate. For nearly a million years, human minds largely had the time and space they needed to process information thoughtfully and thoroughly.

Not anymore.

Today, we are constantly exposed to information through television, radio, Internet, social media, billboards, signs, and everything else you see in the world at large.

I've mentioned filtering. We tend to filter the enormous volume of content entering our senses according to our values and interests. This is a good thing most of the time. At the same time, we want to remain open to other information and ideas so we can expand our understanding. Doing that requires we open our filters beyond our values and interest. This takes a *manual* (conscious) effort, and doesn't happen automatically.

Learning requires an open filter. With that said, you'll want to tighten your filter at times as well.

Contradictory? Let me explain.

There's a lot of garbage out there, and we don't want garbage getting into our programming in the automatic mind. Garbage entering the mind reinforces ugly lie deposits and false beliefs. Tightening the filter to keep out the garbage, just like opening the filter to permit learning to enter, requires a *conscious* effort. It doesn't happen automatically.

Most of us go about our days mindlessly watching TV, engaging in social media, and listening to the radio. When we mindlessly allow content to enter our minds, it's like not having a guard at the door of an upscale theater. The riffraff flow into the theater to cause trouble while the behaved people with tickets might not get a seat. The theater will soon become a mess, and so will the brain if we don't actively and consciously guard what enters it.

Conscious (manual) effort takes more energy. For this reason, it's helpful to limit your exposure to content you can't manually filter for a sustained period. It's true that too much television, social media, video games, Internet, and rubbish reading is like constantly feeding junk food to your brain. What's worse is just like junk food, it can be *addictive*. There are numerous neurological reasons for this, just as there many biological reasons why sugar is addictive. It *is* addictive and it's important to recognize this. You'll want to limit your exposure to what your manual mind can actively manage, which is usually not very much.

There's another reason to guard what content enters your mind; it comes right back out in your communication! If you expose yourself to inflammatory, emotionally charged, controversial content, you can rest assured your communication will reflect this content if you're not careful.

For example, if you watch movies depicting people killing each other over slights, then don't be surprised if you say something such as, "I'm going to kill him if he talks to me like that again."

Now, *you* know you don't really mean it. It's a figure of speech. The problem is you just allowed such language to enter your mind as "just a figure of speech." It's *never* alright to casually talk about harming someone. It's poisonous to your mind and contributes to toxic communication.

In fact, toxic communication is such a widespread problem we have an entire lesson on it.

That's next.

22 TOXIC COMMUNICATION

We learn terrible communication habits from movies, work, school, families, and friends.

The worst and most poisonous of these bad habits is contemptuous language in the form of name calling, sarcasm, ridicule, shaming, belittling, cynicism, and hostile humor. It's *not* alright. You might have been taught differently growing up; unfortunately, you were taught *wrong*.

However, you *can* change. In fact, you *want* to change because adopting more healthy communication habits is a whole lot better for your mind, emoting, behaving, relationships, and outcomes in life. It *absolutely* matters.

Contrary to what is often argued, contemptuous language is not "tough love" or "correcting behavior." Quite the opposite; contemptuous language inhibits growth and learning on both sides. Sometimes, it is truly crippling. It shuts down conversation and harms relationships.

Instead of saying "You're a jerk," try saying, "I feel like you're not respecting my needs. Is that your intent?"

Instead of saying, "Stop being a little (expletive)," say, "I feel you're undermining me and it frustrates me when you don't honor my requests. Can you explain to me what's going through your mind?"

Instead of saying "You rat ___!" say, "I'm disappointed in your behavior. Can you tell me why you belittled your wife in public and made her cry?"

Notice how we leveraged several communications tools. We kept FIFI in mind, we used specific language, and we asked questions to give the other person an opportunity to explain and help us understand. In doing so, we kept the conversation going in a more productive direction.

Other forms of Toxic Communication include blaming, defensiveness, and threats.

Remember, no one wins the blame game.

Blaming is one of the quickest ways to put someone on the defense. Their identity is immediately challenged, they feel negatively about it, and the impact will likely be unfavorable. Instead of blaming, asking questions works much better.

For example, instead of saying, "You wrecked everything!" say, "How do you feel about what just happened?"

Now, sometimes you're the one who's blamed and you might be inclined to become defensive. When you become defensive, this too is toxic communication. Defensiveness is reacting with aggressive language. Understandably, you're trying to protect yourself. There *are* ways to protect yourself without becoming defensive. (We'll talk more about responding to the toxic communication of others in the next lesson.)

The immediate response to someone accusing you unfairly, putting you down, or calling you names is to ask them, "What makes you say that?" or, "Tell me more about why you think that way." Then let them talk themselves till they run out of energy. Try to listen to what they mean to convey (not just their bad words) and to understand the FIFI in action on their side. Once they've spent their energy, it's time to have *your* say.

Threats are attempts to control others. They are *rarely* appropriate and overused too often. The worst threats are what I call the "thermo-nuclear" threats. These occur when someone threatens to utterly disrupt or ruin another's life over some silly or unreasonable matter.

For example, "If you don't get straight A's I'm kicking you out of the house." Or, "If you don't lose weight I'm divorcing you." Or, "If you don't make this sale I'm firing you."

Rarely does anyone *need* to exercise so much control over someone as to warrant threats. If that much control is needed then you should examine why. Most of the time, the issue is not a life or death matter but a matter of preferences. We'll talk about how to manage preferences so they don't manage you in the NEURO-SCIENCE series. For now, it's best to practice communicating without threats or other toxic elements. Your relationships will improve, and your life outcomes will be more favorable once you learn this important skill. Just remember, it will take time. So be patient with yourself.

Finally, if you've ever used toxic communication, you're *not* a rotten, mean, unworthy, awful person. Trust me, I've said more than a few toxic things myself in life and I'm not proud of it. You're a human being who learned some bad habits and is trying to change. The very fact that you're trying is commendable.

23 DON'T ACCEPT SOMEONE ELSE'S SLUDGE

We learn communication habits from others and from society, and we already know those habits are bad. This behavior is not always your fault. With that said, awareness of this matter now makes it *your* responsibility to change. It's no one else's problem. It's yours to own.

The challenge is while you're working hard on your communication, others still have terrible habits. While you can't change them, you don't have to put up with their abuse. You don't want others dumping their toxic sludge all over you. It's not good for your mind and heart, especially when you're working so hard to heal those areas.

Even after having made reasonable attempts to understand someone's side, to leverage FIFI, to use specific language, and admit your contribution through AMUM, you might still experience toxicity in that person. Do not respond to it; you don't have to take it. If you find yourself starting to lose your cool, it's ok to say, "I need to speak but can't right now. I need a moment to get my thoughts together."

Set your boundaries.

If this person continues to call you names, put you down, or threatens you, tell them they have crossed the line. Sometimes doing this much will alter their behavior. Should they continue, the next step is to let them know their communication is toxic and you'll continue the conversation once they've settled down and can be respectful. At this point, they know you're about to disengage and they might alter their tone.

Should that fail, then you fully need to disengage. It's important you disengage to enforce your boundaries. If they throw a tantrum, let them. Stay calm and disengage as best you can.

Hopefully your everyday situations are not this dramatic. What we usually experience from others are toxic moods and feelings more than words. Others might simply be less courteous, less considerate, more grouchy and negative, and more inclined to complain. This is a problem worse than the former because the toxic effects are less obvious. Of course, if someone is shouting at you and calling you names, that's toxic. The less obvious toxicity comes from everyday interactions. Sometimes these interactions come from those closest to you.

The number one thing to remember about toxic communicators is: It's about them, not you. They have issues preventing them from healthy communication.

I once had a grouchy grandfather who used a great deal of foul language. A WWII vet, he was fiercely independent, hunted his own food, and lived alone in a cabin in Montana. When visiting him one morning, I said, "Good morning, Grandpa!" He shot back scornfully, "What's so (expletive) good about it?" I smiled big and said, "You, Grandpa!" He teared up and became silent. I hugged him. We made breakfast and went duck hunting. I knew underneath all that grouchiness was a lot of pain, so I never took his foul moods and bitter criticism personally. He had been through much difficulty in his life, had many regrets, and never learned to communicate.

Sometimes you just have to know who you're dealing with. A little bit of empathy and some kind words go a long way.

24 THE POWER OF NOTICING

Y ou're in a conversation and you're continually interrupted. The other person is dismissive of your thoughts. They don't have time to talk to you. They act upset. They intimidate or bully you. They threaten you.

While such inconsiderate behavior might seem obvious to *you*, it might not be obvious to *them*. That's why you need to *notice* it, and stop it before it goes further.

By noticing, you bring attention to their behavior.

People tend to pay attention to things others notice, so noticing is a powerful technique.

The way to notice is to simply say what you observe about their communication behavior. When you notice, ensure you do so in a non-blaming tone. If you sound accusatory, the technique is likely to backfire. They'll become defensive.

Here are some examples of noticing:

- ☆ "I noticed you interrupted me several times when I was trying to convey my thoughts."
- ☆ "I noticed you dismiss a lot of what I say and I feel unheard."
- ☆ "I notice we seem to run out of time whenever we bring up this matter. Can we set aside time to discuss this fully without interruption?"
- ☆ "I noticed you're acting upset. Can you tell me why?"
- ☆ "I feel intimidated/bullied by your behavior, is that your intent?"
- ☆ "I notice you resort to threats to get your way."
- ☆ "I notice you resort to name calling to make your points."

You could get a wide variety of responses. They might apologize and alter their behavior. They might enter into an explanation as to why they're behaving the way they are, in which case you should listen. They might behave for a time and then fall back into the bad habit (in which case you *notice* it again without rubbing it in.) Or, they might throw a tantrum. Remember, you can't control their behavior; you can only influence it by exercising healthy communication skills.

There's something else you should notice, and that's *good* behavior.

Noticing is powerful, not only to bring attention to bad behavior but to good behavior as well. This is especially important when the person or people you're dealing with are a work in progress, so to speak.

Some examples of noticing in a positive way are:

"I noticed you listened respectfully."

"I noticed you considered my point of view (even though we didn't agree)".

"I appreciate you were honest with me (even if I didn't like what I heard)."

"I appreciate you told me this bad news, even when you knew it would be upsetting to me."

"I liked how you shared your thoughts with me."

"I like how we can disagree and still remember each other's great qualities."

"I like how you expressed yourself without using profanities. I know you feel strongly about this topic."

It's just as important to notice good behavior as it is bad behavior.

When you notice, you bring the matter to their conscious attention. *Noticing* is one of the most effective means of changing or reinforcing behavior. It's a great habit to learn and practice, especially as a leader.

In fact, this technique not only works in communication, it works in nearly all facets of influencing behavior and building relationships.

We'll talk more about this powerful technique in the LEADERSHIP series (volume two).

In the next lesson, we'll talk about when it's best *not* to express your thoughts.

25 WHEN NOT TO GIVE YOUR THOUGHTS

It's a funny thing about communication. On one hand, people are often afraid to say what they think. On the other hand, people say *way* too much!

I'm not talking about revealing too much personal information.

What I'm talking about is keeping your best thoughts, ideas, and advice to *yourself*, as opposed to sharing them with your spouse, boss, troubled friend, student, and such.

Why?

There are times when it's best to let insight come to the mind of others on their own, as opposed to you delivering it to them on a platter through advice, no matter how sage that advice is.

When you give advice, you're going straight to solution without letting the other person come up with the insight on their own.

When others don't own the insight, they're less likely to be motivated by it. People are more likely to be motivated to change, or implement a change, when the idea is self-generated.

Another reason to let others come to their own solutions, as lengthy a process as it might be, is they'll have more respect for you. Respect *is* influence. It's not just a warm and fuzzy feeling. It's power. Respect and influence is something you want to cultivate.

If you're the kind of person who often gives advice, telling everyone what you think, and imposing your views onto others, you're not going to be well liked. People generally find this sort of behavior annoying, if not overbearing. It does not command much respect. By showing deference, that is allowing others to have their insights without you inserting yours, a few things happen.

First, you make them feel heard and understood. That itself is powerful. When you let others feel heard and understood (even if you don't agree with them), you earn respect.

Second, you give them a sense of autonomy. They feel this autonomy because they probably *do* sense you know something, but that you held back and let them have their journey to insight is huge. People treasure their autonomy. When you let others have their autonomy about coming to their own insights, you earn respect.

Let's say a friend is struggling to decide whether to seek a different job. You might have an opinion about the matter, and this might be a time to keep your opinion to yourself. Asking open-ended questions instead can help her think her decision through.

For example, "How do you think a new job will impact your family?" Or, "What are you looking for in a job?" Open-ended questions to help others discover their own insight can be much more helpful than giving an opinion or lending advice.

It can take a substantial amount of self-control and patience to hold back when you want so badly to pipe up. Some people refrain well. Others, not so much.

If you find yourself in the "other" category, don't beat yourself up. Just try to stay aware of when you have an urge to express an opinion, and then decide, "Do I *really* need to say that?"

Most of the time the answer is no.

You can try to rationalize yourself if you want to, and that's fine. At least you're thinking about it before piping up.

Of course, the situation, timing, and other factors play into whether to keep to yourself or convey your thoughts. It takes conscious effort, small changes over a long time, and constant refinement to good at this art.

26 SOUND BITES

With the arrival of the information age, content gushes at us like water from a firehouse. The human brain cannot, and does not, process all that information.

When people are anxious and stressed (and this describes many people), their ability to process information is impaired. So even less content gets through. To make matters worse, the human brain is asymmetrical in its processing. We tend to focus more on the negative than the positive.

Let's say you want to influence someone's thinking about a subject, but they keep bringing up the negative. How do you respond?

First, acknowledge their point(s) with something such as, "I can see why you might think that way." Then reply with three positive points for every negative point.

For example, let's say you want to respond to someone who says, "That's an ugly car." You'll first want to acknowledge their point, then counter with three positive points: "That car gets fifty miles per gallon, has the highest safety rating in its class, and goes from zero to sixty in five seconds."

To land your points, make them concise. Remember, most people can't process a lot of information at once. This leads to the next point.

Complex concepts and scenarios often don't lend themselves easily to concise points. Many try to reduce complex information or concepts into a soundbite, only to succeed at creating a "reductive fallacy." The reductive fallacy is both true, not true, and often misleading.

For example, a statement such as, "We can solve poverty by putting people in homes" is a reductive fallacy. The causes of poverty are many and complex.

176

Many people in poverty already have homes; maybe not good ones, but homes nonetheless. So, "putting them in homes" isn't going to solve the great many other issues related to poverty such as hunger, disease, hygiene, education, work, transportation, and so on.

So how *do* we explain complex information and concepts to others?

The secret is to break the subject down into logical chunks that can be summarized concisely.

For example, "We can reduce poverty by focusing on several key areas," then list the areas in concise, short statements. Next, unpack each area by delivering three to five concise, short statements per area.

When people are in a calm and relaxed state, they might be able to process up to seven chunks at a time.

When people are anxious and stressed (which is usually the case), the maximum number of chunks they can process is *three* at a time. So, you won't want to deliver on every single point all at once. You'll have to deliver in segments.

This method does take a lot longer and requires a great deal more patience, but you'll enjoy much greater credibility and respect from others.

You can apply this concept to your everyday communication and relations. For example, when the matter under discussion is too complex for a single, simple argument, or a single conversation, break it down into chunks, then deliver your chunks no more than three at a time. Wait for another conversation to deliver another three chunks. Continue this pattern until you've exhausted your chunks, then repeat. You'll need to redeliver your points because it can take up to six times before a point is remembered and comprehended.

I've personally found this technique useful to slowly but surely persuade others about a complex topic I care about. It takes time, planning your points, and repetition. The patience and effort to communicate in this way is well worth the credibility, respect, and influence you'll earn.

Now, this technique doesn't work on everyone. Some people are too entrenched to be persuaded by any amount of logic, appeals to values, or clear and concise language. Remember, you can't control, you can only influence.

If words don't work, sometimes body language does. We'll talk about that in the next lesson.

27 / SPEAKING WITHOUT SPEAKING

Studies suggest more information is conveyed through non-verbal means (as high as 95 percent) than by the spoken word (as low as 5 percent). What's more is for most people, non-verbal communication is involuntary and difficult to conceal.

If you said in a perfectly calm, normal tone of voice the house was on fire, chances are people will not pay attention. If you shouted something totally unintelligible in a loud, fearful voice, you'll get people's attention even if they don't know what you're saying.

We all know the old, "there's nothing wrong" line when someone's body language (crossed arms and scowling face) clearly say they're angry about something. Obviously, there *is* something wrong and they're not telling the truth.

In many ways, you can tell if someone is lying or feeling something different than what they say by observing their facial expressions, gestures, posture, and body language. Additionally, non-verbal communication includes the volume and tone of your voice and speed of speech.

The ability to read non-verbal communication is an important life skill. Many people don't know how to read non-verbal communication, so they go through life misinterpreting or missing non-verbal cues altogether. This is a recipe for trouble in relationships in every area of one's life.

People who struggle with empathy for others, or who have low emotional intelligence often have poor skills in non-verbal cue reading. It doesn't mean they're bad people. It means they haven't learned this crucial life skill. Sadly, they're sabotaging themselves in both their personal and professional relationships, and unknowingly hurting others.

People largely broadcast their non-verbal communication unknowingly because it comes from the automatic mind. Your emotional frequency vibrates out into the world for everyone to see whether you want it to or not, largely in the form of non-verbal communication. Your emotional frequency and non-verbals often speak louder and communicate more powerfully than the words you say. If you attempt to hide your emotions, you'll only appear closed off and unapproachable. That's not a good message to send. What's more is when you behave in this way, you're communicating to your automatic mind that you're closed and unapproachable—a poor message to reinforce in your internal programming. You're not likely to manifest good things for yourself with a "closed and unapproachable" program running.

Remember, the second law of the automatic mind is it absorbs all communication (no matter to whom or what) into *itself.* You want your communication to be positive, but if your non-verbals are screaming out negative cues, that doesn't help one bit.

When I returned home from a two-year tour in Afghanistan, people told me I had become aggressive, irritable, and angry. This was a surprise to me because I was overjoyed to be home after two years in a war-torn country. My words were joyful, but my non-verbals were clearly not. This feedback was valuable. I purposed to become more self-aware and catch myself when my mind was headed toward the badlands, even if my spoken words were polite and cheerful. Through awareness of my own emotions and negative non-verbals, and working to turn them around, my relationships with everyone significantly improved.

When people ask, "What's wrong?" and you say, "Nothing." that's a clue to check yourself. You might not realize you're communicating in a negative way, even if your words say something else. Please do not ignore the gift of this valuable feedback. It's an opportunity to recalibrate your automatic programming and manifest a better reality for yourself.

If you smile but aren't happy, then your smile will appear fake. People will know you're not happy even though you're smiling. Your automatic mind is not fooled at all. It knows you're unhappy and your smile is fake.

If you smile and allow it to trigger happiness in you (without resisting it) then your smile will appear real. People will find you more authentic. Your automatic mind, however, might be a little confused for a time because you were unhappy, but now you're happy. In time, if you keep up this behavior, your automatic mind will accept that you're happy and won't be confused. There's real science behind this phenomenon and we'll explore this further later. In the meantime, let your smile help you feel truly happy. Then it will be more authentic.

Now *that* is a great message to send.

28 NON-VERBAL DO'S AND DON'TS

Your non-verbals communicate to the world, and they also communicate to your automatic mind. Remember, the second law of the automatic mind states that all communication, no matter to whom or what, is reflected internally into the automatic mind. Your automatic mind is soaking it all in like a gigantic sponge.

For example, if you smile, you communicate happiness to both the external world, and to your automatic mind. You might not "feel" like smiling, but if you want to reprogram your automatic mind for happiness, then smiling often, even when you don't feel like it, will help. Smiling imprints a positive mood into your automatic mind, which in turn helps to produce positive, optimistic, thoughts. This positivity can mean the difference between giving up on something hard or continuing to persevere another day.

The opposite is also true. If you go around with a serious look, scowling, or looking depressed, you imprint that mood into your automatic mind. When these sour moods get imprinted, your thoughts can enter the badlands, and that's not good. This negativity can set you up to become easily irritated, impatient, or just a drag to be around.

Think of a confident, happy person you know or have seen on television. How do they carry themselves? Chances are they smile often, walk upright with shoulders back, make eye contact, and shake hands firmly. Such non-verbals state to the world *and* your automatic mind that you're confident, attentive, and a pleasure to be around.

If you a scowl, slouch, look away, and/or have a limp handshake, the instantaneous vibe you give off is not that of a confident person. You need to change that. Start paying attention to your own non-verbals and correcting them with your manual mind. Do this often until your new, better non-verbals become a habit (embedded into your automatic mind). Then you won't have to think about them so much. It takes energy to use your manual mind in this way, which we'll explain more about in the NEURO-SCIENCE series. So, don't beat yourself up if you find this difficult to do at first.

Now, with all that said…

You don't want to overdo it either. Smiling when it's inappropriate to do so (like when someone is sobbing over the loss of a loved one) communicates a lack of connection. Walking with too much swagger will make you look over-confident, and *that* will turn people off. You don't want to glare into people's eyes or stare so much as to make others uncomfortable. Finally, when shaking someone's hand, you don't need to break it.

When I arrived at Marine Corps boot camp, one of the first skills I learned was how to walk with confidence. Head erect, shoulders back, spines strong and straight, and no slouching, leaning against walls, or looking lost. It became a habit that remains with me to this day. Whenever I'm feeling a little less than confident, I turn to my Marine walk and I feel better.

I know this might be a bit much for some folks. You don't need to adopt a Marine walk, but know what a confident and balanced demeanor looks like and then adjust yourself to that demeanor. The demeanor will come with a host of non-verbal cues to notice in detail and apply yourself. This might feel awkward at first, and that's expected. Keep it up anyway and soon enough it will become natural to you.

When you travel the world, pay attention to the non-verbals of the cultures you visit. For example, in Japan, it's polite to exchange currency or business cards using two hands. In the Middle East, it's rude to show the soles of your feet (many Westerners tend to sit with their ankle on a knee, thereby exposing the sole of their foot). In Germany, punctuality is respectful. Pointing with a single finger is generally viewed as disrespectful around the world, which is why it's much better to "point" with an open palm.

Even if you don't know all the cultural norms, smiling and showing a respectful, appreciative demeanor is a universal language nearly everyone understands. I have found this to be true no matter where I am in the world.

⭐ 29 COGNITIVE DISSONANCE

Cognitive dissonance happens when a person is under mental stress due to one or more of the following situations:

☆ When confronted with information conflicting with deeply held values and beliefs

☆ When holding two or more contradictory beliefs or values at the same time

☆ When behaving in a manner contradictory to one's beliefs and values

Here are three illustrations.

Sherry is Matt's mom. Matt has been coming home late at night reeking of marijuana. He's been skipping school and his grades are terrible. Sherry believes her son is a wonderful boy and the school doesn't do enough to help him in his classes. She believes him when he says he was out late studying at a friend's house. Lately, she has found money missing from her wallet. She blames the missing money on her poor memory or misplacing her cash. Sherry's neighbor, Nancy, has tried to explain to Sherry that Matt is using drugs and all the signs are there. But Sherry won't hear of it. One day, a police officer comes to the door to inform Sherry her son was jailed for drug use. Sherry completely denied Matt ever used drugs and his arrest was a mistake. Despite the detailed report from the police officer, Sherry refused to believe Matt was using drugs.

Sherry is demonstrating the first form of cognitive dissonance.

Debbie loves her job as a journalist. She also loves her children intensely. She believes mothers should spend as much time with their children as possible. At the same time, she believes in giving 100 percent of herself at work. Her job often takes her across the country, keeping her away from her family for several days.

This situation causes a great deal of mental stress for her because while she loves her job and wants to give her best it, she also loves her children and can't stand to be away from them. She tends to prioritize work over her children, but then puts down other moms who do the same thing.

Debbie is demonstrating the second form of cognitive dissonance.

Allen is trying to lose weight and is on a low-sugar and carb diet. One morning he notices a large plate of cookies in the break room at work. Allen knew he should avoid the cookies, but a thought creeps into his mind, "I'm allowed to cheat every once in a while." He ate several cookies and then tried to justify himself by promising to work out an extra twenty minutes in the gym today. Allen knew this wasn't true, and he knew he should have walked away from the cookies. His behavior was not in line with his beliefs about avoiding sugar and carbs.

Allen demonstrated the third form of cognitive dissonance.

Why is any of this important in communication?

Because you *will* run into it.

When you converse with someone and no amount of facts, logic, or reason will move them from their position, *or* when you see someone say one thing but do something else, or when you hear someone justifying behavior they should not do, you're witnessing cognitive dissonance. This is common, and while the message they give is conflicting and confusing, at least you'll understand what you see.

More important than recognizing cognitive dissonance in others is to recognize it in *yourself*.

If you find you're ignoring important information (because it conflicts with your beliefs and values), or you find you're inconsistent in how you apply rules or values to certain things, or you find yourself making excuses for things you shouldn't do, then that is cognitive dissonance in yourself. When that happens, you'll communicate in a conflicting and confusing way, which does not bode well for commanding influence or respect.

These are examples of the bad kind of cognitive dissonance. We'll talk about the good kind of cognitive dissonance in the next lesson.

30 "GOOD" STRESS

When you do or say something out of line with the beliefs in your programming, you'll feel a little off.

For example, if ugly deposits in your programming say you're not worthy of being fit and beautiful, or of being unconditionally loved, or of admiration and respect, or of having nice things in life, then anything you or others say that are not in line with those beliefs will make you feel uncomfortable. You'll feel a certain amount of stress. This stress is *good*.

Whenever you say or do something not in line with the beliefs in your programming, there's cognitive dissonance. Your brain doesn't like that.

Interestingly, a funny thing happens when you continue to speak and behave in a manner inconsistent with your beliefs. Your beliefs start to *change*. You can force a reprogramming of your automatic mind by persevering in your new speaking and behaving. This is an example of "fake it 'til you make it." You see, your brain doesn't like the ongoing cognitive dissonance, so it will reprogram itself to make it go away.

Keep in mind the second law of the automatic mind, how it takes every communication personally.

For example, if you call someone a nasty name, you call yourself that name too. If you give someone a compliment, you compliment yourself as well.

If you have difficulty accepting compliments, you have cognitive dissonance. Your automatic mind does not believe whatever nice thing was said about you, so you squirm and behave sheepishly, as opposed to graciously accepting the compliment and saying, "thank you." When you don't accept compliments well, you look and act as if you're not confident.

If you tend to use foul language and harshly put down others, that communication is just as bad for you as it is for others. Foul language and condemnation of others is your automatic mind revealing its programming that it believes *you* are a bad and undeserving person. When you curse or condemn someone else, the intensity of that condemnation reveals the intensity of the criticism you have of *yourself.*

That's why cursing and condemnation of others is a somewhat contagious and addictive habit. Everyone has ugly lie deposits in their programming, and any time you reinforce those beliefs through bad language and behavior, the automatic mind then turns around and reinforces the bad language and behavior in a vicious circle.

Foul language and condemnation of others is poisonous to *you* and your *relationships.* Quit this.

Quitting these bad habits will induce a certain amount of "good" stress because your automatic programming believes all sorts awful things about you, but you refuse to acknowledge it through your words and behavior. You refuse to use foul language and condemn others. You refuse to put down or condemn *yourself.* You are worthy of respect, but respecting yourself can be both difficult and even stressful until the programming in your automatic mind changes for good.

Respecting others, even when they do and say terrible things, is respecting yourself. Don't be a doormat, but keep your cool and refrain from inflammatory language. If you need to walk away, that's fine. You still preserve your self-respect.

Let's go back to giving and accepting compliments. Be generous with your compliments. With nearly everyone you encounter, you can find at least one thing you like about that person. Say so! You might feel uncomfortable at first because your automatic programming will resist. That's *good* stress. Be gracious and open in accepting compliments from others. Again, that's *good* stress.

You see, it's all good!

SUMMARY OF THE COMMUNICATION SERIES

Congratulations! You've completed the COMMUNICATION Series.

Communication is largely an automatic process stemming from our internal programming. Our thinking and emoting emerge in the very words we speak and how we say them.

We know society has many poor communication habits, some of them toxic. Negative messages can seep into our automatic minds and reinforce ugly lie deposits and false beliefs if we're not careful. Those negative messages can come right back out in the things we say. We can unknowingly perpetuate a negative cycle. We don't want this.

We want to change ourselves so we can break this cycle. We want to, instead, perpetuate a healthy cycle of humanity, energy, and optimism. We do this through communication.

Unlike the AWARENESS series in which you don't need to memorize all that content, the COMMUNICATION series offers skills to learn because communication is the feedback loop to your automatic mind. Communication is a critical enabler to reprograming your mind. Go over this content as many times as you need until it sinks in.

Below is a summary of the COMMUNICATION Series. You might want to refer to this summary section to remind yourself of the concepts presented here.

Listening is the most powerful form of communication next to actions.

Positive communication = positive influence. Negative communication = negative influence.

FIFI – Facts, Identity, Feelings, Impact – Is present in every conversation, even your own thoughts.

Facts – we notice what supports our values, and disregard what doesn't.

Identity – a challenge to identity can trigger an F3 response from mild to severe.

Feelings – our feelings about Facts and Identity

Impact – our reaction to Facts, Identity, and Feelings.

Listen to learn other's FIFI. Be aware of your own FIFI.

AMUM – Avoid, Misunderstand, Unapproachable, Mindless – Ways you contribute to problems.

Blaming and excuses make you look weak.

Beware not to trigger an F3 response in others or you'll hamper/shut down communication.

Avoid "but" and absolutes like: always, never, all, every, nothing, nobody, everybody, etc.

Present both sides by using the "and" technique.

Avoid toxic communication. Be generous with compliments.

You cannot control another's response, only *influence*.

Be mindful of the messages you allow into your mind

Notice both good and poor communication habits in others to help influence change.

Accept compliments graciously.

Let others have their journey. Sharing all your insights is not always wise.

Be aware of your non-verbal communication and demeanor.

For every negative point, respond with three positive points (soundbites.)

A soundbite is about nine words.

When emotionally charged, people can only comprehend about three points at a time.

Cognitive dissonance – when a person is under mental stress due to:

#1. Being confronted with information conflicting with deeply held values and beliefs.

> Bad: Ignoring evidence of a loved one's addiction.

> Good: Filtering out toxic messages.

#2. Holding two or more contradictory beliefs or values at the same time.

> Bad: "Do as I say, not as I do" mindset.

> Good: Gratitude for what you have, even if it's not everything you want.

#3. Behaving in a manner contradictory to one's beliefs and values.

Bad: Adultery

Good: Courage to do the right thing.

The brain doesn't like cognitive dissonance, so it will re-program itself to make it go away. This is why bad cognitive dissonance is dangerous because bad behavior eventually becomes part of your programming. Good cognitive dissonance is good for you for the same reason; the behavior eventually becomes part of your programming.

PART 4
THE NEURO-SCIENCE SERIES

FIRST, A GENUFLECT TO THE SKEPTICS

1

Welcome to the Neuro-Science series!

This series presents you with facts and widely-accepted theories about the human brain. Modern science has done a great job revealing fascinating information about the brain. Some of that information validates and reinforces centuries-old theories about the human mind. One of those old theories is that of the conscious (manual) and subconscious (automatic) mind. Enter the skeptic...

Throughout this program, I've presented concepts that build heavily on the conscious/subconscious (manual/automatic) theory of mind. The theory states that the automatic mind largely runs the show of our lives. Skeptics of this theory understandably dispute the degree to which the automatic mind rules our lives. Their instincts are well founded. Here's why.

If we say our automatic mind rules our lives, then that *might* absolve us from personal responsibility of our own behavior.

Here's the catch. The automatic mind only rules our lives if we mindlessly *let* it! You see, the *manual* mind is the ultimate governor. When the automatic mind starts in with its shenanigans, the manual mind has the power to regulate it. The trick is your manual mind must know what's going on and exercise no small amount of energy to engage. It takes more brain energy to engage in this way, and it takes a willingness to stand up to your automatic mind when it's been running the show by itself for so long.

You see, the automatic mind does not want to change because change is scary (Third Law), so it will resist. That doesn't mean we quit, nor does it mean we simply blame our automatic minds and declare ourselves helpless. We are *not* helpless.

We cannot let our automatic minds have its way when it's behaving badly. The manual mind has the power to engage. The manual mind can *choose* to exercise this power. Because we can choose, we are ultimately responsible for our behavior. You cannot blame your automatic mind for your bad behavior.

When the manual/automatic mind theory is explained in those terms, most skeptics nod their heads in agreement. What they don't want to hear is we can't control our behavior. Don't worry, guys, I got your back.

With that said…

Education matters. While your manual mind can absolutely put the brakes on behavior such as murder, rape, grand theft, or other heinous wrong-doing, it might *not* know how to regulate subtle, less obvious behaviors.

It might not know how to persevere through setbacks, respond appropriately to rejection, or regulate negative thinking patterns.

It might not know what good communication is, as not to sabotage itself.

It might not be good at understanding its automatic neighbor and how it butts into life.

It might not know how to leverage communication, behavior, and an understanding of others to better develop the human potential of others.

This knowledge is not obvious to most people. This program exists to educate you on how to employ your manual mind in ways to get the most out of your own potential, and that of others.

Sometimes it's easier to jump into the pool with a good instructor as opposed to getting hours of coursework about the physics of water. Doing so requires faith and optimism. That's exactly what I did with you. We jumped into the water together by creating your Reality Show (thank you for your faith and optimism!)

Now comes the neuro-science behind it to advance you from faith to *understanding*.

2 ⭐ THE HUMAN BRAIN

The human brain is fascinating. It's largely the same brain humans have enjoyed for at least ten thousand years (experts vary on this opinion, as many believe the timetable is longer than that.) What that means is we're all born with the same brain as the proverbial cave-man babies of our ancestors.

Regardless of our race, religion, sex, or wealth, we're born with the same brain. It doesn't matter if you were born among the smartphone-free natives of Papua New Guinea or among the elites of a royal family in a wealthy city. The majority of us are born with a brain no different than that of a child in any other part of the world.

Our brains are remarkably similar across the globe. Differences in our brains have to do with the different content that enters them.

Different content enters the brain depending upon where one is born and raised, environmental exposures, and what content one chooses to let in (or not).

Culture plays a large role in shaping human minds, and every culture has its plusses and minuses when doing so. Every culture has gaps, and it's the intent of this program to fill in some of those gaps so you can make better choices on how to shape your mind and that of others' for the better.

The human brain has both an "animal side" and a "human side." Although other terms and explanations exist for those who are much smarter on this subject and like to debate nuances, I prefer to keep things simple. We'll stick to "animal side" and "human side" for now. Stay with me.

Your animal side is what keeps you *alive*. Automatic processes like pulse, breathing, digesting, and hormone release are just the beginning. There's also pleasure seeking, pain avoidance, memories, and emotions. Learning also takes place here so habits and routines become embedded. Once embedded, habits run on autopilot. The parts of the brain that govern these processes are the *limbic system* and *basal ganglia*. It's called the "animal side" because nearly all vertebrate animals have a limbic system and basal ganglia. Automatic processes are governed by these two control centers. Nearly all animals possess these, as well as humans.

In other words, the animal side (limbic system and basal ganglia) is the *automatic* mind.

Human brains are exceptional because of the *neocortex*. It's quite large in humans, and rather small in animals (if it exists at all). The neocortex is our logic and reasoning center. It governs planning and thinking.

The human side (neocortex) is the *manual* mind.

Animals don't possess the conscious capacity humans have. That's why animals largely do not *think*. They largely do not have a manual mind.

Animals mostly react *automatically* according to the direction of their automatic control centers. They have little manual control. When animals are trained, it's because their automatic brains were programmed by the trainer.

Can animals sometimes solve problems? Yes, of course. Does that mean animals don't feel pain when abused or neglected? Of course not.

Our manual mind is also our primary empathy center. It's why we care about animals as well as our fellow humans more deeply than animals care about each other. Can animals *care*? Some can, but not to the same capacity as most humans.

When our manual minds are off-line and we are only using our animal brains (the automatic mind), we are much less empathetic. We effectively turn off our "I care" center.

The automatic and manual minds are *real*, not some made-up idea. They are also interconnected. That interconnection has much to do with how you think and act. We'll cover more of this in the upcoming lessons.

3 SOME BRAIN PARTS CAN REGENERATE THEMSELVES

Scientists say most of our nervous system does not regenerate, except for *three* areas.

The first is the *olfactory bulb* which governs your sense of smell. I'm not sure why this neurological area renews, but I am glad it does. It comes with a personal story.

While serving in the military, I sustained a traumatic brain injury and lost all sense of smell. I thought I would never smell turkey dinner, macaroni and cheese, or *Georgio* perfume ever again. On the bright side, I could no longer smell the body odor of my military cohorts living life in the field for days on end with no shower.

After almost a year, I started to sense a strange odor. The source didn't matter; if there was an odor to be had, it was the same, weird, somewhat unpleasant odor. After another year, odors began to differentiate themselves. Air fresheners started to smell like air fresheners and body eliminations started to smell like their old, familiar self. After three years, I could smell everything like normal again. I can personally attest that the olfactory bulb renews itself.

The second neurological area that renews is the *hippocampus*. (Not hippos camping, which is an amusing image). The hippocampus is part of the limbic system and is involved in memory and learning. Remember, the limbic system is part of your *automatic* control center.

That the hippocampus can *renew* means memories and learning hanging out in your automatic mind can also be renewed. With that said, it's important to note the neocortex, your manual control center, is *also* involved in memory and learning. So, there's an important connection there.

Memories and learning happen in both your manual and automatic minds.

You can leverage your manual mind to reshape what's happening in the automatic mind.

It's not just the resting thought patterns that can be reshaped, the *physical neurons* (in the automatic mind) are continually renewed. This is a nice feature.

The third neurological area that renews itself is the *subventricular zone*. This part of the brain is a mystery. No one knows what it does or why it's there. And no one knows why *this* part of the brain renews itself.

There's a lot of research going on involving this part of the brain with obvious implications for curing all sorts of neurological disorders and injuries. At this moment in time, it's one big, wonderful, fascinating mystery.

There are a few things you can do with a mystery. The first is you can calmly wait to see what the scientists learn—and you might be waiting a long time. That won't do you much good for the time being.

The second is you can come up with your own happy story. It's natural for humans to fill in the blanks with their own "facts" and assumptions. Use your made-up story about the purpose of the subventricular zone, (and why it regenerates) for good if you go that route.

I like to believe this is my "second chance" zone. In terms of health and happiness, whatever yucky thing happened to me in the past can be erased, and a fresh new future can replace it. I don't care if it's true or not right now. That's my story and I'm sticking to it. You're welcome to come up with your own explanation of why this area regenerates, whether it's true or not, so long as it helps you.

The process of neural tissue regeneration is called *neurogenesis*. It's a process that largely happens when you're sleeping. So, go ahead and take a nap. Just make sure you wake up in time for the next lesson. You won't want to miss it.

4 FIVE HARD-WIRED TRIGGERS

Our egos are more than we think they are. Good reasons exist for why we become anxious or upset at things like:

Getting put down in front of your peers – a threat to your *Status* (S).

Not knowing how you're going to pay an unexpected bill – a threat to your *Certainty* (C).

Having a micromanaging or overbearing boss – a threat to your *Autonomy* (A).

Being ejected from your chess club – a threat to your *Relatedness* (R).

Losing your job while the CEO gets a bonus – a threat to your sense of *Fairness* (F).

The reason you get upset at these things is because your brain is hard wired to react. You see, your brain—and remember, this is the same brain our caveman ancestors had—is reacting to these scenarios as though they are life-endangering threats.

Even though we might not experience physical pain in these scenarios, we experience psychological pain. Would you believe psychological pain registers in the *same* place of the brain as physical pain? Psychological pain really does hurt. That's why pain medications work just as well on psychological pain as they do on physical pain.

Sensing these threats helped our ancestors to compete and survive in a dangerous world, a world in which one wrong move meant you where devoured by a gigantic beast or brutally slain by your human enemy.

Our world has changed dramatically, but our brains have not. Today, our threat-sensing brains often lead us to over-react. We stress out, become angry or depressed, shut down, or lash out. Such responses don't help us one little bit today. We are easily triggered.

The problem with being so easily triggered into a negative state is sadly, widespread. If you find yourself in a negative state more often than a positive one, don't beat yourself up. You're hardly alone.

Dr. David Rock is a leadership and neuro-science expert who popularized this theory along with a catchy acronym capturing our five hard-wired stress trigger areas.

That acronym is *SCARF*. It's a great acronym to remember the trigger areas and build self-awareness. What's more is understanding SCARF will help you manage your relationships better so *you* don't become an unnecessary stress trigger for someone else.

Respect and leadership are about building people up, not tearing them down. You build others up with good stress, not bad stress like you find in SCARF. We'll talk more about the good stress/bad stress dynamic in the LEADERSHIP series.

In the next five lessons, we'll go into each SCARF element in detail. As we do, keep in mind that just because we're hard-wired to react to these five areas does *not* mean you cannot manage them or even leverage them in your favor.

An example is leveraging fear and anger. Fear and anger can be powerful motivators when they're aroused for the right reasons and channeled in the right way.

There's a wonderful bright side. We're not just hard wired for threats and negativity. In addition to being hardwired for SCARF, we're also hardwired for love and optimism.

Those are only two words, so they don't need a catchy acronym. But they are important.

Love and optimism were equally as important to the survival of our ancestors as SCARF.

Love and optimism are no less important to us today than they were ten thousand years ago.

We'll cover love and optimism after we cover SCARF so we can end the discussion of our hardwiredness on a happy note.

 **5 STATUS**

Think about it.

Teenagers are embarrassed to have their parents around because it doesn't look "cool."

Factory workers compete on the assembly line to wear the blue smock, indicating they're a "lead."

Military and police officers wear rank insignia and badges to indicate who's in charge.

Some millionaires wear the finest jewelry and drive the fanciest cars to showcase their wealth.

Status is a strong part of our social culture and daily lives. It plays an important function in law and order, in government, and in organizational life. We could not have civilized life without it.

Status becomes a problem when we abuse our power, or when we attach it too tightly to our sense of self-worth. Status gone bad leads to terrible human rights abuses. While Status is an important part of a civilized society, it has a nasty side we must constantly guard against.

In ancient human history, Status within a tribe directly correlated to your likelihood for survival. Higher Status individuals enjoyed access to more resources such as food, water, tools, shelter, and mates.

Just as chickens have a pecking order and dogs have an alpha in the pack, humans naturally align themselves in a hierarchy. Usually those who control the most resources enjoy the higher Status.

Status is a huge part of your Identity. A challenge to one's sense of Status is tantamount to a challenge to one's Identity. It can trigger an F3 response.

It gets even stickier.

If your Facts are challenged, then your Status and Identity as a "right" person is also challenged. That challenge will evoke a Feeling, usually negative. The resulting Impact (F3 response) is likely to be less than ideal *unless* we are mindful.

If we're mindful (that is, paying manual attention) and responding deliberately, then we can influence a better outcome. If we're not mindful and let our automatic minds (animal brain) react as they please, that's when we get into trouble.

If being treated like you're above or better than others is important to you, then any perceived threat to your Status will likely trigger you into a negative state. This is a recipe for leadership blind spots and relationship problems.

If you think you might have a tendency for Status triggers, keep a mental note every time it happens. Chances are, your resulting behavior is causing harm and you'll want to work on yourself to remedy the thought patterns contributing to this behavior.

At the same time, you could be a humble person and still get triggered by someone who belittles you, puts you down in front of others, or blatantly disrespects you. In this situation, assert yourself in a healthy manner to let that person know your personal boundary was crossed. You have every right to be angry, and you can express it in a controlled and self-dignified manner.

There's a range between these two extremes where most of us get tripped up. Losing a game, not receiving a promotion, or less than ideal customer service can get under our skin. In these situations, it's helpful to reframe.

Instead of "losing" a game, be grateful you learned and did your best.

Instead of not getting a promotion, consider something better fitted for you.

Instead of less than ideal customer service, be grateful you don't have their job, which is probably low paying with no benefits.

Your Status is a whole lot better than you might realize. Gratitude for what you *do* have helps bring the true benefits of your current Status into view.

# 6 CERTAINTY

We love to know what's going on and what the future holds.

We also love *control* over…well, just about everything. When we have *knowledge* and *control*, we get a warm and fuzzy feeling inside. This wonderful feeling is both our friend and enemy (frenemy)…*Certainty*.

Our need for Certainty can send us into one of two lands.

The first land is a happy place. It's the land of great relationships and great outcomes. We arrive in our happy land by leveraging Certainty to our advantage. We do that by asserting the right amount of control at the right time for the right reasons.

People who are good at leveraging Certainty in the *right* way are loved and respected. They make fantastic teachers, parents, coaches, and leaders.

The *other* land is sad. It's the land of harmed relationships and unhappy outcomes.

We end up in our sad land by *allowing* Certainty to hijack our behavior and send us right over the high-anxiety-control-freak cliff. We become obsessed with knowledge and control to the point of driving others crazy. Many of us go over the control-freak cliff over and over, like lemmings in an endless nature video loop. Our behavior doesn't have to be this mysteriously tragic.

People who reside in this land often have rocky relationships, and cast the blame on others.

Two things happen when we exert unnecessary control over people or situations. The first is people resent over-controlling from others. Excessive, controlling behavior can trigger an unfavorable response we'll explain in the next lesson.

The second is you waste a lot of precious time and energy on the *wrong* things. The *right* things don't get done very well, if they get done at all.

To justify our behavior, we rationalize how we *must* control whatever it is we must. The reality is we were hijacked by Certainty and she's good at getting her way. We don't need the degree of control we think we need.

On the other hand, avoiding taking necessary control when you *should* exert control is irresponsible. You'll end up in the same land of sadness. Knowing when you should or should not exert control, and to what degree is something we take up in the WISDOM series.

Rocky relationships and inefficient expenditure of your energy bodes poorly for ideal life outcomes. The ripple effect doesn't reach just you; it affects everyone around you. Clearly, this does not make for a better world. We want to change this.

If you think you're not as liked as you want to be, and seem to struggle with achieving your goals no matter how hard you try, and you can't seem to figure out why, you're not alone.

Chances are, you might have *low uncertainty tolerance* (that is, a high need for Certainty).

Low uncertainty tolerance can contribute to a host of problems such as excessive worry, high anxiety, aggressive communication patterns, hyper-controlling behavior, perfectionism, untrusting behavior, and more.

The root cause of your low uncertainty tolerance is largely the shenanigans of your automatic mind. That's why we started with resetting your brain, to clear out the crud that's holding you back and start making fresh, healthier deposits in your programming.

How do we land among those who leverage Certainty for good? Who become highly respected and admired leaders? Who enjoy great outcomes and have a positive impact on everyone around them?

That, my friends, is what this book is designed to do. It takes a healthy running automatic mind, engaged manual mind, good communication skills, and sound wisdom to tame Certainty and make it your friend. We'll cover the "how to" more in the LEADERSHIP series (volume two).

In the meantime, growing into the person you want to be is a journey, and you're on it.

AUTONOMY

There are few things we cherish more than our *Autonomy*. From the time we learn to walk, we want *freedom*—and a lot of it. It's the stuff of families, societies, history, and politics.

The eternal question is, just how much freedom is good?

Too much and we have anarchy.

Too little and we have slavery.

The spectrum between these two extremes is nuanced and wide.

The human need for autonomy is almost as powerful as the need for love. While individuals fight over love, entire nations fight over Autonomy.

Autonomy is siblings with our frenemy, Certainty, because when you have Autonomy, you *feel* like you're in control, even if you're not. For example, if you choose to undergo a stressful experience (like jumping off the high dive), your brain registers that situation more favorably than when you're forced to undergo a stressful experience (such as being dragged up the stairs against your will and thrown off the high dive.)

Choices are important to us. This is powerful information because we can leverage Autonomy to influence. Autonomy can be a pest sometimes, but if we're smart (and we are) we can turn it into our best friend.

How?

First, Autonomy as a pest.

Autonomy can get in the way of your better self when you zero in on the things you *can't* do, as opposed to all the great things you *can* do.

You see, Autonomy is almost like a drug. We get it, and then we want more and more.

It's important to be satisfied with what you have, and use it. A lot of times we don't appreciate the Autonomy we do have until it's lost, like when we can't walk, drive, or feed ourselves. This is where gratitude for the freedoms and capabilities you do have helps to put things into perspective. You have a lot more Autonomy than you even realize.

Now, Autonomy as your best friend.

When you want to influence someone's thinking or behavior, you present them with choices. It doesn't matter if it's your children, boss, spouse, friend, or stranger. When you present choices (ones *you* craft), they usually pick one of those options. When they do so, you influence an outcome.

For example, let your kids know that in your household everyone eats one vegetable for dinner, and they might choose between broccoli, green beans, or yummy spinach. Or let your boss know you're planning a week-long family vacation and these are the weeks you were looking at—which week does he prefer? In both cases, you will likely receive an answer that fits your desired outcome. Both the child and the boss feel like they're in control, but it's really you! Clever, eh?

Remember in the COMMUNICATION series when we talked about letting others have their journey to enlightenment, even if the solution is obvious? The reason going straight to solution is problematic is you infringe upon their perceived Autonomy. It doesn't matter how right you are, or how brilliant your idea is, if you infringe upon another's sense of Autonomy, you will likely face resistance.

If you're idea for solution is to control someone else by telling them what they will or won't do, or how to do it, and that control is not necessary (even if you think it is), then you have hijacked their Autonomy. When you do that, you not only face resistance, you face *resentment*. Over time, resentment can build. Then when you need help or a favor from that person, you might not get it.

I'm not saying to never suggest something or direct an action. The problem is we tend to overdo it. Instead, we want do employ these measures more tactically as opposed to all the time.

8 RELATEDNESS

Most primates bare their teeth when approaching the space of others, indicating they come in peace. If they don't show their teeth, the chance of a confrontation increases. It turns out humans demonstrate similar behavior. Showing our teeth when we meet others is what we call a smile. It has a disarming effect.

Unless we smile or demonstrate some other positive cue that we mean no harm, the automatic default in the mind of others is we're a potential threat. It doesn't matter who you are or where you are. If people don't know you, you're a threat. Even for people who do know you, you must continually reassure them you're not a threat.

In fact, some people need more reassurance than others. You probably already know who they are. I know it's a hassle sometimes, and there are limits to how far you should go (that I'll cover in a minute). You see, we have a hardwired need to know who's a threat and who's a friend. That concept is *Relatedness*. Here's an example.

Let's say you head into a convenience store late one night on your way home from work. You're tired, tense, and frowning as you wander the store, looking for the right drink and snack. When you approach the counter, the clerk seems nervous and treats you uneasily, perhaps a little curtly. You don't understand why and then interpret that experience as another sour note in your day.

Now let's alter the situation just slightly. You figure it's late at night and the clerk, who is alone, might feel a little nervous about crime. Even though you're tired after a long day, you settle yourself with gratitude and a happy thought, muster up a smile and pleasant demeanor and enter the store. You approach the counter and this time, the clerk is more at ease with you. He even gives you a weary smile in return and tells you to have a good evening. Because you approached this stranger in a friendly manner (even when fatigued) you were treated in a friend-lier manner in return. Now, it might not always work out this way, but it is more likely if you try to present yourself as *not a threat*.

Smiles aside, there's a whole lot more going on in the minds of others when determining whether you're a potential threat or potential friend. Your language, word choice, tone of voice, gestures, posture, the way you walk, eye contact, your appearance, your demeanor—all convey subtle information to others and it's not always easy to know how it will be interpreted. The best thing to do is to be sincere, mindful, and aware of the impact you have on others.

Now for the limits.

This does not mean you can't assert yourself at the appropriate place and time, or that you shrink from the fantastic person you are just to make others feel better about themselves. It just means you're aware of the sensitivities of others and know how to calibrate yourself.

When others are at ease with you, you're more likable and people are more willing to do things for you. When people are more willing to do things for you, outcomes in your favor are more likely.

On the other hand, watch for your misinterpretation of others as a threat. Such misinterpretations can lead you to become defensive and less empathetic. It can cause you to dismiss others' ideas and get upset easily. This is not ideal.

At the end of the day, we all want to belong and be accepted, which is why family and friends are so important, and why we join groups.

We feel safest when surrounded by those we trust. When we're rejected, the pain is real! Our analysis and interpretation of such events is something we'll cover in the WISDOM series. For now, it's important to understand that Relatedness is our constant need to know if others are our friend…or not. It never goes away.

9 FAIRNESS

Someone cuts in line. A co-worker receives credit for your hard work. An elderly couple is cheated out of their life savings.

The strongest emotional trigger for most people is a perceived violation to *Fairness*. Why?

Because perceived unfairness can trigger a *revenge* response.

The automatic programming believes revenge makes things "fair" or right again.

Neuro-science experts say the drive for revenge can sometime outweigh the desire for food, money, safety, or sex.

Fairness is an expectation, meaning it feeds into our frenemy, Certainty. So, when unfairness occurs there's a double whammy because both Fairness and Certainty get their shins kicked. It's especially hurtful if the unfairness came from someone you trusted. This is the substance of Academy Award winning drama movies!

Life, politics, and business are notoriously unfair.

If we allowed ourselves to get triggered by every perceived slight we'd be a mess. I say *perceived* because Fairness is largely a matter of perception, which is sometimes right and sometimes not.

FIFI plays a substantial roll in our perception of Fairness.

Our personal world of Facts feeds our perception of Fairness. Remember, Facts are not always "facts" but values and a filtered collection of information.

Our Identity feeds our perception of Fairness. If Identity is challenged, we may somehow interpret the situation as "unfair."

Our Feelings feed our perception of Fairness. Many people believe their feelings justify their views and behavior. So, if they "feel" something is unfair, then to them it must be so.

Finally, the Impact will govern our response to Fairness. If the belief that the unfairness "must" be corrected, then a strong behavior will result. Beliefs about how it must be corrected, and to what degree also determines resulting behavior. That behavior will then have an impact on many other people, who may view the behavior very differently and respond in their own way.

If it's Fair, then we're ok.

If it was not Fair, then this could be a threat. *Could* is the operative word here.

Many times, just because something is or was unfair doesn't mean we should spend our valuable time and energy responding to it to make it "right." I thought better of giving examples of such situations because any example could get touchy.

Fairness is a huge trigger for a lot of people and is highly subjective. If you frequently find yourself getting triggered into a negative state by all sorts of perceived Fairness issues, that's a problem. If you make a battle out of everything, soon everyone will avoid you. Furthermore, you're just plain angry all the time. That kind of persistent anger will come out in your communications, thereby harming your relationships. Persistent anger hinders your smarts, making you less successful. Persistent anger is also poisonous to your health, riddling you with ailments. Some life threatening (more on that in the SELF CARE series, volume two).

With that said…

Some wrongs *should* be righted, and anger is precisely the right emotion to drive the process of justice. For example, sending a child abuser to jail, or feeding a starving population despite warlords, or bringing justice to the people who cheated the elderly couple out of their life savings.

Anger, when channeled correctly, can be powerful. Use it wisely and tactically, not indiscriminately like most people do on an almost routine basis.

Now that you know this little gem, be aware of Fairness in your dealings with people, including strangers. A sense of unfairness is easy to trigger in others.

Ways to navigate Fairness are to have clear rules, follow the rules, and enforce the rules consistently and equitably. Beware of your biases getting in the way. Empathize and make a real effort to understand the view of others. Keep FIFI in mind whenever you communicate.

That's a lot to remember, and you *can* learn it.

Practice, fall off, get back up, practice some more. It gets easier with practice and time.

10 LOVE

L ove is felt in the heart *and* in the brain.

Love releases powerful neurochemicals, causing all sorts of things to happen. One of those things is the increased likelihood of taking risks—risks to please, save, or comfort those we Love. We might risk everything for Love, from a career to our lives.

Humans have been taking risks for those they Love throughout time. Many animals exhibit the same behavior. Some animals bond with their mates for life. Others readily risk their lives for the survival of their young. *Love is instinctive.*

Some people don't show Love well. That's because they bury it. They don't know how to Love because Love can be scary.

In addition to taking risks, Love increases your sensitivity to FIFI and SCARF elements. A perceived challenge to your Facts (values), Identity, and Status might trigger a more defensive response than usual. Your Feelings are all over the place. Certainty is more enemy than friend if you become more controlling and anxious. There's a loss of Autonomy because we're obligated to commit to those we Love, and because Feelings are stronger. You might misinterpret others as a threat more often than appropriate. Your sense of Fairness might be heightened, inducing you to overreact to perceived unfairness.

Love seems to make of mess of us.

When we feel more sensitive to FIFI and SCARF (because of Love), we feel more *vulnerable* overall.

Some people can handle this feeling of vulnerability, while others are scared to death of it. Their fear of vulnerability sabotages their ability to fully Love. It's sad. Those who live and know Love are truly happier, live higher quality lives, live longer, and are more successful than their less Love-experienced brethren. It's probably why Love is hardwired in us.

Love helps us not only to live, but live *well*.

On one hand, Love makes no sense because we become more vulnerable to others.

On the other hand, Love was and still is critical to the survival of humanity.

If everyone were always out for themselves and no one ever bothered to care for one another, we would be a sad animal indeed, and probably wouldn't survive long.

The most notable aspect about Love is it is high on the value scale. In individuals, families, organizations, and nations, Love forms the foundation of our perception of happiness, well-being, and righteousness.

There's a reason why most novels, plays, and movies showcase Love prominently. There's a reason why we celebrate weddings and high school graduations, and why we mourn divorces and deaths. The reason is Love represents the fabric of our lives.

Imagining a completely loveless life is like imagining no life at all.

The reason why violations to FIFI and SCARF put us in a negative state, and why AMUM puts others in a negative state, is because such perceived violations go against our instinct of Love. Everything about our lives and our being is Love energy. When our Love energy is dampened, darkened, or damaged by life events, perceptions, or negative beliefs, it *hurts*.

When we hurt, we're not our best selves, and everything about our lives and our being is impacted. That is why we react.

It's not that we're bad or silly people. It's that our Love energy, the energy that runs our lives and makes us who we are, was impinged. When you react in a negative way, you impinge upon the Love energy of others. That is precisely what we want to avoid.

Instead, we want to build up the Love energy in ourselves and in others. We do this by developing in ourselves a healthy mind and body, practicing mindful awareness and communication, and being the best we can be while empowering others to do the same.

11 OPTIMISM

Have you ever had a friend or relative who was a little bit *too* helpful?

You know they mean well, and much of the time they're great to have around. But sometimes, they screw things up for you.

I think kids fall in this category. For your birthday, they made you breakfast in bed, but they sure made a mess in the kitchen. Or it could be the cat bringing the dead, flea-infested rat into the house as a gift to you. You love them so much (and they love you), and yet they can be so frustrating at the same time.

Everyone has such a friend hardwired in their brains. Her name is *Optimism,* and she's the queen of hope.

Optimism loves you—to a fault.

On one hand, Optimism is the driving energy behind your willingness to try and to persevere despite overwhelming odds. Optimism compels you to keep up the good fight, and to inspire others to do the same.

When challenges or setbacks occur, or when the situation is bleak, Optimism helps you see the possibilities of alternative futures, and to expend the right energy in the right ways to manifest those preferred futures.

Optimism, next to Love, is one of the most important factors behind the success of our ancestors, as well as to humans today.

Optimism truly has your best interests at heart.

With that said, she can sure make a mess of the kitchen! This happens when Optimism is not realistic, or makes us lazy. Here's how.

First, Optimism can be unrealistic.

There's no further example needed than hoping you'll win the lottery. Your chances of winning big are about the same at setting your cash on fire, throwing it in the waste bin, and then expecting the bin to explode with thousands of one-hundred dollar bills fluttering delightfully to the ground all around you. Yet every hour of every day, people buy lottery tickets hoping for exactly that outcome.

Second, Optimism can make us lazy by putting too much reliance on hope.

There's a common saying among senior business and military leaders: "Hope is not a course of action. You must have a plan."

We "hope" things will magically get better or that everything will turn out ok. We rely on hope as the lazy way out of doing the hard work of thinking, planning, and doing. This is a recipe for failure.

There are times when there's truly nothing we can do to help a situation or help others. In those cases, hope is all we have. Optimism gives us that hope. In those cases, Optimism helps ease our minds during highly stressful situations. She keeps us sane with her loving moral support.

The most important thing you can do with your overly helpful friend is to recognize when Optimism is helping and when she's not.

When she helps you to see possibilities and motivates you to work hard, take full advantage of her help.

However, when Optimism is unrealistic, suggesting you expend your valuable, limited resources on a true impossibility, or when Optimism lures you into laziness such that you procrastinate or fail to plan, that is when you say, "No thank you!" and kindly ignore her.

Don't worry, she won't get upset, but she'll continue to tug at your sleeve and tempt you.

Optimism is remarkably persistence, and that's a good thing. We just should be smart in how and when we let her help.

12 KNOW YOUR HANDICAP

The AWARENESS series included a lesson on Hot Buttons.

Hot Buttons are situations that put us in a negative state of mind. When we're in a negative state of mind, we're impaired.

Negative thoughts burn up valuable energy and can cause *exhaustion*. That is the last thing you need. You don't have time for tired. Many people simply reach for a caffeinated drink, which might give them a boost of fake energy, but their thinking is still impaired.

It's impaired because it doesn't promote a learning state of mine. You're less creative, less productive, and less able to see the reality of the situation in a holistic, healthy manner.

Not to mention, chronic negative thinking causes biochemical changes in your body that over time can lead to health problems. We'll talk more about the mind-body connection in the SELF-CARE series.

On the other hand, positive, healthy thinking and emoting is *energizing*. You can still enjoy your caffeinated drink if you want, but you won't need it as much as you would if you were exhausted by negative thinking.

Back to Hot Buttons.

We presented ten Hot Button categories (U-HIDE-CUPID) each with numerous triggers. As you can see, there are many potential triggers. It's a jungle out there, and you'll want to remain aware of your emotions so they don't enter the badlands.

Unsurprisingly, all Hot Button categories are linked to one or more of the five hardwired SCARF elements. That's why Hot Buttons are such triggers for many of us; they link to our hard-wired, primitive self. They also feel like a threat, even though they're usually not.

Here's a list showing the SCARF element followed by the Hot Button categories falling within the element.

Status: Unfair, Hostile, Inconsiderate, Embarrassing

Certainty: All Hot Buttons (U-HIDE-CUPID) can fall in here.

Autonomy: Unfair, Disruptive, Controlling, Painful

Relatedness: Hostile, Inconsiderate, Embarrassing, Disappointment

Fairness: All Hot Buttons (U-HIDE-CUPID) can fall in here

Some Hot Buttons might be more powerful than others, depending upon your unique vulnerabilities.

For example, if you're prone to feeling inferior, you might have a heightened sensitivity to Status-related Hot Buttons. Things like losing a video game or changes in your work hierarchy could arouse a threat response.

We size each other up on Status with clothes, cars, watches, mannerisms, age, male, female, and it continues every day.

However, if ever you *feel* inferior, you aren't. Those feelings are due to ugly lie deposits in your automatic mind. SCARF hardwired elements lay in wait in your automatic mind looking, for the opportunity to be triggered.

Do you see why we started off with resetting your brain? It's not your fault those ugly lie deposits are there, or that SCARF elements are hardwired, or that your automatic mind actively looks for "threats." Any self-flagellation you do to yourself for over reacting to a Hot Button only makes it worse.

Instead, acknowledge what happened without judgment, make friends with your automatic mind, and make peace with yourself. I know that's a lot to ask because it's a lifestyle change.

The SELF-CARE series has many lessons designed to help you make those lifestyle adjustments. But you'll have to wait for volume two.

13 WHEN FEAR AND ANGER HELP

We're about to enter some advanced stuff, and I think you're ready for it. Normally when we think of fear or anger we think of them as negative emotions. When manifested in the wrong way, they're negative. When manifested in the right way, they can be powerfully positive.

It's like playing with fire. When you don't know what you're doing with it, you can cause a lot of destruction. When you do know what to do with it, you can do some pretty amazing things.

Fear and anger can be fantastic motivators. For example, you're angry you lost the track meet race so you use anger to fuel your workouts, put in more effort, and win the next race. You're fearful for your child's safety in a rough neighborhood, so you take the time to walk him or her to the bus stop.

In cases like these, fear and anger can help us make smart decisions about our behavior and our priorities. If we felt absolutely no fear or anger, we wouldn't be motivated to do much at all. The key is to have just the right amount of arousal coupled with sound thinking. This combination of emoting and thinking is what drives the best of our behavior.

Over arousal is not good because then your emotions are in control. Sound thinking doesn't happen as much, and you're not your best self.

Under arousal is not good because then there's no drive. Being driven doesn't mean you never rest or relax. It means you're focused, balanced, and committed to your decisions.

For example, let's say you're battling a serious health matter that leaves you exhausted most of the time. Fear of dying or anger you can't do what you want with your life are powerful motivators to keep you going during the times you do feel relatively well, as opposed to just giving up. It gives you the will to keep fighting.

The pressures of life, and the pressures we put on ourselves, create feelings of fear and anger that manifest themselves as *stress*.

There's a certain amount of stress people can tolerate. Some stress is good (like studying for an exam), while others are harmful (like getting a divorce.)

Good stress is more tolerable than bad stress, however; too much stress of either type is not good for a few reasons.

First, when you're under high stress, you're usually not as mindful. Your communications and relationships suffer.

Second, chronic high stress is taxing on your health. Be careful you don't let fear and anger drive your stress to unhealthy levels. We'll discuss this in the SELF-CARE series (volume two).

Excessive stress ruins relationships and kills people. Yes, some people can handle extraordinary levels of stress. Some are unusual beings, and some have learned to tolerate increasing levels of stress over a long period of time. You can do that too, so long as you stay mindful.

After all this talk about how negative emotions are bad, we now discover that when channeled in the right way, negative emotions can serve an important purpose.

One of the reasons why having emotional awareness is so important is because you need to know when you're feeling fear or anger.

The next step is to ascertain if that fear or anger is working for or against you.

If it's working against you, reframe the situation to something less arousing.

If you think the fear or anger could work for you, that's the time to think how to properly channel this powerful energy.

Channeling the energy properly is important to do, because you don't want this superpower running rogue on you.

That would not be good.

14 THREATS AND OPPORTUNITIES

I've mentioned several times how the automatic mind works its shenanigans to sabotage you.

For example, it retains old, ugly lie deposits and then operates as though they were true.

It makes up information to fill in the blanks of what you don't know.

It keeps its antenna out looking for revalidation of ugly lie deposits, ignoring information showing otherwise.

It houses all our vulnerabilities, such as FIFI), our Hot Button categories (U-HIDE-CUPID) and our hardwired vulnerabilities (SCARF).

It actively scans the environment for perceived threats to any of the above-mentioned residents.

Do you see how your automatic mind operates in your life now? That's why it's so important for your manual mind to understand what the automatic mind is up to and manage it appropriately.

As if all that weren't enough, there are *three* more pieces of unhappy news about the automatic mind. I'll tell you what they are and how to deal with them. This is advanced information.

The first we'll explain here.

The second we'll explain in the next lesson.

The third we'll explain in the WISDOM series (volume two) because that is much more advanced stuff.

The first piece.

It probably comes as no surprise that your automatic mind is biased. After all, you already know it filters out information that doesn't conform to whatever deposits are in your programming. If the deposits are negative, then your automatic mind will reinforce the negativity, which affects your thinking, emoting, and behaving. If the deposits are positive, it will do likewise.

So, what happens to this filtering process when we're aroused by a perceived threat, such as a Hot Button trigger?

The filtering goes into high gear to the point where arousal of a threat can blind you to *opportunities*.

For example, let's say you're terrified of public speaking, and a friend invites you to play a small role in a local theater play she's directing. You fear looking bad in front of others, disappointing your friend, and having to interact with people you don't know, so you decline the offer. The opportunity to improve your social skills, speaking abilities, and build your confidence is missed. Not to mention all the fun you'll miss.

High gear filtering also takes place when you're aroused to a perceived reward.

In this situation, you are blinded to the *risks*. Many of humanities' vices such as gambling, drinking, and unprotected sex are Exhibit A of this phenomenon.

It's important to understand your automatic mind operates in this way and that you can leverage it in your favor.

For example, when you set a goal you want to achieve, you'll start to notice little things related to that goal.

Let's say you want to become an NBA player, a world-class chef, or a Kung Fu grand master. Your mind will automatically tune in to anything related to these subjects.

Maybe you want to be a parent. You'll start to focus on children a lot more.

Let's say you want to get married. All things related to weddings will grab your attention.

That's because your brain automatically orients toward your values. When your goals align to your values, you're much more likely to achieve them.

Everyone's automatic mind operates in this way. This is good to know because if you also understand the values of others, then you have great potential to influence them. The hope is you'll use this power for good, to lead, and to inspire.

I'm confident you will.

15 INTRODUCING TODDLER

Hold on. I'm about to reveal to you the most shocking secret of the automatic mind.

This is advanced stuff and it's going to make you do a lot of thinking. That's a good thing.

You might not like this news at all, so much so you might reject it. I hope you won't, because it's for your own good to understand the truth.

Here we go.

The brain of a newborn to four-year-old relies heavily on its "animal," or automatic mind because its neocortex is still developing. Over time, the manual mind begins developing along with the neocortex. This is why we don't remember much from our toddler years. We simply reacted according to the pre-programming of our automatic mind with little manual control.

The development of the manual mind depends in large measure on the child's environment, education, and life experiences. This process continues into adulthood when our manual mind is fully formed and we become fully responsible for ourselves.

Toddler years reveal what's happening in the automatic mind, because their manual minds have not formed.

Forgive me if this next part sounds harsh at first, but I will present a much brighter side. Bear with me.

Toddlers are notoriously selfish, narcissistic, insecure, dependent, and prone to expressions of rage called *temper tantrums*. They're hypersensitive. They don't give a hoot about anyone else, and they want what they want right now. They need constant reassurance and attention. They can be exhausting creatures.

Does this make them bad people? Of course not! In fact, we love them dearly, unconditionally—well, if you're their parent you do.

Even if we're not the parents, we understand every toddler is like this.

Patience, boundaries, love, and reassurance help these poor creatures through a tough time in their lives. They're learning the world is a stressful place and they can't take it all at once.

Over time, the manual mind develops and puts the automatic mind's outrages into increasing check. We enter our adult years as well-mannered, polite, considerate, nice people, unlike the toddler we once were (most of us, anyway.)

There's just one teensy, weensy problem—the toddler is *still* there! The manual mind might have entered it into a maximum-security prison, but little miss or mister Toddler with all its selfish, narcissistic, insecure, and dependent ways is still there.

Oh, and it still has fits of rage. Sometimes this rage bubbles into the manual mind and we wonder why we're angry, sad or fearful for no apparent reason. Often, we make something up to explain why, but our made-up reason is rarely the truth.

What's going on is your Toddler is upset. The problem is we don't want to acknowledge our upset Toddler because that would reveal the selfish, narcissistic, insecure, and dependent side of us we absolutely do not want to come out—nor should it. We don't want to accept we have this side of us because that would make us rotten people.

What do toddlers want more than anything else? You know—*attention*. That doesn't mean the toddler gets its way. What it means is if you give a toddler direct, firm, and loving attention, it goes a long way toward settling it down. That is the point.

So, how do you do that with *your* Toddler? That cute little, needy creature that's still inside of you?

The first thing to do is to recognize and accept it. Don't ignore or reject it anymore. It might be difficult to accept you have a selfish, narcissistic, insecure, hypersensitive, and dependent side. It's also super important to do.

Next is to acknowledge your Toddler is upset, reassure it everything will be ok, and say you love him or her unconditionally. That's what we do with real toddlers to settle them down without letting them have their way. That's exactly what you do with your Toddler. The Toddler is *you* before your manual mind was formed.

As unflattering as it can be, Toddler is actually your *friend*.

How?

Toddler is fearless, has abundant energy, and loves to help. It wants to be part of your life.

All you need to do is accept it, love it unconditionally, and allow it to help. Toddler can actually be quite helpful. We'll talk more about asking for the Toddler's help in upcoming lessons.

For now, understand you have this *other* element in your automatic mind. You have your deposits built into your programming (first element), *and* you have Toddler (second element).

There is also a *third* and final element to your automatic mind, but that will have to wait until the WISDOM series (volume two).

16 "PREFERENCES" HELP YOU THINK RATIONALLY

In the last lesson, we had a good look at Toddler. Toddler is hypersensitive because all your Hot Buttons plastered all over it with a bright red, light flashing, "Push me!" When a Hot Button gets pushed, Toddler enters tantrum mode.

These tantrums are distracting to our better thinking and emoting. We learned it's better to acknowledge and settle Toddler instead of letting it scream and yell and distract us. Once we've given Toddler some attention (but do not let it have its way), it'll usually calm down. What's next is to enter Rational Thinking mode. That is the subject of *this* lesson.

Rarely does an event or someone else's behavior *cause* us to react.

For example, your husband did not cause you to shout angrily at him when he criticized your cooking. Your daughter did not cause you to give her the silent treatment for two weeks because she was disrespectful toward you. Your boss did not cause you to become depressed because of a poor performance evaluation.

What's causing you to behave the way you do is your *beliefs* about these events.

Beliefs such as, "He must never criticize my cooking," "My kids must always respect me," and "My boss must always be fair to me," are behind your outbursts.

Beliefs such as these are *irrational.*

Why?

Because there's no law of the universe that *requires* your spouse to not criticize you, your kids to respect you, or your boss to be fair. That's why your original beliefs are irrational.

Irrational beliefs stand right in front of your Hot Buttons, pushing them at will. Holding on to irrational beliefs is a surefire way to get your Hot Buttons pushed frequently. This is not good.

The good news is there's a simple technique to reframe beliefs so that they're *rational*, and aren't as likely to push your Hot Buttons.

The technique is to reframe beliefs in terms of *preferences*.

For example, "I prefer my husband not criticize me," "I prefer my kids treat me respectfully," "I prefer my boss is fair with me."

When you reframe beliefs into a rational context, there's much less emotional baggage. You're less likely to get triggered.

Must/should never and *must/should always* preclude a large number of irrational beliefs that lead us into the unhappy land of the triggered. Toddler enters tantrum mode. When your Hot Buttons are pushed and you allow yourself to react accordingly, you're not your best self. You might think you're thinking clearly or behaving appropriately, but rest assured you're likely not. When you're in a triggered state, you're not in your right mind, and you'll likely say or do things to hurt others, hurt yourself, or you'll later regret.

Remember, you can only influence behavior with good communication. You cannot control.

If you prefer your spouse not criticize you, your kids respect you, and your boss be fair with you, now might be a good time for a difficult conversation.

Remember to keep in mind your own contribution to the problem and the presence of FIFI. I know this is a process that takes time and patience, but you'll like the outcome much better.

Most people have similar preferences.

For example, we prefer others drive courteously and safely. Alas, many do not and we're grateful to those who do.

We prefer others are considerate, honest, and fair. Alas, many are not and we are grateful to those who are.

We prefer to sleep in and have more time off. Alas, we are grateful to have a job, and soon enough the weekend will come.

These are powerful ways to reframe and stay in your right mind. Reframing is so powerful and important to re-programming your mind, it's one of the wonderful options we have in Ground Control.

Speaking of Ground Control, now is a good time to learn how to use Ground Control when Toddler is acting up. That lesson is next.

TALKING TO TODDLER WITH GROUND CONTROL

When your emotions are aroused and you can't quite explain why, chances are Toddler is acting up. That's when you need to have a special conversation with Toddler using Ground Control.

Remember, Ground Control is our important tool to help us get back to our right mind: notice the thought or feeling, take a deep breath, then exercise one of several excellent options.

Chances are, the emotion coming out of Toddler will be an "icky" one, even though they are perfectly normal and part of being human: jealousy, anger, neediness, impatience, rage, selfish, greedy, arousal, etc. We don't like these emotions, so we usually lock them away in the Super Max and ignore Toddler.

We are *not* going to do that anymore.

The first step in Ground Control is acknowledging the emotion. In the case of Toddler, it is *critical* to do this without judgment, justification, and especially without shaming. In fact, if you shame, you could actually do more harm than good!

By acknowledging the emotion without judgment, you give Toddler exactly the attention it is craving. Simply saying, "I know you're feeling ____ right now" is perfect. This initial attention goes a long way toward calming Toddler down.

The second step in Ground Control is taking a deep breath. In the case of Toddler, it is also critical to tell Toddler "I love you" while you're taking this cleansing breath. *All* real live toddlers need to hear those three words often. Your Toddler is no different. If you rarely or never heard those words when you were an actual toddler, this could be a break-through moment for you, so brace yourself. That little guy or gal is still there waiting and longing to hear those words. They may as well come from you. Think of yourself as an adult talking to yourself as a toddler, and loving that little, cute, guy or gal with all your heart.

The third step in Ground Control is one of several options (gratitude, Happy Place, etc). You will continue to do that as before, except in the case of Toddler, you'll invite it *with* you. Ask it to join you in gratitude, or to a trip to your Happy Place, or to reframe to find the learning point or opportunity. This experience should feel like you're the adult embracing yourself as a toddler and taking it along for the journey. At the same time, Toddler is exhilarated and feeling warm and secure hanging out with this amazing, cool adult.

At this time, both you and Toddler have settled down and you might like to take things one step further. Asking Toddler to *help*.

You see, Toddler is actually your friend. Toddler is full of curiosity, energy, and a thirst for adventure. Its mind is wide open and it learns like a sponge. These qualities are missing in many adults, and we could do well to acquire these beautiful traits once again. But you have to encourage Toddler to help. It needs your encouragement to bring these qualities out.

For example, let's say you're nervous about speaking in public. Initially, Toddler might be scared and throwing a little fit to run away. An internal conversation might look like this:

"Hey, I know you're scared. I agree, this is scary stuff…and it's exciting! It's so exciting it could be fun and you'll want to do it again." Now Toddler is curious and enticed by the adventure. Toddler becomes a help rather than a hindrance.

Here's another example. Let's say you're studying for a difficult exam. Toddler is angry because it wants to go outside and play, not sit around all day looking at math equations. You might not feel angry. Instead, you'll likely feel a mix of anxiety and resistance as you distract yourself with unimportant tasks. An internal conversation might look like this:

"Hey, I know, I know. You're mad at me right now. I'd love for you to help me. Can you help me? We can pass this exam together and that would feel exhilarating! What do you say? Let's do this thing together, shall we?"

In this conversation, acknowledged the feelings of anger. Toddler wanted to go out and play, but we enticed it to help.

You see, Toddlers love to be involved and to feel useful. Inviting Toddler to help and be part of the process has a calming effect.

18 SUBCONSCIOUS BIAS

You might be surprised to learn we unknowingly treat people differently based on what we think we know about them. For example, if you think someone is wealthy, famous, or smart you'll treat them differently. If you think someone is dangerous, dishonest, or unintelligent, you'll treat them differently.

People who go to great lengths to be open minded and unbiased are surprised when psychological tests reveal they aren't much better than the rest of us.

For example, if you take two ordinary kids and tell a school teacher one of them is "gifted" and the other one is "not gifted," studies show the teacher will absolutely treat these students differently, even though they have the same level of intelligence. In time, the student who was treated as "gifted" will advance beyond his peers and the student who was treated as "not gifted" will fall behind.

Do you think this subconscious bias has implications with gender and race? You bet. People who are treated as if they're weak and fragile, even though they're not, can sometimes manifest that destiny. People who are treated like they're criminals, even though they're not, can sometimes manifest that destiny.

People tend to become how they perceive they are treated. When people are treated as intelligent human beings with great potential, they're more likely to manifest a happier destiny. This makes an important point: you can make a difference in the world when you treat *everyone* as a decent, smart, and worthy human being.

With that said, subconscious bias is a two-way street. Everyone, and I do mean *everyone*, has subconscious bias in one form or another. Now, just because you or others have subconscious bias does not make you racist, sexist, or rotten people. What earns you one of those ugly labels is when you're consciously biased.

Subconscious bias resides in your automatic mind and is thoroughly mixed in with the deposits of your programming. In the case of subconscious bias, deposits such as "when people walk a certain way, they're dangerous," or, "when people talk a certain way, they're not smart," or, "when people don't share my values, they're a threat," can lead you to treat people differently. It's not your fault those deposits are there. You might not even know about them. It takes a lot of focused energy from the manual mind to pick up on these things.

Here's another fact of life. *Everyone* is a victim of subconscious bias.

If you perceive you have it worse than others, remember you have your own subconscious bias going on that doesn't help matters. Your own automatic filters might see more bias against you than there is, thereby feeding your subconscious bias against others. Worse, it could evolve into conscious bias. In a world of mass media and rampant toxic communication, it is easy to trigger the automatic mind into this mode of behaving.

Good people can be lured into a much more biased mindset than they ever thought possible. This is why it's so important for you to be your best self, to not judge others, and to communicate in a healthy manner.

You are a fantastic person no matter how others treat you. Be aware to avoid letting others' behavior lure you into thinking and behaving in a manner inconsistent with your Reality Show, especially your *Who I Am* statements.

Finally, consciously assume the better intention in others instead of assuming the worst. Most people are good and decent, even if their actions and words don't always seem that way.

19 HIGH SPEED PROCESSING AND GUT INSTINCTS

You sold your car and were paid a large sum of cash. You count the money; it's all there. The buyer is eager to shake your hand and drive off with the car. He didn't negotiate much, paying nearly your asking price. He wore sunglasses the whole time. He seemed overly friendly. You're happy about how easy the transaction went, but something doesn't seem right.

When you get to the bank, you fill out the deposit slip and hand the cash to the clerk. She uses her special pen on each bill and hands them back to you. "I'm sorry, but these bills aren't real." The entire wad of cash is counterfeit $100 bills.

The one thing we can thank our automatic mind for is its high-speed processing of seemingly disparate information. Our automatic mind picks up patterns, sees scenarios, and reads people much faster than the manual mind. It's extremely good at this. It's a gift we could do well to appreciate more.

Your automatic mind is following its programming. A huge part of that programming is constantly scanning the environment for clues that could impact you.

Your automatic mind rapidly scans and *defaults* to FIFI (communication elements), U-HIDE-CUPID (Hot Buttons), and SCARF (hard-wired elements). It can pick up instantly things that would take your manual mind many hours to analyze. Your automatic mind is trying desperately to tell you the answer, but often our slow, analytical manual mind won't hear it.

When you get a weird feeling that something is out of place but can't put your finger on it, pay attention. Your automatic mind is trying to tell you something. Additionally, you'll probably feel something in your gut. That's because there's a connection between the automatic mind and the gut. Your mind and gut are actually connected which is why when you feel a certain way in your mind, you also feel it in your gut. We'll talk more about the mind-gut connection in the

SELF-CARE series. For now, it's sufficient to know that you "feel" something in your gut when your automatic mind is on to something. It's what is commonly known as "gut instincts."

To "hear" the message of your gut instincts, you must have a good relationship with your automatic mind. Building that relationship takes strong mental habits of awareness and reflection. Over time, your understanding of your automatic mind will strengthen, and the once unintelligible messages of your gut instincts will become clearer.

A technique to help you with awareness and reflection is asking *why?* at least five times about things you would ordinarily take for granted. Using our example from earlier, you might ask, "Why do I feel uncomfortable with this transaction?" "Why is he eager to leave?" "Why is he paying me in cash?" "Why does he never remove his sunglasses?" "Why is he so friendly to me?"

Chances are you might answer every one of these questions with an assumption like, "I'm just anxious." "He's excited about the deal." "Some people carry wads of $100 bills like that." "He's sensitive to light." "That's just his personality."

When you notice you're making too many assumptions, that's when you should challenge them. Try to come up with three possible answers for each. If any of the answers indicate a red flag, it might be wise to heed that flag. Slow down and check it out.

If you get accused of not trusting, use your "And" technique. "I trust you *and* I must verify."

If they threaten or belittle you, then that's definitely a red flag something is wrong.

Follow with, "I noticed you're threatening or intimidating me," or "I feel you're threatening or intimidating me, *and* I don't like that." Their response will be telling.

Your gut instincts are there to keep you safe. They are a gift, so learn to listen to them.

20 WILLPOWER STRENGTH TRAINING

Willpower is your strength in *self-control.*

Humans have always known the more self-control you have, the more success and happiness you enjoy.

If we know this to be true, why is self-control so difficult?

For example, why do we procrastinate? Eat too much? Watch too much TV? Not exercise? Say bad words? Smoke or drink? Struggle with negative thoughts? Have trouble focusing? Resist change? Have emotional outbursts?

The reason?

Willpower is a *finite* resource of strength.

Neuroscientists equate willpower to a muscle. You can strengthen it if you use it. It weakens when you don't use it, or *overuse* it.

Using willpower throughout the day will deplete it. Just like a weight lifter will get tired hauling heavy weights around all day, even strong people with a lot of willpower will have their strength depleted at some point.

For example, let's take a person who eats healthy food, exercises daily, doesn't smoke or drink, makes his bed every morning, and is usually easy to talk to and work with. Now imagine that same person's child has a terrible disease. On top of that, he has high medical bills, a bad neighbor who plays loud music at night, and a micromanaging boss. Still, he deals with it all with strength and courage. One day, a person aggressively cuts him off on the freeway and nearly causes a wreck. Something triggers inside him and now he's in road rage, driving like a maniac. He has lost his self-control. His willpower, although strong, was depleted and he is not in his right mind.

Everyone has a threshold when their willpower is depleted. Ideally, you want to increase your willpower threshold to a level that helps you cope better with the setbacks of life, and help you achieve greater satisfaction with yourself.

The primary consumer of willpower is the manual mind. Whenever you activate the manual mind to:

☆ Notice and manage your thoughts, emotions, or impulses,

☆ Make decisions, whether big or small

☆ Adapt to changes, like new habits, or

☆ Focus on something difficult

You're using up willpower.

That's why you come home tired from work. You've used up willpower being nice to co-workers, putting up with yours boss, staying on task, focusing on difficult work, not eating the donuts, and dodging traffic on the way home. Something as simple as deciding what to have for dinner uses up willpower.

Is it possible to strengthen willpower so a normal day isn't so depleting? So you have more energy to do other things?

Yes! That's the good news, anyway. But it takes time, and you need to do it in small doses.

Start with little things you know you can do to build successes. For example, try just making your bed every morning. That's it. Doing that for three months will make it a habit. Once something becomes a habit, it no longer depletes your willpower like it once did.

Then move onto the next *little* goal, like not saying bad words. That's it. Do that for three months. It becomes a habit. Move onto the next.

Try breathing more deeply throughout the day. Or three minutes of stretching every morning. Or going to bed earlier. Or eating smaller, more frequent meals. Or spending a certain amount of time every day doing something toward your goals.

Over time, little habits add up to a lifestyle of excellent self-control. This is a recipe for success.

Here's the point.

The changes you undertake to become your best you require exactly this process.

Changes use willpower, so create your new habits over time and congratulate yourself for every little step of success.

21 THE TEN-THOUSAND-HOUR RULE

A popular theory says it takes ten thousand hours of dedicated practice to master something.

That means if you want to be a world-class chess player, safe cracker, or Kung Fu champion you'll need to put in up to ten thousand meaningful hours of practice consistently to achieve this level of mastery.

The more you practice something, the more it embeds into the automatic mind.

For example, let's say you're practicing dodging knives. Over time, your automatic mind will pick up the subtle moves of your opponent. Picking up this information allows you to make the split-second decision on where to move.

Or, let's say you're learning a new language. Over time, an increasing amount of the new language will become embedded into the automatic mind so you no longer have to manually translate it.

The more we embed a skill into the automatic mind, the faster and easier it becomes. Remember, the automatic mind processes information much faster than the manual mind, but it takes time to train the automatic mind to move fast correctly.

What's more is if you truly want to master something, it's important to dedicate yourself to that *one* thing. If you try to master more than one thing at a time, your chances for success decline.

I'm not saying you can't improve at both tennis and speaking Latin at the same time. What I'm saying is winning at Wimbledon while publishing peer reviewed articles in Latin, when you're not good at either one right now, is probably not a realistic goal.

Here's another tidbit. The quality of the time matters because it's not enough to just be good, you want to be the best.

Being the best requires continuous improvement with stretch goals added over time. You want your goal challenging but *achievable*. Each new goal requires your full concentration and effort, followed by reflection, refinement, and repetition. When you achieve the goal, you're elated. Then you're excited about achieving the next goal.

The one thing children and successful people have in common is they both know fear and failure. They understand they must experience and handle both because fear, and the chance of failure is always there. Our fear of failure is usually what holds us back from trying at all. We fear we might look stupid, or wreck our image as a smart or athletic person, or that others will judge us poorly, or that we'll judge ourselves poorly.

While these fears all seem irrational, they are real. They're also your biggest enemy to success.

Imagine if a child gave up trying to walk because it fell so many times. It's a good thing you didn't, or you would still be crawling on the floor.

Are you going to fail sometimes? Of course! Your self-control to not let your own thoughts and emotions derail you when a set-back or failure happens will determine a great deal about your success and happiness in life.

Maybe you don't want to be in the *Guinness Book of World Records* for dodging knives, but you do want to get better at math, public speaking, cooking, teaching, business, surfing, or playing the guitar. The point is these skills won't come out of a cereal box. It still takes practice; maybe not ten thousand hours (or ten years) to achieve a level of competence to which you're happy, but many hours nonetheless.

In the next lesson, we'll go into the land of two mindsets. The first helps you achieve your goals, and the other mindset sabotages you.

22 TWO MINDSETS; TWO OUTCOMES

If you're naturally gifted at something, don't count your blessings just yet.

The problem with natural talent is it can seduce you to laziness. You won't put as much effort into practice. You'll be less humble and open to learning. It's a recipe for less than ideal outcomes.

If you're not naturally gifted at something, and want to be good at it, then you'll put in the hard work and *effort* to get good.

You're open to constructive criticism and to learning. Eventually, you'll beat the naturally gifted person who doesn't try. It's almost a law of the universe. The ability to do something well isn't magic. It's effort and practice.

Psychologists and neuroscientists have a name for this phenomenon: *Fixed versus Growth Mindsets*. It's a concept popularized by Dr. Carol Dweck.

The Fixed Mindset is the "I can't change" mindset. It assumes you are who you are and that's that. Effort and learning are a waste of time.

The Growth Mindset is the "I *can* change" mindset. It knows with hard work, effort, and learning, a person can change. Effort and learning are worth every minute.

Often, we call someone who is extraordinarily good at math, science, teaching, coaching, running, playing the violin "talented" or "genius."

By using those labels we're letting ourselves off the hook. They're "natural" and we're not.

We overlook the extraordinary effort these people invested to achieve their abilities. We too, can be just as good if we put in the work.

The following quote is attributed to Henry Ford, but has been stated in one form or another since the Roman Ages: "If you think you can or can't, you're probably right."

The key is to have the attitude you're never fully satisfied, because there's always a way to get better. This attitude comes from passion.

Passion helps you persevere even though some things are tedious, boring, dirty, frustrating, or painful.

Passion isn't something you wake up with. It's a combination of discovery, continued interest, sustained engagement, and further development over time. Passion takes time to cultivate and a conscious decision to stick with it. Passion is fuel for a Growth Mindset.

Fixed versus Growth Mindsets play a role in how you deal with challenges, criticism, and the success of others.

If math becomes hard, do you quit? If someone criticizes your joke, do you melt down? If a friend of yours got promoted and you didn't, do you get jealous?

The Fixed Mindset says yes to all three.

The Growth Mindset says, "I'll get a tutor and try harder," "I can learn from this criticism to improve," and, "I'm happy for my friend and want to learn what she did right to get the promotion."

The Fixed vs Growth Mindset isn't a black or white matter, it's a continuum. That means a person can be Fixed in some ways and Growth in others.

For example, "I could never live in another country to be with my true love," is a Fixed Mindset that can reside simultaneously with, "I know I can find a way to improve sales," which is a Growth Mindset.

With all that said, it's ok to quit or avoid something to pursue something of higher value more fully. Quitting the right things for the right reasons so you can devote more time, energy, and focus to the things you're passionate about is a smart move.

23 YOUR OLD SELF MAY CLING

Negative thought patterns lead to negative emoting and behaving. You know that well now.

You've also been working to reframe your negative views into positive, more productive ways of thinking. You've been working to create a new, better, more happy and successful model of yourself.

Some of you are off to the races, while others might be down in the dumps or feeling anxious. If that's you, don't worry.

Your reaction is typical of those who are undergoing positive changes, relinquishing their old, negative ways of thinking, emoting, and behaving. It's a well-known phenomenon among psychologists.

Remember the Third Law: *The automatic mind resists drastic change.*

Letting go of your negative, old self is like a grieving process. You're losing one identity and taking on another.

Even though the new identity is much better than the old one, your automatic mind is still saying, "Oh no! You're leaving! You can't leave me! I'll be crushed! It's not fair! I've known you all my life! You can't just *leave*!"

Your clingy Toddler in the automatic mind feels abandoned. It does not like one little bit the uncertainty of the new "you," so it rebels by making you feel sad, anxious, or just plain weird.

When you feel this way, you might be tempted to return to your old ways. Resist this temptation with every ounce of your being. Will you slip up and be you're "old" self sometimes? Of course! *Don't stay there.*

In time, your new self will become embedded in your automatic mind.

Your Toddler will become increasingly familiar with the new you and grow more comfortable. It'll take less manual effort to stay positive, reframe negative thinking, communicate in a healthy way, emote in a productive way, and behave accordingly.

In time, your automatic mind will adjust and do great things for you—automatically. It doesn't happen overnight, but with time and persistence, it does happen.

At some point, your new, better you will feel completely natural. And those pesky feelings of sadness, anxiety, or just plain weirdness will fade away.

When you don't feel right and don't know why, understand it's just a phase. Sometimes the phase is short, and sometimes it might last a while. Every time you make another positive, incremental change in yourself, the process becomes easier. Your automatic mind will start to play along a little more nicely.

Sometimes it helps to give a name to your "lesser" side and to your "better" side.

For example, you might call your lesser side (I will use my own name here) "Toddler Val" or "Anxious Val" or "Insecure Val." You might call your better side "Champion Val" or "Millionaire Val" or "Director Val."

When you see "Insecure Val" subtly making her way to the manual mind, acknowledge her, tell her she's ok, and "Champion Val" has got this.

Or maybe "Toddler Val" is acting up because she's jealous of a friend. Acknowledge her, let her know she's loved, and then ask "Millionaire Val" to come out and applaud your friend.

Yes, I know. For several lessons now I've encouraged you to have these little conversations with yourself. You might think it's strange.

But you've already been talking to yourself all your life!

You might not have realized it before, but you have. The difference now is you're aware of it and take control of the conversation.

These conversations are important because they help reinforce your new deposits, challenge old ugly lie deposits, and transform your automatic mind.

They help you change your life.

24 INTRODUCTION TO BRAIN WAVES

Ok, everybody! Hold on to your hats and glasses because we're about to take a ride on some waves—the scientific kind.

Whenever we talk about energy, frequencies, and vibrations, we're basically talking about the same thing—waves.

All energy is made of waves.

What differentiates energy is the size, length, and speed of the waves.

If all energy waves were the same, the entire universe would be one giant blob of goo. There would be no planets, stars, asteroids, bouncing rubber balls, cute puppies, video games or anything else.

Because we seem to have an infinite amount of different "things" in the universe, this tells us the how number of ways waves can differ from each other is also infinite!

Your thoughts, emotions, and energy are all an expression of different waves.

For example, the waves of negative thoughts and emotions have a different signature than positive thoughts and emotions. Those different wave signatures then shape your reality in different ways.

Think of the waves on a beach. Large, fast-moving waves dumping right on the sand will shape the shoreline and experience of beachgoers differently than small, slow-moving waves breaking further out in the water.

Think of ocean waves as your thinking and emoting, and the shoreline and experience of beachgoers as your external reality. The waves you deliver to the shoreline and beachgoers is like the thinking and emoting you deliver to your world. As you shape the shoreline and experience of beachgoers with the waves you deliver, so too you shape your world.

Your brain is a virtual wave-generating machine. It generates five different types of waves, each with a different impact on your mental and physical state. Scientists have given each these different waves a name:

Gamma Waves: These are the smallest and fastest of the brain waves. Scientists are still learning how these waves affect our emotions and physical state. Gamma is somewhat of a mystery. Scientists know a lot more about the other four types of waves, which we'll discuss next.

Beta Waves: These waves are small, but move fast and forcefully. Beta Waves are associated with alertness and typically dominate our day. When we're "working," that is, engaged in cognitive tasks, we're in Beta. We need Beta to get through our day and achieve our goals. But there's a dark side to Beta. It's also associated with fear, anxiety, insecurity, anger, sadness, and all the yucky emotions that often sabotage us. Think of bees. They busily do the good work of pollinating plants and making honey. But they're also hyper alert for any perceived threats. If they react to a threat, they'll swarm and sting you with little thought that *they* will die as a result of the sting. Beta can leave a lot of negative baggage during the process of doing its necessary work, that's why you need Alpha Waves to come in and take out the garbage. That's next.

Alpha Waves: These brain waves are large but slow and gentle. Think of happy elephants enjoying a peaceful life moving from one water pool to another in an easy, confident way. Alpha waves are associated with calmness, confidence, focus, safety, peace, relaxation, creativity, and learning. When you do brain hygiene (meditation), you enter your brain into this wonderful state. Alpha helps to take out the garbage produced during the Beta state.

Theta Waves: These waves are even larger and slower than Alpha Waves. Think of blue whales; gentle giants roaming the oceans in a slow, hypnotic way. Indeed, these are the brain waves associated with hypnotism, dreamy sleep, and deep meditation. Your automatic mind is wide open for re-programming during this state.

Delta Waves: These are the "big daddy" of the brain waves, even bigger and slower than Theta! They're associated with deep, dreamless sleep. These waves play a huge role in physical and mental rejuvenation.

A different biochemistry takes place in your body during each of these brain wave states. This biochemistry significantly impacts your mental and physical health. It's fascinating stuff, but you'll have to wait until the SELF-CARE series (volume two) to learn the details.

25 ⭐ GETTING YOUR NEUROTRANSMITTER "HIT"

In this lesson, we'll put on our lab coats and goggles to enter the fascinating world of brain chemistry.

Not only does your brain give off waves, it produces different chemicals too. These chemicals play a critical role in your thinking and emoting.

The chemicals I'm talking about are called "neurotransmitters." You might have heard of dopamine, serotonin, and oxytocin—or not. They're scientific words for several different neurotransmitters. There are many other neurotransmitters, but these are the ones that play the largest role in feeling good and being happy.

Whenever you do something pleasurable, like hugging someone you love, eating your favorite food, or winning a video game, your brain gives you a neurotransmitter "hit." In other words, it releases a tiny bit of this "feel good" chemical. When you feel good, your thoughts and emotions are positive, and you enjoy the power of the moment.

Humans need to have lots of daily hits of feel good neurotransmitters. If they don't get enough of them naturally through exposure to people they love, and enjoying things in life such as pets, meals, learning, seeking and finding, laughing, exercising, hobbies, being with nature, and other healthy ventures, then their brains won't make enough of the feel-good neurotransmitters. They won't get enough hits. When that happens, their thoughts and emotions enter the badlands, and they become depressed and anxious.

What's worse, when humans don't get enough feel-good neurotransmitter hits in natural ways, they might be prone to destructive behaviors in a sad and desperate effort to get their hits. Those behaviors might include drugs, pornography, excessive alcohol, gambling, and other unhealthy addictions. When they engage in destructive behaviors, they reprogram their automatic mind the wrong direction. They become even more depressed, angry, irritable, selfish, and less empathetic toward others. Their relationships further erode, perhaps becoming toxic altogether. It also takes a serious toll on their health. They'll become more open to illness and prone to disease.

As you can see, it's not a pretty picture.

Chances are you've seen or even experienced this sad state of affairs.

Many people don't know how to get their feel-good neurotransmitter hits in healthy, natural ways. That's because *humans learn by watching others.* If they see others getting their hits in destructive ways, they're prone to do the same themselves.

You can make a huge difference in your life by identifying the habits and behaviors giving you your hits but do not help you reach your goals. Such habits can include engaging in toxic social media, watching too much television, drinking, smoking, or gambling. Replace these behaviors by pursuing healthy interests such as cooking, sports, auto mechanics, robots, coding, hiking, body building, surfing, crafts, flowers, gardening, archeology, astrology, horses, butterflies, painting, creative writing, psychology, karate, or anything else that sparks a healthy interest.

When you pursue your interests, the "seeking and finding" gives you a natural and healthy feel good hit; that is, your brain releases a nice little shot of feel good neurotransmitters.

In time, your interest could become a passion and you might become so immersed as to become an expert. When that happens, you continue to give yourself a healthy daily dose of hits while opening yourself to a potential employment or business opportunity. How cool is that?

What's more is others are watching and learning from you getting your hits in healthy ways. Don't be surprised if some people, especially children, mimic your behavior. In fact, when others model you, you can be proud of yourself (yet another hit) that you're making a wonderfully positive impact on the lives of others.

If you want to further your positive impact on others, you can help them get their hits by paying them sincere compliments, noticing what's right, and helping them grow and pursue their interests. When that happens, you're both getting your hits at the same time. And that's a beautiful thing.

26 WHAT DOES "RIGHT" LOOK LIKE?

As humans, our manual minds can overrule the impulses of our automatic minds. Animals and young children largely *cannot.*

As children grow, their manual minds develop with increasing capability to regulate.

Ideally, by the time we become adults, our manual minds would have instilled sound habits in the automatic minds. Our adult manual minds would have us practicing courtesy, respect, good communication, and rational thinking in every aspect of our lives. We would be fantastic role models to children to help them in their development journey. We would have our priorities straight. Our work ethic and morality would be clean and strong. We would eat healthy, exercise, and enjoy life with those we love. We would handle setbacks and failures with dignity and grace.

Of course, we know that is far from the case.

Why, if we have these amazing brains, do we not use them in all these positive ways?

The reason is the manual mind is heavily dependent on role models to know what "right" looks like.

If it does not see enough good examples of emotional regulation, healthy communication, self-control, or rational thinking, it doesn't know what it looks like.

If it doesn't know what it looks like, it has a hard time "correcting" the automatic mind. Correct it to what?

Also, the manual mind must choose to want to improve. This is an individual choice requiring no role models (although role models do help).

Many young people grow up surrounded by terrible role models (gangs, drugs, crime, cruelty, neglect) and yet choose, "I'm not doing that—I don't know what

I'm doing, but I'm *not* doing *that!*" At that moment, something clicks inside them and they actively look for the better alternatives. Do they struggle? Certainly. But they usually end up much better off than the poor role models who once surrounded them.

The yearning for positive role models doesn't stop once we become adults. As adults, many of us (not everyone) continually educate our manual mind as to what "right" looks like. Many of us *want* to be better people. We just need a little help. We love good role models and are disappointed at the poor ones.

Throughout this program, we talked about *mindfulness* in its various forms. Mindfulness is your manual mind at work. Mindfulness is awareness of your own thoughts and emotions, awareness of the feelings of others, empathy for others, openness to listening, situational awareness, and rational thinking. That is a lot to ask of the manual mind!

It takes *willpower* to sustain a high degree of mindfulness. Remember, willpower can be depleted, but it can also be strengthened with practice.

Our social behavior and communication is largely scripted by the programming of our automatic minds. When we are *mindful,* we engage our manual minds to regulate the automatic programming. When we are *mindless,* our manual minds are not engaged, and our automatic mind is governing.

Mindfulness levels correlates with physical, mental, and spiritual health.

Remaining focused on mindfulness takes persistence and practice. The more often you do it, the easier it gets. Over time, your manual mind becomes stronger and better able to program the automatic mind in a more positive way.

Strengthening your mindfulness is a social journey. Spend quality time with positive people who share your values and goals for success, and avoid negative people who don't.

This could be a good time to re-order your social life and surround yourself with good role models.

27 YOUR REALITY SHOW – THE SEQUEL

We started this book with the BRAIN RESET series to start clearing out old, ugly lies in the programming of your automatic mind, and refilling it with fresh, healthy truths. We created a vision for yourself highlighting what you want to do and the kind of person you want to be. Then we created your Reality Show. Your Reality Show is as an essential tool to help manifest the best version of yourself.

We then started building your awareness of different personality types, emotional intelligence, change types, and hot buttons. From the information you gained in the AWARENESS series, you hopefully learned some things about yourself you didn't know before.

The COMMUNICATION series presented insight on the dynamics of communication—the interplay between the automatic mind and the words you speak. Your words reinforce the deposits in your automatic mind, which is why it's so important your communications are healthy, positive and rational.

The purpose of the NEURO-SCIENCE series was to explain the science behind the two minds (manual and automatic). There, you saw a clear connection between the information in the NEURO-SCIENCE series and everything that came before.

You've come a long way and have learned a tremendous amount about yourself. Now is a great time to reflect on the work you did in the BRAIN RESET series. You might wish to review everything you produced—your statements, your values, and your deposits. How might you refine them now?

You might find yourself making a lot of changes, and that's wonderful. You might find yourself refining and adding some things. That's perfectly fine too. Or you might find everything looks just fine the way it is. There's nothing wrong with that.

Now consider your life goal for a moment. If you revised it recently, terrific. What are some of the intermediate goals you need to achieve to achieve your life goal?

Now, here's an important question…Let's say you have multiple goals for yourself. What are your thoughts on focusing on just the top three to five, and tabling the rest (at least for now?)

The reason I ask is because too many goals become distracting. It can also burn you out. When you're burned out, that's a dangerous place to be because you're susceptible to reverting to your old ways. We don't want that.

The next thing you might want to do is rate your top three to five goals in order of importance. Just because something is not #1 does *not* mean it's not important. It just means it's not the top priority right now.

This is important because once again, you have a finite amount of willpower. While you can strengthen your willpower over time, it's still finite. You want to keep some willpower in reserve for when those setbacks and disappointments happen. Cars break, kids get sick, the dog runs away, the roof leaks, auntie passes away, lay-offs are announced, your beehive is stolen. The list goes on.

Events like these, which are normal life occurrences, will stress you. Knowing the priority of your goals when your energy is limited will help you make good decisions about where to dedicate your precious time and energy.

Finally, make sure your Reality Show speaks to resilience, persistence, and staying strong during setbacks. You know yourself and your weak areas better than anyone else. The deposits in your Reality Show should be specific and tailored to you. They should be realistic, honest, and aligned to your values.

Most importantly, make sure you continue to watch or engage your Reality Show often, if not daily. You might refine your Reality Show even further after the WISDOM and LEADERSHIP series. You'll find those in volume two.

28 SUMMARY OF THE NEURO-SCIENCE SERIES

Congratulations! You've finished the NEURO-SCIENCE Series!
Now you understand much better why people behave the way they do. Understanding the science gives you tremendous power and influence to lead yourself and others in a positive way. This information will become increasingly relevant as we move forward in volume two.

Below is a summary of the NEURO-SCIENCE Series. You might want to keep a copy of it handy to remind you of the key concepts.

☆ Two brain parts: animal and human.

☆ Animal = Automatic Mind, limbic system, basal ganglia, keeps you alive, does not think, high speed processing of information, connected to the gut, "gut instincts."

☆ Human = Manual Mind, neocortex, thinking, planning, reasoning, analyzing, very slow processing of information, *empathy* center.

☆ Regenerate: olfactory (smell), hippocampus (memory & learning), subventricular zone (mystery).

☆ Five hardwired F3 triggers by Dr. David Rock, SCARF:

☆ Status – need for being right, better, higher ranking, in charge, privileged, good, respected, admired. Rogue Status = must be right, never apologizes, won't admit fault, wants to be in charge, won't take direction, arrogant, self-important, can't stand criticism, overly defensive.

☆ Certainty – need for knowledge and control. Rogue Certainty = worry, anxiety, controlling behavior, perfectionism, untrusting, aggressive communication, low tolerance, can't accept "no.".

☆ Autonomy – need for choices, freedom, and independence. Rogue Autonomy = uncooperative, rebellious, violates rules, non-team player, disobedient, disrespectful, discourteous.

☆ Relatedness – need to know if friend or foe. Rogue Relatedness = needy, clingy, low trust, jealous, demands loyalty, can't stand criticism, needs compliments and praise.

☆ Fairness – was it fair, right or just. Rogue Fairness = makes a battle out of just about everything.

☆ Poor leader triggers bad SCARF: S – "I'm in charge," puts people in their "place." C – Withholds important information from people, keeps secrets. A – Micro-manages. R – Cold and uncaring. F – Arbitrary decisions that hurt people.

☆ Good leader stimulates good SCARF: S – Values people. C – Shares information, listens. A – Lets you do things your way (in line with the mission). R – Truly cares about your well-being. F – Open, transparent decision making duly considering all stakeholders.

☆ Love makes us feel vulnerable, but contributes to quality and longevity of life.

☆ Optimism – bad side: lazy/unrealistic. Good side: motivates/see opportunities & possibilities.

☆ Negative thinking and F3 triggers – impair smarts and make you tired.

☆ Positive thinking and managed F3 – improve smarts and energize you.

☆ Fear/Anger – Are like fire, powerful when used *correctly*, dangerous otherwise.

☆ Reframe threats as opportunities.

☆ 2 of 3 elements of the automatic mind = deposits in programming, Toddler. 3rd element in Vol 2.

☆ Toddler houses unflattering feelings, is you before your manual mind formed, *still* there.

☆ Toddler is your *friend* – highly curious, open minded, energetic, wants and loves you.

☆ Manage Toddler – #1 don't ignore, acknowledge its feelings without letting it have its way; #2 – no judging or shaming, love unconditionally; #3 let Toddler help with its curiosity and energy.

☆ Rational thinking – replace "must/should" with "I prefer."

☆ Everyone has subconscious bias, is victim of it. Don't assume ill will, leads to sabotaging behavior.

☆ Automatic mind and gut are connected, "gut instincts." Learn to listen to it.

☆ Strengthen willpower over time by adding small, new habits incrementally. If deplete, can cause set-back, burn-out, regression.

☆ Manual mind uses willpower. When habits form/move to automatic mind, less willpower used.

☆ Manual mind uses willpower whenever you: notice and manage thoughts, emotions, and impulses; make decisions whether large or small; adapt to new changes, habits; focus on something difficult.

☆ Mastery requires 10k hours/10 years of constant, incremental improvements.

☆ Brain waves: Gamma – fastest, mystery; Beta – working, thinking; Alpha – daydreaming, meditation; Theta – meditation, REM sleep; Delta – deep sleep, slowest. Need all in right amounts.

☆ Neurotransmitter "hit" when do/get something that makes you feel good. Seeking/finding = "hit."

☆ Surround yourself with *good* role models to see what "right" looks like, get support.

☆ Prioritize top 1-3 goals. Too many goals leads to burn-out/regression.

☆ Mindsets: Dr. Carol Dweck. Fixed: "I can't" – gives excuse, protects self, pessimistic. Growth: "I can't" – reframes, finds possibilities, opens self, optimistic. *Continuum* between Fixed/Growth.

A PEEK INTO VOLUME TWO

You have completed volume one! This is a huge accomplishment for you.

Your next step is to start right in with volume two in order to take your learning to new, advanced levels.

The material in volume two builds upon the material in volume one. You will find value in having the summary pages from volume one by your side as you progress through volume two.

In volume two, you'll learn:

☆ Startling revelations about rational thinking that could completely alter your personality – for the better.

☆ The third dimension of the automatic mind, and how to deal with it.

☆ The GEMS model of leadership: what it means, the power behind it, and how to live it.

☆ How to influence others without manipulation.

☆ What *not* to do when in a position of leadership.

☆ How to deal with a subordinate who's a better leader than you.

☆ Examples of different leadership philosophies you can tailor for your own situation.

☆ How to create a *Group Reality Show* to make lasting change with your team or organization.

☆ Why becoming a role model to others is critical for you to achieve everything you want in life.

☆ How to fearlessly become a highly admired and respected role model that people emulate and love.

☆ How to confront people effectively and constructively.

☆ Three powerful techniques to push past fear.

☆ The right and wrong way to push yourself and others.

☆ How to get commitment and high performance from people, even when conditions are difficult and compensation packages are uncompetitive.

☆ Exactly what "Lead with Results and Grace" means.

☆ The connection between the perception of stress and your smarts.

☆ The connection between the perception of stress and your health.

☆ The five environmental areas that play on your genetic expression, and how to navigate these areas for optimal outcomes.

☆ Why focusing on your brain health is the best bang for your buck when it comes to your overall health.

☆ Many inspirational stories, and much more!

Thank you for taking this journey, and choosing to be the very best you can be. I look forward to seeing you in volume two.

Other works and content available:

☆ Online courses, webinars, live workshops, speaking engagements, group mentoring, and corporate consulting available at www.teemingwithtalentllc.com or berubeteam.com

☆ Follow me on Face Book at Valerie L. Berube

☆ Follow me on Twitter @ValerieLBerube

☆ Follow me on LinkedIn at linkedin.com/in/Valerie-berube-b835b871

☆ Follow me on Instagram at teemingwithtalent

☆ Follow me on Tumblr at vberube

☆ Email me at teemingwithtalent@outlook.com

ACKNOWLEDGEMENTS

I am deeply appreciative to my editor, Anna Floit, whose patience and expertise polished this work beyond my expectations; to Terry Whalin, who encouraged and mentored me during my journey as a first-time author; and, to the Morgan James Publishing team, whose faith and support earned my admiration and gratitude. Most important of all, my deepest appreciation goes to my husband, Brian, who sacrificed several years of evenings with me as I poured myself into this work. His love and support made this book possible, and his fun and playfulness made this journey a joy.

ABOUT THE AUTHOR

Valerie was born in California in 1968 to teenage parents. After graduating high school in 1987 she enlisted in the USMC Reserves and attended college. She took on odd jobs to pay for her education and noted significant differences between civilian and military philosophies on leadership and workforce development.

After graduating college, she entered the USMC full time and was commissioned an officer in 1996. She led thousands of diverse people in arduous conditions around the world, and advanced her leadership knowledge through senior military schools, a master's degree program in leadership, and a substantial amount of self-study. After retiring as a lieutenant colonel in 2017, she re-entered the civilian world full time and once again noted the stark philosophical differences in leadership and workforce development. Most notably, she noticed that most junior and mid-level employees were not set up for success in their careers or personal lives by their employers or schools. She saw an opportunity to make a difference and endeavored to write books, develop courses, and offer workshops to fill this critical gap.

In 2017, Valerie started Teeming with Talent, LLC., to serve both individuals and businesses in their quest for individual and organizational excellence. Valerie and her husband Brian live in Phoenix, Arizona.

REFERENCES AND RESOURCES

Dr. Daniel G. Amen
Psychiatrist, neuroscientist, professor and brain health expert. Authored several best-selling books and has appeared on many popular television shows. Helped millions of people improve their brain health. *www.danielamenmd.com*

Dr. Roy F. Baumeister
Social psychologist and prolific author of numerous books and articles specializing in the areas of willpower, self-control, and self-esteem. *www.roybaumeister.com*

Jack Canfield
Motivational speaker and author of numerous best-selling books focused largely on self-confidence and what makes people successful. CEO and founder of the Canfield Training Group. *www.jackcanfield.com*

Dr. Vincent T. Covello
International expert on high stakes communication; author; founder & director of the Center for Risk Communication. *www.centerforriskcommunication.org*

Dr. Angela Duckworth
Psychologist, CEO of the Character Lab, and best-selling author of *Grit*. Studies focus on why some people work harder or have better self-control than others. *www.angeladuckworth.com*

Dr. Carol Dweck

Psychologist specialized in human motivation, particularly in children. Authored several best-selling books; one of the leading experts on mindset. Creator of the "Fixed" versus "Growth" theory of mindset. *www.mindsetonline.com*

Dr. David Eagleman

Neuroscientist, best-selling author, adjunct professor at Stanford. Founder and director of the Center for Science Law (*www.neulaw.org*); writer and presenter of PBS television series. *www.eagleman.com*

Dr. Albert Ellis

Psychologist; creator or Rational Emotive Behavior Therapy (REBT); considered one of the most influential psychotherapists in history. Author of several books and founder of the Albert Ellis Institute. *www.albertellis.org*

Malcolm Gladwell

Journalist who investigated the science behind human behavior. Wrote several international best-selling books on his findings. *www.revisionisthistory.com*

Dr. Daniel Goleman

Psychologist and science journalist who popularized the term "Emotional Intelligence." Authored several best-selling books; co-director of the Consortium for Research on Emotional Intelligence (*www.eiconsortium.org*); co-founder of the Collaborative for Academic, Social, and Emotional Learning (*www.casel.org*). *www.danielgoleman.info*

Dr. Chip Heath and Dan Heath

Brothers, best-selling authors, speakers, and experts in the field of organizational behavior, particularly in the areas of change and decision-making. Dan founded the Change Academy (*www.changeacademy.com*). Chip is a professor at Stanford Graduate School of Business. *www.heathbrothers.com*

Dr. Daniel Kahneman

Psychologist, professor emeritus at Princeton University; founding partner of the TGG Group. Nobel Prize winner in economics; author of best-selling book *Thinking Fast and Slow*. *www.tgggroup.com*

Dr. Carolyn Leaf

Cognitive neuroscientist; best-selling author; world leader in the science of thought. International speaker on diverse topics. *www.drleaf.com*

Dr. Bruce Lipton

Developmental biologist, author and producer of several books and films. Pioneer in science of epigenetics (how thoughts affect genes/DNA). *www.bruceliption.com*

Dr. Leonard Mlodinow

Theoretical physicist, best-selling author and screen writer for several popular science-fiction works. *www.leonardmlodinow.com*

Dr. Gabriele Oettingen

Professor of psychology at New York University; author of *Re-Thinking Positive Thinking;* creator of the *WOOP* mental strategy model. Her work focuses on revealing the right and wrong way to leverage positive thinking. *www.woopmylife.org*

Christopher Peterson, Steven F. Maier, & Martin E. P. Seligman

Psychologists and authors of *Learned Helplessness: A Theory for the Age of Personal Control.*

Dr. Steven Pinker

Cognitive scientist and psychologist, Harvard professor, and author of several books focusing largely on language. *www.stevenpinker.com*

Bob Proctor

World renowned author and motivational speaker whose work largely focuses on the mindset of prosperity. Proctor popularized his long-held instincts on the power and workings of the subconscious mind, much of which is now supported by modern science.*www.proctorgallagherinstitute.com*

Dr. David Rock

Social neuroscientist and best-selling author focused on the neuroscience of leadership. Coined the word "neuroleadership;" created the SCARF® model; CEO and co-founder of the NeuroLeadership Institute. *www.neuroleadership.com*

Dr. John E. Sarno

Professor at New York University, author of several books, and leading expert on pain management and the mind-body connection. *www.johnesarnomd.com*

Douglas Stone, Bruce Patton, & Sheila Heen

Communication experts from Harvard University. *Authors of Difficult Conversations: How to Discuss What Matters Most. www.stoneandheen.com*

Dr. Richard H. Thaler & Cass R. Sunstein

Psychology and economic behaviorist experts; authors of *Nudge: Improving Decisions about Health, Wealth, and Happiness.*

The Myers & Briggs Foundation

Continues the work of psychology pioneers Katherine Cook Briggs and Isabel Briggs Myers, a mother daughter team who developed the Myers-Briggs Type Indicator ® Instrument. *www.myersbrigs.org*

Morgan James
Speakers Group

www.TheMorganJamesSpeakersGroup.com

We connect Morgan James published
authors with live and online events
and audiences who will benefit
from their expertise.

Printed in the USA
CPSIA information can be obtained
at www.ICGtesting.com
JSHW022216140824
68134JS00018B/1084